Quest for Self-Knowle
An Essay in Lonergan'

The theme of self-knowledge, introduced by classical philosophers, was taken up and extended by Bernard Lonergan in his major work, *Insight.* In this innovative and complex study, Lonergan worked out a systematic method for understanding the development of self-knowledge. Joseph Flanagan shares with Lonergan the premise that the problem of self-knowledge can be resolved methodically. The purpose of this book is to introduce teachers and students to this difficult subject and to provide readers with a transcultural, normative foundation for a critical evaluation of self-identity and cultural identity.

Flanagan elucidates the complicated historical context in reference to the emergence of Lonergan's positions; in particular he relates Lonergan's thought to the development of modern science. He then retraces the main arguments of *Insight* as they relate to the theme of self-knowledge, and invites readers to discover and verify within their own conscious experiences a foundational identity that they share with all knowers in an ever-expanding search for truth. This method of self-appropriation not only reveals a new philosophical method, but also transforms the traditional science of metaphysics by subsuming it into a richer and more comprehensive ethical context.

Quest for Self-Knowledge establishes new ground for philosophical and religious dialogue and demonstrates how Lonergan's philosophy provides a context that complements and enriches the analytic and phenomenological approaches that dominate Western schools of philosophy.

(Lonergan Studies)

JOSEPH FLANAGAN, SJ, is director of the Lonergan Institute and a member of the philosophy department at Boston College.

JOSEPH FLANAGAN

Quest for Self-Knowledge: An Essay in Lonergan's Philosophy

UNIVERSITY OF TORONTO PRESS

Toronto Buffalo London

© University of Toronto Press Incorporated 1997
Toronto Buffalo London
Printed in Canada

ISBN 0-8020-0866-6 (cloth)
ISBN 0-8020-7851-6 (paper)

Printed on acid-free paper

Lonergan Studies

Canadian Cataloguing in Publication Data

Flanagan, Joseph, 1925–
    Quest for self-knowledge

    (Lonergan studies)
    Includes bibliographical references and index.
    ISBN 0-8020-0866-6 (bound)
    ISBN 0-8020-7851-6 (pbk.)

    1. Lonergan, Bernard J.F. (Bernard Joseph
    Francis), 1904–1984. Insight. 2. Self-knowledge,
    Theory of. 3. Self (Philosophy). I. Title.
    II. Series.

    BD161.L6513F55 1997   126'.092   C96-932367-0

University of Toronto Press acknowledges the financial assistance to its
publishing program of the Canada Council and the Ontario Arts Council.

This publication was assisted by a grant from the Trustees of Boston College.

To the memory of Bernard Lonergan
who bequeathed to the world a rich and inspiring legacy

Contents

Acknowledgments

This is a book with many authors. For more than fifteen years, I have been a member of a weekly seminar that meets to discuss the writings of Bernard Lonergan. In many different and, I am sure, unsuspected ways, these ongoing conversations have become part of the texture of my own thinking and part of the text that thinking has produced. While I am unable to disentangle the particular sources of my ideas, I can certainly thank the members of this group for their collaboration and acknowledge their considerable contributions to this project. The members of this group – Pat Byrne, Mary Ann Glendon, Charles Hefling, Tom Kohler, Matt Lamb, and Fred Lawrence – come from different professional backgrounds, and the diversity of their perspectives has certainly enhanced the range of topics that I have been able to discuss in the following pages.

During the early stages of this work I served as chair of the Philosophy Department of Boston College, and throughout this time I had the delightful support and professional services of our department administrative assistant, Peggy Bakalo, and of our two department secretaries, Louise Dietenhofer and RoseMarie DeLeo. They were always indulgent of my obsessive lapses into philosophical perorations, and I am deeply grateful for their continuing friendship and encouragement.

As every teacher knows, students give back a good deal more than our own cherished phrases. And so I would like to thank my students for their deeply thoughtful exams, essays, and comments. In many subtle and unexpected ways, their ideas have become part of this book.

During the time the material of this book was germinating I had five different graduate assistants: Harry Otaguro, Paul Kidder, Jeff Nielsen, Paul Bruno, and Mark Goodman. I team-taught a number of courses with these gifted doctoral students. They not only assisted in arranging and administering the courses, but also regularly shared insights and ideas gathered from teaching them. In addition, they assisted me in a number of ways in preparing this manuscript. I am delighted to thank them for their generosity and enthusiastic support.

Both Joseph Appleyard and Charles Hefling read the first draft of my manuscript, and their critical comments helped me avoid more than a few mistakes. Several other members of the Lonergan seminar read chapters and offered suggestions that have been included in the final version. I am also indebted to the reviewers of the University of Toronto Press who suggested several structural changes that have made this book much better organized and more readable. Linda Biesenthal's careful editing of the text should be warmly appreciated by its readers.

Along with a wide range of her other responsibilities, Kerry Cronin, director of the Lonergan Center, found time to assist me with the final preparation of the manuscript as well as with proof-reading and other details.

A very special word of thanks is owed to John Turner, who not only organized the index and prepared the diagrams, but also made a number of important editorial improvements.

Finally, I thank my family who graciously listened to much more talk about this book than they really wanted to.

The reader will find an excellent glossary of Lonergan terminology compiled by Carla Mae Streeter in *Communication and Lonergan: Common Ground for Forging the New Age*, edited by Thomas Farrell and Paul Soukup (Kansas City: Sheed and Ward, 1993).

Quest for Self-Knowledge:
An Essay in Lonergan's Philosophy

Introduction

1

Who am I, really and truly? Each of us has many different identities: we identify ourselves by our family name, for example, and we have cultural and ethnic identities, as we recognize ourselves as Japanese, or French-Canadian, or German-American, and so forth. As well as these more personal and social identities, each of us shares with every other person a human identity that is our most comprehensive and foundational one. To discover and appropriate this human identity has been the goal of a philosophical quest in Western history since philosophy's early beginnings among the Greek scholars.

If we consider the results of this philosophical quest in terms of the present state of philosophy, we will be very disappointed. For some, philosophy has reached a dead end. For others, philosophy has had to hand over its search for self-identity to history and the social sciences. For still others, the quest goes on, but it does so by retrieving forgotten questions or by discrediting the mistaken and hidden assumptions that were involved in asking and answering these questions about our identity during the past two thousand years.

This book offers a different alternative, as well as a different interpretation of why philosophers have had so much difficulty in searching for our common identity. I see myself as returning to the original question asked by the early Greek philosophers, but I do so to demonstrate a continuity with that tradition and, more important, to invite the reader to develop a critical interpretation and evaluation of his or her own basic identity. One foundational assumption behind this book is that the problem of self-knowledge that has oriented the Western quest for our common human identity can be resolved methodically. Another assumption is that the history of philosophy has failed to achieve more successful results in this quest precisely because it has lacked such an overall method for dealing with the perennial questions that philosophers have asked and attempted to answer. If we look to the history of the natural sciences, we will find a dramatically different story.

From the time of Galileo, the history of mathematics and science reads like a remarkable success story. The reason, I will argue, is that mathematicians and scientists developed at that time new methodical procedures and directions, which included clarifying just what their common objective was. During the nineteenth century, scientists developed two more methods with different procedures and different objectives. During the nineteenth century as well, the human sciences, which had been gradually emerging since the Renaissance, came up against their own problem of method. Just what is a human science? How are such sciences related to the natural sciences? How are sciences like sociology and history related? Such questions are still unresolved.

After the natural sciences broke away from the controls of philosophy during the Renaissance, philosophers found themselves in a crisis as they faced a pressing need to develop a new method for philosophizing. Descartes responded with his methodical doubt and an invitation to scholars to direct their attention to the subject's own awareness of herself or himself as a thinker. From that time to the present, there has been a series of different methodical procedures and differing philosophical positions, a situation that today causes some philosophers to despair of discovering a method for seeking answers to such problems as our common human identity. An alternative interpretation is that these different attempts to find a method have served to clarify certain basic questions and basic mistakes, and that it is still possible to work out a foundational method for interpreting and critically evaluating both philosophical methods and other methodical procedures and objectives of the natural and human sciences.

Before outlining how I will proceed to develop such a philosophical method, let me make a few preliminary remarks about what I mean by the term 'method'. A method is not a plan or program that begins by setting forth its desired results along with the best means for achieving them. It is not a set of rules – for assembling a new bookcase or a barbecue – nor is it a recipe. A method is a procedure for discovering an unknown. Moreover, it is a normative procedure which certainly seems like a paradox since the object we are seeking is unknown. Finally, a method leads to results, not only once but repeatedly. These results are not guaranteed, but they are probable, and the probabilities can be shifted from lower to higher expectations. A brief example from the history of mathematics will provide a preliminary sketch of this meaning of 'method'.

François Vièta, a French lawyer and mathematician, was responsible for pioneering a number of new mathematical procedures during the Renaissance. He was the person who first proposed the simple method that most of us learned in high school algebra: in any mathematical problem, we begin by clarifying what we know and do not know, then we let x equal the unknown variable and proceed to discover what we do not know in terms of what we do know through simple arithmetical operations. Scientists and human beings in general have always employed what they knew to discover what they did not know, but they did not proceed methodically, as Vièta. Once this method was clarified and expanded, mathematics took off and is still producing 'cumulative results.' The same thing happened as the natural sciences took advantage of the advances in mathematics to enhance and clarify their own related, but somewhat different, procedures and objectives. The new scientific method initiated by Galileo did not guarantee that Newton would produce a new world-order, but it did make it more probable. And those probabilities shifted dramatically as Kepler, Huygens, Boyle, Descartes, and others who followed this new method made it more and more probable for Newton to move to the center of the intellectual stage and construct his new ordering of the entire universe.

There is, of course, a vast difference between the method of the natural sciences and the human sciences, as well as between the human sciences and philosophy. Such differences will be dealt with in the following chapters. The point I am making here is that the discovery of a method does change the way knowers proceed and, while a method does not guarantee results, it does significantly alter the chances of success.

Some recent advances in mathematics provide another example of method. In simple algebra we are seeking an unknown number or magnitude, in coordinate geometry we are seeking two geometrical or numerical unknowns that are known to be 'coordinate' unknowns, but in the nineteenth century a dramatic advance was made with the discovery of group theory. Whereas before mathematicians had been seeking the properties of unknown numbers or magnitudes, they now shifted to discovering the properties of the operations that generated these unknowns. Once this step was taken, mathematicians could begin to examine an entire system of mathematics by studying the properties of the operations that generated the system. This, in turn, led them to the study of different systems and the way one system builds on a prior system, incorporating the prior lower system in a more extensive, effective, and higher integration. Again, a simple example will illustrate this advance.

Once you develop a formula, you can find maaa answers

When mathematicians state $a + b = b + a$, they are not primarily interested in the unknown a or b since these are considered to be variable values. The mathematician instead focuses on the property of the operation of adding and, in the process, discovers that this operation combines numbers or variables in such a way that different orderings of the numbers will not change the results (the commutative law of adding). When we say $2 + 4 = 4 + 2$ the focus is on the numbers, but when we say $a + b = b + a$ the focus shifts to the operation of adding that generates the sum of any two or more numbers. These discoveries have some remarkable implications since they can be generalized to include all the different fields of meaning. Most importantly, they make possible operational definitions by which philosophers can distinguish between what is known immediately and what is known only mediately through certain defined operations. This advance also revealed a basic and recurrent mistake in human knowing.

Whether in scientific or ordinary forms of knowing, there is a recurring tendency to assume not only that reality is already known, but that it is known infinitely and absolutely. This mistake pertains to notions of reality, and also to the basic constituents of reality, such as space and time. For two thousand years scientists tended to assume that they knew what space and time were and that our physical universe was contained within an infinite and absolute space and time. This was Newton's basic assumption in his explanation of how our universe was ordered, and it was the foundational assumption of every major scientist up to Einstein who finally reversed this basic mistake by drawing attention to the significance and properties of the measuring system through which the scientists had been mediating their empirical observations, without being aware of that 'mediation.'

A very similar mistake plagued the history of mathematics, as is brilliantly recounted by Carl Boyer in his *History of Calculus*. Boyer shows how the early Greek mathematicians were already struggling with the basic problems of calculus, such as the analysis of an infinite continuum which Zeno's paradoxes made famous. Even after Newton and Leibniz had discovered how to do calculus, they were unable to define what it was they were doing. For two hundred years after Newton, the best mathematical minds struggled to produce a consistent and coherent account of the basic terms and relations for the science of calculus, and failed. When they did finally generate an accurate and rigorous set of definitions, it led to some surprising discoveries. They realized that for two thousand years mathematicians had mistakenly assumed that the infinite was immediately known, only to realize that, in mediating this assumed notion of infinity, they had to limit what they had presumed was unlimited. Just as Einstein discovered that infinite space and time were actually limited, so mathematicians also had to reverse their own basic assumptions concerning the notion of the infinite. What makes Boyer's account of the history of mathematics so important and helpful is the way he underscores the recurring tendency of the best mathematicians to assume the infinite through various forms of imaginative picturing of an endless space or time. Only when the mathematicians of the nineteenth century shifted from imagined meanings to strictly intelligible meanings were they able to bring their basic concepts under control. The two-thousand-year history of physics and mathematics, therefore, teaches a basic lesson to all who want to know what they are doing when they are knowing. For this reason I will examine this history in the second chapter.

My purpose will be not to focus on the mathematical or scientific contents, but to invite the reader to pay attention to his or her own mediating operations of knowing through which such mathematical and scientific meanings become known. My concern is quite different from that of mathematicians and scientists who are interested, not in their own conscious mediating operations, but in the contents that become known through these operations. My further concern will be to appropriate the operational method that the scientists themselves developed during the scientific revolution of the seventeenth century, as well as the two other methods they developed during the nineteenth century.

It would seem that the scientists who developed these methods would be the ones who should know what these methods are. But such an assumption is a repetition of the basic mistake just sketched above. There is a foundational difference between what you know immediately and what we know mediately through our operations of knowing. Certainly the scientists were aware of what they were doing but, as we shall see, awareness is not knowing; it is only a condition for knowing. These scientists had an immediate awareness of what they were doing, but to know what they were doing would involve shifting their attention away from the known contents and attending to the operations through which they were mediating these known contents. Descartes provides a good example.

Descartes made major contributions to both the science of physics and mathematics. He also made a major contribution to philosophy as he shifted the philosopher's attention away from an object-centered philosophy to his or her own operating subject; he invited knowers to pay attention to their own conscious activity of thinking. However, as we shall see in the second chapter, while Descartes opened up a new philosophical field of inquiry, he also made some serious mistakes, confusing the method of doing philosophy with the method of doing science and mathematics.

In the seventeenth century the Royal Society set down a number of new methodical procedures for doing science, including the requirement that every hypothesis must be experimentally verifiable or sensibly testable.

Descartes put forth a theory of vortices or rotating fluids to explain the orbiting motions of the planets; these swirling fluids were invisible and could not be experimentally verified. Newton developed a theory of vortices that proved that Descartes's theory was incorrect; more important, Newton's theory was sensibly and experimentally verifiable. The same thing happened a century later when the caloric theory of heat, which involved an assumption of heat as a weightless fluid, was also 'methodically' eliminated. My point is that the scientific method had many parts, and it took some time for them to be clarified. In the long run, however, the method proved very effective because its normative procedures led to 'cumulative and progressive results.'

While the methods of science were limited to sensibly verifiable data (excluding the data of consciousness), philosophical methods, as initiated by Descartes, did appeal to the data of an individual's awareness of thinking. Again, as we shall see, to appropriate and verify within your own conscious experiences, what you are doing when you are thinking is just as difficult as discovering that space and time are not unlimited.

One final example of this difference between philosophical and scientific methods can be found in Aristotle's *Physics*, which dominated the field right up to Descartes and Newton, largely because Aristotle's physics could handle so many different problems in systematic fashion, and to replace it required constructing a new and more comprehensive system. A contemporary scientist would be surprised to find that the last book of his *Physics* addresses theological questions, and that his treatise on the soul includes an analysis of the souls of plants, animals, and human beings. The problem of the methodical difference between the natural and human sciences would not become an issue until the nineteenth century. For example, the term 'object' for Aristotle meant 'cause'; it did not mean 'object' as we use this word, namely, as the term of an intentionally conscious act. This latter meaning only emerged as Descartes shifted philosophical attention from Aristotle's general theory of causes to a study of the data of his own consciousness. In other words, Descartes was appealing to empirically verifiable sense data as a scientist, and to the empirically conscious data of his own subject as a philosopher. However, he did not have this shift from one empirical method to a very different empirical method under control. It is my purpose to invite the reader to develop precisely such normative controls.

It is possible to achieve a methodical understanding of our philosophical identity as human beings. The core of this method is to shift our attention away from what we know about ourselves or anything else, and to begin to pay attention to the conscious operations by which we know. The foundational problem in this journey of self-discovery is to realize that we do not know the reality of anything, including ourselves, immediately. The reality that we do know is known in and through the mediating operations of knowing. This implies that we do not know reality, infinity, space, time, or any other basic constituent of reality, except in a very limited way. While we have, as Aristotle said, an unlimited ability to come to know, none of us, nor all human beings together, have actualized our human capacities. We do not know who we really are in any complete sense. We are, as Nietzsche said, 'incomplete' realities.

2

In the first five chapters of this book, I attempt to answer the question, What am I doing when I am knowing? Having answered that question, I will then turn to the question, Why do I do these acts of knowing? Or posed in another way, What is my goal or objective? The answer to those two questions will give us the methodical foundation for establishing, first, a theory of objectivity or epistemology and, secondly, a theory of metaphysics. In pursuing this method, we will arrive at two major discoveries. First, knowing is not a single-level activity, but involves three different, but functionally related, sets of activities. This discovery not only explains why knowing ourselves as knowers is so difficult to achieve, but it also suggests why so many different accounts of knowing can be interpreted as part of a developing, dialectical process leading to the goal of knowing our own knowing. Once this goal is achieved we can proceed to identify the different forms and objectives of specialized patterns of knowing and to integrate them into a search for a unifying objective. That objective will be to know our own reality and the way in which that self-knowing can provide the normative foundation for knowing any and all things. The second major discovery resulting from this methodical pursuit of self-knowing is that the sciences of epistemology and metaphysics that we will develop will turn out to be much more limited than the traditional metaphysics set forth by Aristotle and medieval scholars. This method will also lead to the surprising position that a moral epistemology and a moral metaphysics are much richer and more comprehensive sciences than the traditional sciences of metaphysics and epistemology.

Traditionally, speculative wisdom was considered to be the higher and more perfect way to pursue the philosophical life. The practical wisdom of the statesman engaged in political life was thought to be a less perfect way of living. Rousseau, Kant, Hegel, Kierkegaard, Marx, and their successors have changed that traditional interpretation and evaluation of speculative and practical wisdom. Praxis, not theory, now holds the preeminent position. Or, I shall suggest, our identity as choosers subsumes, transforms, and incorporates our identity as knowers. Only in moving from a methodical metaphysics to the higher and more comprehensive study of ethics can the philosopher come to a methodical understanding of herself or himself as a historical being.

In chapter 7 I will turn from the question of knowing to the question of choosing and ask, What am I doing when I am choosing? And then, Why do I choose? What is my goal and basic objective in choosing?; These questions will open up the more controversial study of human motivations and the newly emerging need for a logic of images and emotions. In the first five chapters which focus on our coming to know, our 'images' keep getting in the way, as they subtly mislead us into mistaken assumptions; in the last two chapters, the problem of developing images and appropriating the way they evoke and control our feelings will become a central problem. It is in this context that I will refocus the question and invite the reader to appropriate his or her cultural identity. Culture, as we shall see, is not just the manner and mode of a people's behavior. More significantly, culture is why a people behave the way that they do. If institutional, cooperative schemes are what people do, culture is why they do it. Culture is, as Montesquieu and Tocqueville realized, an expression of the spirit of the people. Our cultural habits are not primarily habits of the mind, but habits of the heart; they express the attitudes and motivating meanings of our behavior. Thus, to appropriate our cultural identity, we need to critically interpret and evaluate the cultural meanings and values we have inherited.

These reflections on culture will lead us to a more comprehensive and concrete definition of ourselves as 'symbolic animals.' The role that symbols play in cultivating our personal identities is pervasive and concretely operative throughout our lives. These reflections will help us to integrate and organize the 'hermeneutic of suspicion,' which is set forth in several chapters of this book. This hermeneutic of suspicion raises dialectical questions not only from Freud's, Marx's, and Nietzsche's points of view, but also from the traditional perspective of moral impotence, going back to Augustine and the biblical tradition. It is in this context that our methodical approach will lead us to pose the religious question in a very untraditional way and, at the same time, to take advantage of the developments in the history of religion during the past century. These considerations will further clarify the basic purpose of the book, namely, to provide each reader with a transcultural, normative foundation for critically evaluating his or her present cultural identity. However, our cultural identity is not known through our own immediately generated knowledge. Rather, we know our cognitive, moral, and religious identity primarily because we believe it.

There are two ways of knowing: one is by our own immanently generated knowledge; the other is by believing someone else's knowing. We are, for the most part, familiar with knowing by believing in religious matters, but it may come as a surprise to find that we know most of what we know about our own identity because we believe it. Even more paradoxical is Einstein's statement that most of what a scientist knows he or she knows by believing it. If this is true, as I propose, it will further explain and underscore the importance of addressing the historical sources of our cultural identity. This may seem like a very roundabout way of coming to know who we are, but if, as Aristotle said, our identity is potentially unlimited, then it is only in dealing with human history and our identity with that history that we will come to realize how incomplete our present identity actually is.

3

The title of this book, *Quest for Self-Knowledge,* is taken from what I consider to be the central theme of Bernard Lonergan's major philosophical text, *Insight: A Study of Human Understanding.* My basic purpose in this book is to summarize the successive chapters of *Insight* as they are related to this theme of self-knowledge. To do this, I follow the main argument and structure of Lonergan's work as they are related to this theme of self-knowledge, with two exceptions. In summarizing chapters 2 and 5 of *Insight,* I provide the reader with a brief history of mathematics and science because these chapters have proved to be a stumbling block for many of Lonergan's readers, and it seems to me a less rigorous theoretical approach will assist the reader in appropriating the major themes of these chapters without presupposing the strong mathematical and scientific background that Lonergan demands of his readers. The second exception will be in the material set forth in chapters 7 and 8 where I introduce certain major developments in Lonergan's thought between the publication of *Insight* in 1957 and his second major text, *Method in Theology,* published in 1972. In these final two chapters, I combine material from *Insight* and *Method in Theology* to round off my study of self-knowledge in terms of the self as chooser and lover.

I have chosen not to mention Lonergan's name in the text (my sources will be identified in the notes) because I want to provide the reader with continuity in expression, and also because Lonergan himself always insisted that his purpose was to put people in touch with themselves so that they could learn to philosophize out of their own concrete, actual experiences. To emphasize this personal dimension of Lonergan's method, I have addressed the reader directly by using the pronoun you. I hope you, the reader, will not find this too disconcerting.

Finally, a note on Lonergan's position in the contemporary philosophi-

cal scene. Lonergan did not philosophize in either of the two major traditions operating in the twentieth century – analytic philosophy and
phenomenology. His own philosophical roots were in Scholastic philosophy, but because of his own quite original understanding of the achievement in modern mathematics and science and his own retrieval of
Aristotle's and Aquinas's thought, he was able to build an entirely new
foundation for the philosophical tradition in which he had been brought
up. It is my hope that this present work may communicate this new foundation to scholars working in phenomenology and in analytic philosophy.

4

Following is a summary of the fourteen themes of this book.

(1) The fundamental question is: Who am I? It can be answered in many
different ways, since we have a number of different, emergent identities.
However, our foundational identity is that of a concrete, contingent
knower, chooser, lover.

(2) Our present, actual cultural identity may be in tune or out of tune
with our own basic transcendent identity. → who we are for all eternity

(3) The relation between our actual cultural identity and potential transcultural identity can be methodically examined, interpreted, and evaluated.

(4) That method involves appropriating what we are doing when we are
knowing, choosing, and loving, as opposed to what we may assume we are
doing when we are knowing, choosing, and loving.

(5) This method proposes that our religious assumptions are dependent
on our moral assumptions, and that our moral assumptions are dependent
on our cognitive assumptions. These functionally related assumptions can
be appropriated, either beginning with our religious assumptions and
working back to our cognitive assumptions or the other way around. I have
chosen to move from cognitive to moral and religious assumptions because
of what I consider to be the basic problem in our quest for self-knowledge,
or in appropriating our basic transcending identity and reality.

(6) That basic problem is our concrete operative assumptions about
what makes reality real, objectivity objective, and knowing knowing. These
concrete, lived assumptions concerning reality and objectivity are dependent on how we answer the question, What are we doing when we are
'doing' knowing?

(7) The solution to this problem involves a conversion from one set of
assumptions about what we are doing when we are knowing and why we are
doing it to a precisely defined and opposed set of assumptions. However,
we cannot 'convert' other people, nor can we argue them into changing

Who I om ↓ *What I ought to do* ↓ *What God is*

their basic set of assumptions. We can, however, in a somewhat Socratic manner, invite them to examine and reflect on whether their basic assumptions square with their own spontaneous tendencies or with their naturally given experiences.

(8) Such an intellectual conversion is an extremely difficult and stubborn problem to resolve because it arises from the ontological structure of the person and from the way we develop as human beings both in our personal lives and in our collective, historical lives. The complexity of this problem can be best exemplified, from my point of view, by the history of mathematics and science. That history not only explains the tenacity and obstinacy of the problem, but also provides a set of conditions for solving the problem.

(9) The core of the problem lies in the way our notions of reality, objectivity, and knowing are connected to our notions of space and time. The history of mathematics provides an extraordinary testimony to the continual inability of mathematicians to formulate logically satisfying definitions of such terms as infinity, number, limit, function, derivative, and integral, or of the set of terms on which the science of calculus can be grounded. The history of physics shows, first, how difficult it is to comprehend and formulate a coordinate system for measuring physical spaces and times, and secondly, the difficulty of understanding that physical spaces and times mutually condition one another, that they are not independent or infinite realities, but the very opposite, dependent and limited. Besides clarifying the nature of the problem, the history of these sciences also reveals the way the problem was, in fact, resolved, as both sciences developed new methods showing human knowers successfully operating in new, dynamic, and cumulatively successful methods. It was these methods that provided philosophers with the opportunity of clarifying their own methodical procedures and of identifying within themselves the invariant structure of human knowing. Having appropriated that invariant structure, we may then proceed to identify within our own cognitive experiences what the other patterns of knowing are and how they may be integrated into a science of metaphysics. Appropriating our own basic identity as a transcendent knower enables us to construct a metaphysics that will allow us to anticipate knowing the reality of all the different kinds of reality and how they may be ordered and united to one another. In constructing such a metaphysical world-order, however, it is important to underscore the fundamental similarities and differences of the earlier Scholastic and Aristotelian world-orders.

(10) The fundamental difference between the traditional world-order and the one I articulate in chapters 4 and 6 is method. By 'method' I mean a normative set of operations that can anticipate unknown goals, advanc-

ing toward them in effective ways, while generating steady and progressive results. In a word, method is our own performing mind, or any other human mind, or all of them working cooperatively. All the different methods we shall discuss are specializations of our own performing intellect. Such methods have three basic characteristics: operational, heuristic, and transcendental.

(11) By *operational* I mean that method proceeds from our own concrete operations of knowing, abstracted from their contents in order to emphasize the activities that generate, and thereby mediate and explain, the cognitional contents they produce. This characteristic of method underscores the difference between a science that is strictly explanatory and one that is a mixture of descriptive and explanatory relations and differences. The latter has not yet reached the stage where the explanatory relations and differences are clearly differentiated from the descriptive relations and differences. The metaphysical world-order I set forth in chapter 6 is strictly explanatory, while traditional ontological world-orders are a mixture of descriptive and explanatory perspectives without any explicit way to control the differences between these perspectives.

Methods are also *heuristic* in that they anticipate a goal that is unknown; they are not plans or programs or blueprints. A plan has an explicit goal along with a sketch of the means to reach that goal. Method is just the opposite. The objective is unknown; what is known are the intending operations through which we will generate or cause the object to come into existence, provided that the conditions for these operations are given. These operations, therefore, are normative-orienting intentions, directing us toward a known-unknown. These operations have an operator, namely, you the subject who not only will direct these operations, but also will be constituted in and through the performance of these operations. Finally, these operations are transcendental in the sense that they take us beyond any achieved results, as they invite us to pursue still yet unknown objectives. The classic instance of transcendence is the question, since it moves us as questioners beyond ourselves as observers toward an understanding of our observations. But there are different forms of questions and different forms of interests or intentions which initiate and govern the orientations of questioning that quietly and persistently direct us toward different unknown objectives. The answers to these questions may be formed into the rounded whole, which we will call a 'system'. A chief characteristic of a system is the range of questions that it is able to incorporate and bring under control. But as the system develops, it tends to become more specialized, clarifying its own boundaries, thereby setting the conditions for new transcending questions which will eventually incorporate and comprehend more extensive transcending operations and fields of interest.

(12) Our transcendental identity is first revealed in the levels and stages of knowing, but there is the more penetrating and intimate identity in our choosing and, especially, in our loving. Transcendental method means appropriating our own dynamic interiority, as we seek still further aspects of identity with ourselves and others.

(13) Love can be experienced as a total transcendent mystery that can, in dramatic, ecstatic, or very silent ways, take us out of ourselves and raise us into new horizons of belief and trust. But, while transcendental, religious experiences may go beyond prior levels and stages of our identity, they do not leave behind our past operating identities and unities, but rather draw them into more perfect modes of personal existence and of being with others, including the totally 'other' that we will identify in and through religious experiences. Transcendental method, however, does not lead to taking sides when it comes to different religious traditions or differences within the same creedal tradition. Rather, it leads the philosopher to discover in his or her own transcending identity the ground from which these different religious traditions have evolved.

(14) Finally, philosophy is a way of life; it commits us to an existential question that deals with the total reality of our own self-identity as known and lived, and as still unknown and unlived. The question is whether our present identity is in tune with our own potentially unlimited capacities, that is, are we existing cognitionally, morally, and religiously in an authentic way? To answer this question in a methodical way we must be able to interpret and evaluate our present cultural identity in a developmental and dialectical way. Our present cultural identity as knowers, choosers, and lovers depends on the historical situation in which we were born and the linguistic community in which and through which our experiences have been, and are being lived and mediated. Any linguistic community will have a history of past knowing, choosing, and loving which has advanced and/or obscured and blocked the transcending identity of past cultural communities. The philosopher, who has appropriated his or her own transcultural identity and the various specialized methods that are grounded in, and generated by, a transcendental method, can cooperate with historians and social scientists to discern the concrete operative sources of the present authentic and inauthentic trends that are actually operative in their culture. Thus they are setting the conditions for their cultural identity and the different ways they are or are not in tune with their own transcending identity.

1

Insight

1   Insight

You look at a *New Yorker* cartoon, read the caption, look back at the cartoon, and wonder, What does it mean? You keep looking and looking,
assuming that the cartoonist has provided a clue that you are too slow to
grasp. Finally, after several minutes of puzzling, you get the point and feel
reassured that you are among the select audience that appreciates the sub-
tlety of *New Yorker* cartoons.

   This moment of catching on, of getting the point, is a familiar and fairly
frequent event in the course of our mental lives. Thus it may seem almost
preposterous to suggest that this activity of catching on can provide the
foundation for a whole new approach to philosophy, as well as for the basis
of a new method for reaching agreements about scientific, moral, and religious questions. This act of insight has been noticed by a number of philosophers, but it has never been made the explicit center and foundation of a
new method of philosophy. If insights are so important, why have philosophers failed to appreciate their remarkable importance? Before attempting to answer this question, let me describe certain characteristics of the
cognitional event referred to as 'insight'.

   The most remarkable aspect of an insight is that it transforms you, quite
suddenly from being stupid to being brilliant. Once you get the point of
the cartoon, the impenetrable drawing is suddenly penetrated and its
meaning becomes perfectly clear, leaving you to wonder how you could
ever have missed the point. To shift to a much more dramatic and complex
example, once Newton had grasped that problems of quadrature were the
reverse of ordering tangents, he could not understand how Fermat and

Pascal could possibly have missed this point. After all, Newton mused, it was lying right there in the diagrams on the paper in front of them.[1] He assumed that they must have had 'bandages over their eyes.' The difference between Newton and his fellow scientists was an insight. Diagrams are not insights, but they may evoke insights in a properly disposed thinker. This leads us to the second characteristic of our sudden, intellectual illumination.[2]

Insights occur in ready minds and what readies your mind is a question, a wondering. Wondering is a wanting, a desire to understand, to catch on. To be in a state of questioning is to be conscious in a quite remarkable way. In the first place, when you ask a question you orient yourself toward an answer; you reveal to yourself that you do not know the answer, and also that you have the ability to arrive at an answer. That is why, as questioner, you can make the paradoxical claim that you know your own not knowing and simultaneously you know your ability to arrive at the answer. The key to your ability to arrive at the answer is the way your question orients you toward that answer, even while not knowing what that answer is. In other words, the answer is not simply an unknown; rather, it is a known unknown. The question reveals your questioned experience as a possibly intelligible experience which your expected insight, when it ocurrs, will transform into an actually intelligible experience.

This point can be further clarified if we focus on a third aspect of an insight: its relation to experiences, either outward sensible experiences or inward imaginable experiences. It is one thing to see the *New Yorker* cartoon and quite another to see it intelligibly. Seeing is not understanding, but what you see can be made intelligible. In wondering about the meaning of the cartoon, your questioning reveals that the cartoon is a sensible object that can be transformed by an insight into an intelligibly sensed object. Cats can see cartoons, but they do not see them as possibly intelligible because they do not question them.

There is a very old and famous example of what I am talking about here. In *Meno*, Plato describes Socrates speaking to a slave boy about the problem of doubling the area of a square. He draws a diagram of a square and begins asking the boy different questions, attempting to lead him to discovering the answer. After shifting the diagram and posing the problem in different ways, the boy finally catches on and solves the problem. He has had an insight. This is a marvelous illustration of how the emergence of an insight depends on two conditions: the questioning and the diagrams which are made possibly intelligible by the questions. Socrates was not able to make the discovery for the slave boy, but he was able to make its emergence more or less probable by the way he asked the questions and drew the diagrams.[3] Teachers can evoke insights in students by asking more sug-

gestive questions or by multiplying examples that express the same problem from different perspectives. In *Meno* Socrates uses the example of
teaching geometry to the slave boy to suggest that the boy had learned his
answers in a previous life, and so his insights were not acts of understanding but a recollecting of the soul's prior knowledge. Aristotle was not
impressed by the argument, and pointed out that the key to discovery was
not remembering prior learning, but an act of understanding by a mind
made ready by intelligent questioning and appropriate images. Remembering plays a role in getting insights, but the key is the question and the
evocative image that may trigger an insight.

Insight is a personal act of understanding which is a response to appropriate questioning and is dependent on suitable images or sensations. In
addition to the activities of questioning, imagining, and sensing that may
evoke understanding, there are other activities such as remembering and
feeling that also come into play. For the moment, however, I wish to focus
on the interplay of questioning, imagining, and sensing as they condition
and lead to insights. Questioning is the key activity since the sensible data
without the questions will not encourage a person to try to transform sensible diagrams or cartoons into intelligible ones. Questioning directs and
sustains the whole process, generating the tensions that will find their
release in that sudden illumination we call insight or understanding. In an
instant what before seemed impossible to understand is suddenly transformed into an obvious intelligibility. But the process does not stop with an
insight. It is one thing for you to have an insight and quite another to state
clearly just what it is that you have understood.

2   Defining

It is important to keep in mind that understanding depends on questioning and that questioning depends on a desire or interest in knowing. In
general, people are not interested in clearly defining just what it is they
have understood. Thus, in my first example of getting an insight into a cartoon, there is no problem of communicating such an insight. The language for expressing such insights does not have to be discovered, and it
does not require a precise and exhaustive statement of understanding.
However, if you wish to appreciate just what you are doing when you are
understanding and how understanding differs from remembering, imag-
ing, and sensing, then it is important to state clearly and precisely just what
it is you have understood. The first person in Western culture to attempt to
do this was Socrates.[4]

Aristotle states that Socrates was the first person who attempted to form
universal definitions. To appreciate just how difficult it is to do so, we need

only read Plato's dialogue *Euthyphro* where Socrates tries to lead Euthyphro into forming a definition of what it means to be holy. The problem is that Euthyphro is well aware of what it is to be holy in particular cases, but he is unable to generalize from his understanding of particular meanings of holiness to form the more general understanding that would cover all such cases and only those cases. Socrates was searching for a new type of insight because he was asking a new type of question, and his questioning, in turn, was conditioned and directed by a new and quite different desire to know.

Ordinary knowing is oriented to, and motivated by, desires for practical knowledge. Socrates, on the other hand, was pursuing knowing for its own sake; he was attempting to interest the Athenians in developing a 'disinterested' interest in knowing – a desire to know that would be free from, and purged of, practical interests. To know what you are doing when you are defining, it is important to realize that there are different purposes and patterns of knowing. There is a theoretical pattern of knowing in which you are pursuing the ideal of discovering what you know and do not know. You can accomplish this by defining precisely the content of your understanding, as opposed to the contents of your sensing, remembering, and imagining. Socrates knew what he was trying to do, but he was unable to realize his goal. Where Socrates failed, Aristotle succeeded. In Aristotle's ethics are not only definitions of the different virtues and vices, but also a systematic way of relating these virtues and vices and of distinguishing one from another.

An important clue to Aristotle's success was an insight into his own questioning, especially the difference between a what and a why question. Here an example will help. You may ask, What is a house? Or, Why is this material object constructed the way that it is? The second question for Aristotle assumes a material object, the house, and wonders about the way the builder has patterned the parts of the house into a unified whole. Why did the builder unite the roof, walls, windows, and doors into this particular design? To ask this question, you must first apprehend the pattern in the design and then abstract that pattern from the material parts in which the pattern is embodied. You must also be aware that the same design could be embodied in quite different materials. Thus we refer to the design or 'form' as an abstract pattern of relations existing in and through the material parts. For example, Frank Lloyd Wright referred to the basic pattern of houses as a box design, and he set out to 'break the box design,'[5] to reconstruct the parts of the whole into a new type of design or pattern. To do this requires, first, abstracting the design or pattern from its material parts and, then, rearranging the parts into a new pattern. There will still be a roof, walls, windows, doors, and floors, but they will be formed into a different design. An architect may have any number of abstract designs in mind and find any number of instances of them within a neighborhood. To define a house or a circle, therefore, is to understand what a house or a circle is and to abstract the why – the form or pattern – from the sensible instances. The problem then is to conceive of this 'why,' or pattern, as an abstract or immaterial form within the mind, apart from its sensible embodiment.

It may serve to clarify the activity of defining if it is looked at as a process of abstracting. Abstracting is usually thought of as an activity that is opposed to the concrete, and is mistakenly taken to be a process that involves a thinning out, or reduction, of an assumed concrete reality. The reason for this mistake is that abstracting involves two different activities, namely, leaving out and putting in. You leave out of your definition whatever you decide is not required in order to get the point, or get the insight. For example, in order to write an abstract of an article you must pick out the primary ideas while putting aside secondary ideas. Two things should be noted: abstracting is a conscious activity, and it is an activity that depends directly on your understanding. If you do not understand the article, you will not know which are primary ideas and which secondary. Abstracting is not an unconscious, hidden activity; it is a conscious activity proceeding from your own prior conscious activity of understanding. As a medieval scholastic might say, it is an act proceeding from an act.

Abstracting is deciding what is relevant and what is irrelevant for the purpose of understanding, not for the purpose of imagining.[6] You need images to understand, so you select certain images while putting others aside, because you decide that certain images will probably evoke the insight. Abstracting, therefore, is an activity with a negative aspect, but this negative putting aside or leaving out depends on the positive and remarkably enriching aspect of the act of understanding. The more you understand, the better you can pinpoint what is essential in setting the limits of a definition and what is not.

As an example, let us consider four different definitions of a circle.

(1) A circle is a line that goes around and meets itself.
(2) A circle is a set of coplanar points equidistant from a center.
(3) $x^2 + y^2 = r^2$
(4) $x^2 + y^2 + Dx + Ey + F = 0$

The difference between these four definitions of a circle is the insight that grounds their respective formulations. The first definition is not a definition in any technical sense, but merely a description that permits you to understand the word 'circle' and talk about it or name something as circular. Such a definition may be called 'nominal.' The second definition is

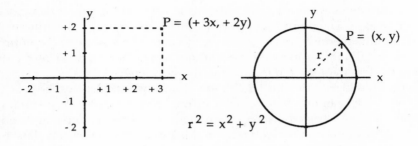

Figure 1.1 Coordinate system of perpendicular axes

essentially Euclid's definition, which not only states what a circle is, but also explains why a circle is what it is. The first statement does not explain why a circle is round, but the second definition tells you why the circle is perfectly round – because all the points that make up the circle are the same distance from the center point. Equally important in Euclid's definition is the word 'coplanar,' which means that the set of points must be on the same plane. The circle is a two-dimensional figure, not a three-dimensional one – it is not a sphere. This is an essential part of the definition because, if you trace the points of the continent of Africa on a globe, there is a set of points along the coast that are all equidistant from the center of the globe, but they do not form a circle. In other words, in your definition of a circle, you must exclude what is not a circle as well as include why a circle is what it is. The problem here is your imagination and the need to appreciate the difference between imagining and understanding.

Though you need images to understand, understanding is not imagining. To differentiate clearly and precisely the difference between those two activities, you must set the limits of (i.e., define) your act of understanding in such a way as to exclude images. Understanding goes beyond imagining, but to clarify what this means requires examining the third definition of the circle. The third definition goes far beyond Euclid's definition by eliminating the problem of mistaken or hidden images that limit understanding in unsuspected ways. It makes a complete break with the ordinary language system, inventing a new symbolic system that allows the systematic thinker to exercise precise control over the different terms that are defined through this symbolic language. In the next chapter, I discuss in more detail this symbolic language, but here I wish to stress how it allows us to appropriate the distinctions between understanding and imagining. There is no mention of 'points' in this third definition, since the points have been transferred into positions within a coordinate system of perpendicular axes named x and y (Figure 1.1). This coordinate system permits the geometer to indicate the way every point on the plane between the axes is correlated to those axes. The point is transformed into a coordinate of two numbers which simultaneously are related to the two major axes, while the centering point signifies the primary intersection of the two major axes. The r^2 indicates the length of the radius, which can be any length.

The advantage of the third definition is the way it emphasizes the activity of your understanding as it frees itself from images, even while it employs these images to trigger its act. Points have no size, neither length nor breadth nor thickness, yet you tend to think of points as very tiny dots. By conceiving or defining these points as positions that are simultaneously co-ordered to the major axes x and y, you underline that their intelligibility is immaterial and unimaginable. You can imagine a relation of x to y and a relation of y to x, but you cannot imagine both relations simultaneously. Correlations and coordinates are not imaginable. In other words, insights reveal their ability to transcend images in the way you conceive of your understanding in various concepts or definitions. Images condition insights but they do not cause them, whereas your insights do cause your ideas, concepts, or definitions. Definitions, then, are the expressions of the intelligibility that you grasp by your insights into images. The act of understanding needs images. You question spontaneously and immediately, but you understand *mediately* in and through images. If you focus on the ideas or definitions that come forth from those images, you will find yourself with immaterial ideas of circles and you will begin to wonder, Where did these immaterial ideas come from? They seem to have emerged immediately and directly 'out of the blue,' since they transcend any particular sensible or imaginable circle.

This was Plato's dilemma concerning the 'forms' that emerged in the mind apparently out of nowhere – no *sensible* where, since sensible things are limited while forms (i.e., ideas, concepts, definitions) are not limited to particular things, times, and places, but are universal and immaterial. What was missing in Plato's theory of forms was the insight by which you grasp the intelligible form in the imaginable or sensible data and, thereby, are able to conceive that intelligibility apart from the limits of the imaginable or sensible forms. Insights form the pivot between your lower activities of sensing, remembering, and imagining and your higher activity of conceiving or defining. The higher activities transcend the lower but are still related to these lower acts.

Furthermore, in the account of the first three definitions, we find the meaning of universal, general, or comprehensive changes from one definition of the circle to the next. The third definition is more universal, general, or comprehensive than the second. And the fourth definition is even more general than the third since the third, $x^2 + y^2 = r^2$, has a limited centering at the zero position of the intersecting axes, whereas in the fourth definition the center can move to any position within the system of coordinates that is employed. Definitions or ideas, then, may be more or less comprehensive. The generality of ideas depends on the power of the insight that grounds their intelligibility, and the power of that insight reveals itself in the type of concepts it is able to generate.

Another feature of insights is that they coalesce or unite.[7] A single definition may involve a number of different concepts but only one act of understanding, because the prior, isolated acts of understanding come together to form a single insight that understands these many different concepts simultaneously. For example, you may begin with the first definition of the circle and gradually come to understand all four definitions through one and the same act of understanding. The definitions remain distinct, but the insights fuse into a single, comprehensive understanding. This ability of insights to complement, correct, and enhance one another, simultaneously forming more universal and general insights, is especially evident if we shift to a study of the notion of 'higher viewpoints.'

3   Higher Viewpoints

It is important to keep in mind that it is one thing to have an insight and quite another to be able to understand what it is you are doing when you are actually engaged in the act of understanding. Similarly, you may move from an understanding within one context to an understanding within a new and more comprehensive context that includes the prior understanding in a much richer and broader context. A good example of such a distinction can be found in Piaget's theory of the cognitive development of children.[8]

Piaget suggests that there are three periods in the development of a child: the sensory-motor stage that lasts from birth to two years of age; the concrete operational stage that covers ages two to eleven; and the formal operational stage of ages eleven to fifteen. Each subsequent stage presupposes, complements, and extends the previous stage. Development occurs in each stage through a process of cognitive adaptation, which consists of acts of assimilation and accommodation. Children acquire new skills in adapting themselves to their environments, assimilating new objects or situations into their prior operating skills, and by expanding the range of these skills through a process of trial and error (adjustment). Most significant in Piaget's analysis of cognitive development is his use of the notion of a mathematical group to specify the completion of development within any given stage or period.

The child completes a period of development when any operating skill or combination of operations can be reversed by the opposite operation or combination of operations. For example, in the first period the child develops his or her sensory-motor intelligence to the level where a range of bodily movements within a physical environment has been mastered, which enables the child to move from one place to another and return to the starting place with ease and familiarity. In the second period, children enter into the world of language and begin to mediate their immediate, physical world within the wider world constructed of linguistic meanings. However, Piaget would argue that during this concrete operational stage, children are not yet able to abstract from their concrete, actual circumstances and to consider other possible situations that might emerge if different courses of action were followed.

Only in the formal operational stage are children able to develop their capacity to abstract from concrete, actual circumstances and consider alternative cases or courses of action. Piaget refers to this new development as the ability, not just to use a language, but to begin to argue within that language and to try out different ways of coming to conclusions by varying the assumptions. Children who have reached this stage can operate with meanings, and can also begin to operate on the operations through which they make their meanings. This allows them to combine sentences into different patterns as they try out a range of alternative meanings.

This notion of learning how to 'operate on the operations' is the central issue in understanding what we mean by 'higher viewpoints.'[9] In moving from the concrete operational stage to the formal operational stage, the child passes from a lower to a higher viewpoint and does so, not only by learning to extend the range of objects he or she deals with on the lower level, but primarily by shifting from the objects of the lower level to the operations by which she or he dealt with those objects or contents. This transformation can be further clarified if we consider higher viewpoints in mathematics, since it was from mathematics that Piaget took his notion of a group. A group is characterized by a set of elements and a set of operations that can construct those elements in various combinations, as well as deconstruct them within a certain range. Mathematicians had formed the notion of the group by analyzing the way mathematical operations were being carried out in various systems of numbers. Piaget grasped the possibility of applying this same idea of a system to physical operations like sitting, standing, walking, and running. He suggested that just as children learn how to add and subtract numbers so they learn how to walk back and forth, in and around their house until they can go anywhere and return home within a certain range. Similarly, the mastery of a language system can be understood as a process similar to learning arithmetic or algebra. Just as children learn how to add, subtract, multiply, and divide numbers, so they learn how to form attributive and actional sentences which they order in past, present, and future tenses; just as they are able to set out and return to their homes, so they learn how to construct their past, present, and future meanings within certain ranges of verbal activities.

How was Piaget able to make so many fertile suggestions? The key was that the mathematicians made a dramatic shift in the history of doing mathematics when they learned how to abstract from the concepts and definitions of mathematical meanings and focus instead on the operations that generated these concepts or terms of meanings. To make such a powerful 'abstraction' means grasping that the concepts or definitions are not relevant to getting the new higher insight. The person who made this step possible was Descartes, who discovered the mathematical notion of a variable. This discovery is discussed in more detail in the next chapter, but here I will simply sketch the notion to show the difference between defining a mathematical term like a circle or triangle and the process of defining a system like arithmetic or algebra.

Students start out thinking that numbers have a single, fixed meaning, such as the number 4 which gets its assigned meaning from being counted or numbered after 3 and before 5. But, if you think of 4 as a sum (i.e., $3 + 1 = 4$), then you are paying attention to the way the number is generated, which means that you have shifted attention away from the number and focused instead on the process of generating numbers through different operations. In this context the number 4 may be transformed from a sum ($3 + 1 = 4$) into a remainder ($5 - 1 = 4$), or into a product ($2 \times 2 = 4$), or into a quotient ($8 \div 2 = 4$). Once you understand that numbers are the way they are because of the operations that generated them, you can make the dramatic shift from defining terms or concepts to defining the operations that generate the terms or concepts. Instead of asking about the properties of a circle, you can ask about the properties of the operations that make circles to be the way they are. Thus, the definitions $x^2 + y^2 = r^2$ may be identified as an equation in the second degree where the term 'second degree' refers to the type of operation that generates such geometrical forms as circles or squares or, more generally, numerical terms such as powers and roots.

This is what happened to mathematics in the nineteenth century. Mathematicians shifted their attention away from (i.e., abstracted from) the different types of numbers and started paying attention to the operations that generated those numbers. Thus, they made the discovery that the operations could be correlated to one another into a group, and that different groups generated different classes of numbers and had different ranges or powers of systematizing these objects. Finally, they grasped that there was a series of systems – like arithmetic, algebra, analytic geometry, and calculus

– where successive systems were built upon prior systems by extending the range of objects that could be generated and combined with one another.[10]

Such a series of systems that transformed and transcended prior systems provided scientists with the possibility of defining the notion of development in a radically new way. It was this possibility that Piaget and contemporary evolutionary theories have explored. More important, it is this distinction between an operation and the contents formed by that operation that has made possible the method that we are pursuing of inviting you to study your own operation of understanding, where attention shifts from 'the understood' to your own activity of understanding, which generates and forms the contents that you have understood. It is my purpose in this work not to study mathematics or science, but to study this act of understanding that has mediated and made possible the remarkable advances in these and other fields.

Besides the kind of direct insights that we have been examining here, there is the rare, but even more unique, type of insight called 'inverse insight.'

4   Inverse Insight

In inviting you to appropriate your own act of understanding, I have placed considerable stress on the significance of wondering or questioning. Just as understanding or insight is a preconceptual event, so too questioning is prior to understanding and directs your attention toward the unknown that you seek to understand. But what if you are asking the wrong question? What if you are asking questions about something that does not even exist? Is it possible that your whole line of questioning has been completely misdirected, that you have been on a wild goose chase?

Once again we turn to Aristotle for an example. Aristotle argued that infinite space was a contradiction because space was a limit, and to assume that a limit is unlimited is to assume a basic contradiction. Yet a series of remarkable minds in Western intellectual history not only made such an assumption, but argued that infinite space existed. In fact, most of the scientists in the Western world, from Democritus to Einstein's predecessors, held that space was absolute and absolutely infinite. Einstein rejected this assumption not by proving that infinite space did not exist, but by arguing that it could not be detected, observed, or measured, and thus such suppositions were contrary to the normative procedures of scientific method. How a genius like Newton could suppose that space and time, which are limits, could be unlimited is a question that I will answer in the next four chapters. Here I wish only to illustrate how an inverse insight is a very rare type of insight which leads not primarily to new understandings, but to new lines of questioning, thereby opening up a whole new horizon of intelligibility.[11]

A brilliant example of an inverse insight can be found in Robin Collingwood's *Idea of Nature*. Collingwood suggests that the pre-Socratic history of the study of nature can be summed up as a shift from a mistaken line of questioning to a correct way of wondering. Instead of asking, What is the basic stuff out of which things are made?, these pre-Socratic thinkers should have been questioning the way the Pythagoreans did: What are the forms that make the basic, indeterminate stuff come to be and to behave in the determinate ways that it does? In other words, the pre-Socratic thinkers were assuming that there was some sort of underlying, formless matter that took on different forms, whereas it was just the opposite. Matter is simply not understandable in itself; it becomes intelligible in and through the different forms that make such matter come to be what it is and to behave as it does. The 'nature' of things is to be found in their forms, not in their formless matter or in some underlying primitive substance. This dramatic reversal was primarily a reversal not in thinking, but in questioning. The pre-Socratic thinkers were questioning with a false assumption, but they were unaware of the assumption and that it was false.

When the pre-Socratics asked, What is the basic stuff from which all things are made?, they were asking an unanswerable question. Thales, however, tried to answer the question by suggesting that everything was made out of a primeval water, while his fellow Ionians proposed that primeval air was the formless matter from which all things were made. The Pythagoreans did not reverse these answers; rather, they started Greek thought off on a whole new line of inquiry by making new discoveries. For example, if you d‍   ‍th of a musical string in half, it will vibrate twice as fast and   e way it sounds by an octave; if you divide it into a third   ll likewise change the behavior of the string. As the   overed, changing the ratio changes the way the string   nt on to similar discoveries and ended with the startling   he world could be explained by numbers or ratios. My   xamine Pythagorean theories, but to indicate how they   ek line of research from one way of wondering or ques-   y opposite. Instead of asking about the matter or stuff of   n wondering about the forms or proportions that made   ome to be the way they were. Plato and Aristotle differed   about what 'forms' were, but they were still both   way they wondered.

          are very rare, and when they happen they result in   remarkable advances in human understanding. The history of mathematics and physics, which I sketch in the next chapter, has several dramatic examples of inverse insights. But let me conclude my treatment of this unusual type of insight with a final example from Freud.

Before Freud, a person observing certain abnormal forms of behavior might ask, Why does that person behave in such a strange and unreasonable way? After Freud's discoveries, the question shifted to: Why do reasonable people prevent their reasoning from operating so that they can act as if they had no reason? To question unreasonable behavior as if it were reasonable is to ask the wrong question. But to wonder about the ways we successfully repress and block out our ability to reason is an extremely fertile line of inquiry. Freud gave us new ways of wondering about abnormal human behavior, and his suggestions have continued to prove productive ever since his first discoveries of the various ways we sidetrack and censor our understanding of ourselves and others. Put in a simple form, Freud taught us that we should not ask, Why does an inebriated person act unreasonably? Rather, we should wonder why a reasonable person would place himself or herself in a mental state in which his or her reason could not function properly.

5   Insight as Self-Constitutive

Thus far I have considered insight (1) as an activity that brings about a sudden illumination; (2) as an activity that is correlated with our wondering; (3) as an activity that is preconceptual, that grounds our activity of defining and thereby mediates between the abstract realm of concepts and ideas and the world of concrete, particular experiences; (4) as an activity that cumulates and expands into a stable system or viewpoint only to be destablized by further questions that cannot be answered within the range of the system and thereby tends toward a new and higher system that will subsume and enrich the prior system; and (5) as an activity that can reverse the way in which we wonder. Besides these five aspects of insight, there is one further insight into insight that needs to be appropriated and appreciated.

Insights, once they have occurred, do not disappear; they are your insights and they can recur almost whenever you want them to. In the traditional Scholastic vocabulary that goes back to Aristotle, we could characterize them as producing *habits* of understanding. Habits are usually defined as dispositions or tendencies that become a somewhat permanent part of a person's character and dispose that person to respond in certain recurrent ways. In this case, what recur are specific acts of understanding.

Insights occur in particular places and times and with reference to particular problems. Nevertheless, single insights complement or correct prior insights; they also accumulate and become the basis for continual learning. Thus the child begins by learning how to count numbers but later learns how to add, subtract, multiply, and divide them; in other words, the child forms the habit of doing arithmetic. Such a habit results from the gradual accumulation of many different insights which are constantly expanding. These accumulated insights may eventually form the rounded whole that we named 'systematic understanding' and, from there, move on to higher systems.

As a knower, then, you are continuously transforming yourself from a questioner into an understander. Further, it is not just insights that occur but, as we shall see, it is you that exist in and through these recurrent patterns of understanding. And so in appropriating your activity of understanding and the ways in which this activity cooperates with your other activities of sensing, imagining, and remembering, you are coming to a knowledge of yourself as an understander, an understander who comes to be an understander in and through your acts of understanding.

6   Empirical Residue

In the foregoing sections, I have invited you to begin to appropriate what you are doing when you are understanding. As we proceed in the following chapters, we will discover how difficult it is to distinguish your understanding from your imagining. This problem recurs in the history of mathematics and in the sciences primarily because, while you cannot understand without using images, these two quite different activities occur on two different levels of knowing. The insight is the pivot between these two different levels – the level of sensing, remembering, and imagining and the level of understanding and conceiving or defining.

Defining is a process of generalizing or universalizing, and the richer your insights, the more general or universal or comprehensive your definitions will be. The ability to classify things into genera requires a more universal or comprehensive understanding than is required to group things into species. The terms 'concrete' and 'abstract' must be carefully understood. As we shall see in a subsequent chapter, the concrete is both particular and completely comprehensive, and to be a completely concrete thinker means moving toward more and more comprehensive forms of defining. The point to be stressed here is that the opposition between the intelligible and sensible worlds, between universals and particulars, between the abstract and the concrete, can be resolved through understanding your own activity of understanding which mediates and correlates these opposite but related realms.

It should be noted that images may play pivoting roles. Besides scientific and mathematical insights, there are also symbolic and artistic insights. While scientific understanding moves steadily away from imaginable realms, the abstracting insights of symbolic and artistic patterns use images to transcend the sensible realm in a very different way. However, it is not imagination that primarily explains symbols, rather, it is the way such images are formed under the control of a person's own understanding.

Finally, there is the important category of the 'empirical residue,' which refers not only to the acquired habits of abstracting that we find among theoreticians or artists, but also to the more prevalent and spontaneous abstracting that is common to all human knowers.[12] There is a type of abstracting that occurs without your noticing it, and it happens because there are aspects of your experience that you spontaneously brush aside, consider irrelevant, and do not even bother to question. Nobody wonders why this tree is 'this' tree. You may ask, 'What is this tree,' but you do not ask about its 'thisness,' about its individuality as individual. Certainly you can sense the individual tree, and you do so immediately, but when it comes to wondering about the tree, you wonder about it as a tree, as a thing. In other words, there are aspects of your sensible experiences that are not puzzling; you pass right over these aspects, and focus instead on those qualities that are to be understood, that are intelligible. Particular places and particular times as particular are not intelligible even though they are sensibly experienced. Nobody asks, Why is now now? Or, Why is here here? You may ask, What is time? and What is space?, but those are questions about the intelligible relations among different times and different places. The difficulty in discussing the empirical residue is that you never pay attention to it even though you sense it, which makes it very difficult to discuss.

'Inverse insights' is an easier topic to discuss. With inverse insights, you pay attention, ask questions, and expect answers, when in fact there are no answers. The Greeks were convinced that there was some whole number or fraction which when multiplied by itself would equal 2, that is, $a^2/b^2 = \sqrt{2}$. Their mistake was that the $\sqrt{2}$ was actually a new kind of number, and in posing the question, What is the $\sqrt{2}$?, the Greeks had mistakenly assumed that they already knew what numbers were. In other words, they were incorrectly assuming that they had an unrestricted notion of numbers, when what they had was a very limited understanding of what numbers were. The inverse insight revealed their mistaken assumption. This is a type of 'Socratic discovery.' The Greeks disclosed a limit in their actual knowing, a limit they were unaware of. Inverse insights, then, are about the discovery of limits that are operative within your horizon, but limits you are unaware of.

The category of empirical residue is also about limits, but it is a much broader category since it refers to any and all limits that can be discovered through the activity of understanding. Certain limits are passed over or put aside so spontaneously that you hardly notice them. For example, how many different hydrogen atoms there are is a question that does not worry scientists because they spontaneously put aside the individuality of the atom. They abstract from this individuality because they do not anticipate that there is anything to be understood in it. Another example: the question of how many different places and times there have been in the universe since the first moments of its existence did not concern Einstein when he attempted to understand space and time. He attempted to grasp and explain the intelligible ordering of any and all spaces and times, but he did not attempt to explain this endless multiplicity. Rather, he spontaneously assumed that there was nothing to be apprehended in these particular times and places. While believing that there was such spatial and temporal diversity and multiplicity he did not anticipate that there was anything to be understood in such differences. What Einstein assumed was that there was an intelligible way to order all these different spaces and times in relation to one another. This meant that the differences would be 'left over' but that there would still be a cosmic design that united these differences.

The empirical residue cannot be defined directly because it cannot be known directly. It becomes identified as a difference or limit through the insights that apprehend what is to be left out, and it is left out because you consider it irrelevant for discovering the intelligibility that you are seeking to define. The reader familiar with Aristotle's notion of matter or potency and especially with his notion of prime matter will find a direct parallel with this notion of empirical residue. Matter is not intelligible in itself, but only becomes intelligible through the 'form' (i.e., the intelligibility) that realizes or actualizes that matter or potency.

This chapter has introduced you to your own activity of understanding and to the exercise of distinguishing that activity from other conscious activities closely related to it yet notably different. This process of understanding your own act of understanding has been approached by presenting many different types of insight or understanding that characterize human knowers. In the next chapter, I focus on the way insights have accumulated and brought about dramatic changes in the history of mathematics and physics.

2

Heuristic Structures

In *The Origins of Modern Science*, Herbert Butterfield suggests that the most significant event in Western history since the birth of Christ was the scientific revolution of the sixteenth and seventeenth centuries.[1] Not only did this scientific revolution overturn ancient and medieval sciences, but it also broke up the medieval tradition of Scholasticism and precipitated the rise of modern philosophies by such thinkers as Locke, Descartes, Hume, and Kant. In the previous chapter, I invited you to begin a process of self-appropriation by trying to understand what you are doing when you are involved in the activity of understanding. Now I wish to build on that preliminary foundation and invite you to appropriate how this activity of understanding was responsible for the scientific revolution of the seventeenth century.

I have already indicated in chapter 1 how Renaissance mathematicians developed a new horizon or viewpoint in mathematics which set the conditions for the remarkable expansion of mathematics in the succeeding centuries. Now I wish to trace that history in more detail and then do the same for the history of physics. Obviously, such a history will have to be selective. The norm of this selection will be to get a deeper insight into insight and the way developing understanding grounds the history of human progress. But, as we saw in chapter 1, besides insights culminating in higher systems, there are the opposite inverse insights that reverse short or long sequences of mistaken questioning and thereby open up new and extremely fertile lines of inquiry. Significant turning points in the history of mathematics and science have been greatly affected precisely by such inverse insights.

1   History of Mathematics

The mathematical success of the early Pythagoreans led to the emergence of a problem they could not solve within the context of what they already knew. In attempting to measure the diagonal of a square by taking as their measuring unit a small part of one side, the Greeks discovered that no matter how small or how large they made the measuring unit it would not fit a fixed number of times within both the side and the diagonal. The unit turned out to be either too short or too long.[2] To their chagrin, they realized that the diagonal was not measurable by the side, nor was the side measurable by the diagonal, and so they named them 'non-measurables' or 'incommensurables.'[3] The Greeks had been assuming a notion of measurement or equality among magnitudes that was quite limited, but they were unaware of what these limits were. The genius of Eudoxus, one of Plato's pupils, was to transcend these limits by redefining the meaning of a mathematical proportion as a relation between ratios that could be more, less, or equal, without stating exactly how much more or less that relation actually was. To state exactly how much more or less would require a theory of fractions which the Greeks did not have. What Eudoxus's definition did was bypass the problem.

These advances by Eudoxus are especially evident in Euclid's *Elements* and in Apollonius's *Treatise on Conic Sections*. In the first thirty-three theorems in Book I of Euclid's *Elements*, two triangles are considered equal to one another: one triangle is placed on top of the second triangle so that the two triangles coincide.[4] In other words, geometric figures are equal to or like one another if they have the exact same shape. In the thirty-fifth theorem, there is a surprising shift: two geometrical figures are considered equal even if their shapes are not congruent, provided they have the same area (Figure 2.1). Further on in Book V a dramatic new meaning of equality is introduced. Book V opens with the famous definition of proportions worked out by Plato's disciple, Eudoxus.[5] Using this definition, Euclid argues that geometrical magnitudes and figures can now be considered equal even though they may have not only different shapes, but even different sizes, provided they are 'proportionate' to one another. In the earlier books, Euclid had demonstrated how known circular figures could be used to explore and explain unknown rectilinear figures, as well as the reverse procedure. But in Book V, and in the later books, he opens the door for thinking in a series of figures related to one another in diminishing or increasing sizes. If we ask how small or how large these figures can be, the central question in the science of calculus emerges namely, how to fix the limits of a changing series of numbers or magnitudes. Euclid did not discover calculus and, before Newton and Leibniz could do so, there

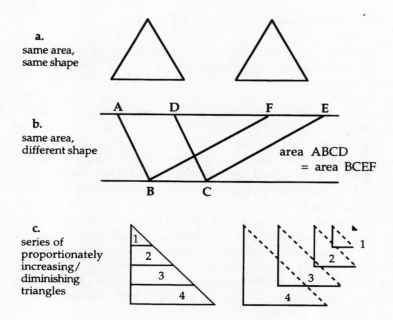

Figure 2.1 Notions of equality

would be more than a thousand years of remarkable discoveries. Why it took so much time will become clear as we proceed.

The most significant advance in the ancient world beyond Euclid was taken by Apollonius in his *Treatise on Conic Sections*.[6] Before calculus could be discovered, coordinate geometry needed to be invented, and it is in Apollonius's work that the beginnings of Cartesian coordinate geometry can be found. Following Euclid's lead in thinking in geometric proportions, Apollonius demonstrated how the familiar conic sections – parabola, ellipse, and hyperbola – can be analyzed by proportioning rectilinear figures to one another (Figure 2.2). Setting up a series of diminishing rectilinear figures is a preliminary step to learning how to graph problems, and it was by exploring this potential that late medieval thinkers set the stage for Galileo's dramatic advances in physics. In the next section, we move on to the second stage in the history of mathematics, namely, the development of symbolic algebra, coordinate geometry, and calculus.

1a Renaissance Mathematics

The pioneering figure in Renaissance mathematics was François Vièta.[7] He was the first Western thinker to say with complete generality: Let *x* equal

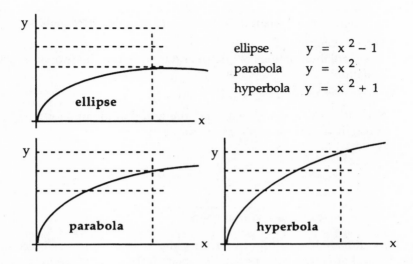

ellipse $y = x^2 - 1$
parabola $y = x^2$
hyperbola $y = x^2 + 1$

Figure 2.2 Defining the hyperbola, parabola, ellipse by co-ordinating rectilinear figures

the unknown. This simple procedure, which we all learn in school algebra, allows us to: (1) name the unknown; (2) form an equation between what we know and what we do not know; and (3) solve for what we do not know by what we do know, using simple operations of adding, subtracting, multiplying, dividing, and finding roots (Figure 2.3).

This three-step process, which seems very rudimentary, provoked a revolution in mathematical thinking. In a number of Euclid's theorems, the way he constructs and alters his diagrams provides the crucial clue for solving a number of his theorems. We saw in the first chapter that a properly presented image or an evocative way of diagramming a problem can trigger an insight. Getting the insight makes the proof suddenly luminous. But how did Euclid arrive at his insight and thus know how to draw his diagrams in such suggestive ways? In some cases, Euclid got his solutions from earlier geometers who had the original insights. But how did these original thinkers get their insights?

Vièta was convinced that the Greeks had a secret method, that they refused to reveal because they wanted to impress their audiences. In fact, what the Greeks had was theoretical wonder that transformed their sensible or imaginable experiences into potentially intelligible experiences, which eventually led to insights, insights that transformed these potentially intelligible experiences into actually intelligible experiences. Their method was a trial-and-error procedure, and while the Greeks relied on

Find a number which when doubled and increased by 10 equals 32.

(1) Let x = the number
(2) Translate the relations of known and unknown terms into an equation:

$$2x + 10 = 32$$

(3) Solve the equation by discovering the values of the unknown through known arithmetical operations:

$$2x + 10 = 32$$
$$2x = 32 - 10$$
$$2x = 22$$
$$x = 11$$

Figure 2.3 A methodical approach to mathematics

what they already knew to find what they did not know, this reliance on their prior knowledge was not an explicit, normative procedure as it became with Vièta. With his discoveries, Vièta initiated a new way of doing mathematics, namely, doing mathematics methodically. As a preliminary definition, 'method' simply means a way of discovering what you do not know. It is not a plan because planning is organizing or reorganizing what is already known. As I am using the term, 'method' emphasizes that the goal you are seeking is unknown, that you cannot plan it, but you can discover or invent it. And since all discoveries or inventions are the result of insights, we may say that method is a way of making insights more probable. Insights are made more probable when what you already know is employed as an anticipatory or heuristic structure that guides you toward a particular type of insight. How did Vièta know how to anticipate knowing the unknown? He began by naming what he did not know, which sounds strange because names are usually thought of as referring to what is already known. The name that Vièta gave the unknown was taken from a brand new language which was just emerging, the language of symbolic algebra, the language of equations in a, b, c, and x, y, z.

It is somewhat difficult to read Vièta's text because his formulations are written using both prose mathematics and symbolic mathematics. A radical decentering takes place in the shift from doing mathematics in ordinary language (prose mathematics) to thinking in abstract symbols. Certainly for Vièta this was a very difficult transition. John Wallis, a Renaissance scholar who influenced Newton, suggested that Vièta's legal background was an important asset when it came to naming the unknown since Vièta named that unknown as the member of a class. The unknown was an unknown magnitude, but it was also a member of certain known classes of magnitude (e.g., sides, squares, cubes). It was as if Vièta were saying, Let us bring a suit into court for all sides, magnitudes, or all square magnitudes – what today we call a class action suit. The unknown that Vièta was seeking was a particular side, square, or cube, but that particular unknown belonged to the general class of sides, squares, or cubes. Next Vièta arranged these genera in a hierarchical or ladder series beginning first with a side, second with a square, third with a cube, fourth with a squared square, fifth with a squared cube, sixth with a cubed cube, etc. Having established a way to classify different types of unknowns, he went on to explain how to operate on these different 'ladder magnitudes.' Thus a square divided by a side gives us a side, or a cube divided by a side gives us a square. A side multiplied by a square gives us a cube, or a square multiplied by itself gives us a squared square, and so on. It is obvious that Vièta's method is to operate on geometrical magnitudes the way we are taught in high school algebra to operate on known and unknown numbers.

While this is a remarkable advance, it also underscores the major weakness in Vièta's method, namely, his inability to abstract from geometrical images expressed as 'a square multiplied by a side gives a cube.' Today we would simply write $x^2 \cdot x = x^3$ and, for most students, the unknown x would represent a numerical variable and not a geometrical magnitude. Vièta was moving in this direction, but he was unable to abstract from geometrical images and think more abstractly, and thus more universally or in a more comprehensive fashion. There is a second weakness in Vièta's method: his inability to think in terms of two unknowns that are correlated to one another. Thus his algebraic geometry is a significant distance away from being a coordinate geometry. This point needs to be emphasized, because it is frequently assumed that analytic or coordinate geometry is simply a combination of geometry and algebra. Vièta, however, was able to combine algebra and geometry employing algebraic operations on geometric magnitudes, but because he named his geometric quantities lines, solids, and cubes, he encouraged his readers to visualize cubic and quadric equations in stereometric images (i.e., simple, readily measurable, geometric solids), rather than inviting them to think in graphic representations, which would mean thinking horizontally and vertically at the same time.

When Vièta multiplied a line by a line he got a square. Descartes, in the first section of his *Geometry*, multiplied a line by a line and got another line.[8] Descartes had began to think of geometrical quantities as replaceable by numerical quantities – another stunning leap forward. While the Greeks set up a proportion such as $A{:}B{::}C{:}D$ (i.e., $A/B = C/D$), Descartes changed it to $1{:}B{::}C{:}D$, which may be transformed into $1D = BC$ or $D = BC$. Descartes substituted unity or one for a geometrical quantity so that he no longer had to picture geometrical quantities as limited to certain shapes or even extensible quantities. The result of such a remarkable abstraction was to shift attention from the quantities or extensions to the operations that generated these extensions to the operations of adding, subtracting, multiplying, dividing, and other higher powers. But before such algebraic operations could be considered as operations in a coordinate geometry, another major step had to be taken.

There are two basic problems in analytic geometry: first, given an algebraic equation, find the corresponding locus; second, given a locus defined by a set of geometric conditions, find the corresponding equation. The first problem gives us an algebraic equation, and asks us to transform it into a geometrical solution, while the inverse problem gives a geometric locus, and asks us to transform it into an algebraic equation. Vièta was working on both problems, but he limited his unknown to a single unknown x. What was needed for analytic geometry was two unknowns that were known to be ordered to one another (co-ordered).[9] The two general unknowns were the ordinate (y) and abscissa (x), or generally located lines that could serve as general reference positions for any and all specifically positioned magnitudes. This would mean that 'Euclidean points' were no longer points but had been transformed into positions, and lines could be transformed into a series of extended and directed positions. Further, the extremities of lines were no longer points but terminal positions, and the extremities of planes were no longer lines but a series of positions. Finally, proportions were a similarity or identity no longer between ratios but between positioned or directed ratios. Thus, correlations were transformed into coordinates, which means geometric, scalar quantities became vector quantities. (Scalars and vectors, however, are much later discoveries.)

Just how difficult it was to achieve this series of advances can be seen in Descartes's own inability to think in negative coordinates. To define a point as a position without magnitude means conceiving an intelligibility that refuses to be limited by images. Images have size, but positions without magnitude have no sizes, not even infinitely small sizes. The intellect has broken through to the realm of pure intelligibility, yet intellects still need images to think even though they can and do transcend these images. The trick is to grasp that the images are simply heuristic or pointers. In breaking with a linguistic geometry and conceiving a symbolic geometry expressed in algebraic equations, Descartes transcended the limits of his own imagination. But this is not entirely true because, while Descartes accepted positive and negative number series, he could not accept positive and negative geometrical quantities. He could not conceive what a negative quantity could be. This meant that Descartes's geometry tended to be

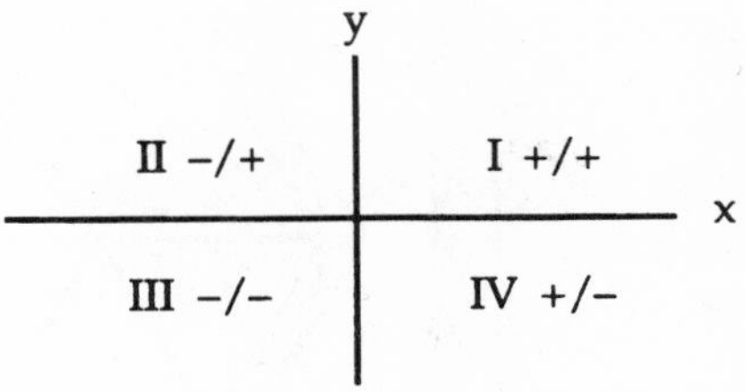

Figure 2.4 Quadrants (x,y)

restricted to the upper, right-hand quadrant and is more properly called an 'ordinate geometry' (Figure 2.4). Descartes did not invent the geometry named Cartesian coordinate geometry. The first person to use all four quadrants in a systematic fashion was most likely Newton. To what extent Newton's ability to transcend the imaginable limits that held Descartes back depended on his own discovery of calculus is an open question. But when considering what a critical step 'reversible coordinates' are in the discovery of calculus, it would seem there would be an important connection between the discovery of calculus and the ability to think in all four quadrants.

At the core of calculus lies a marvelous example of an insight. There were two familiar problems in Renaissance geometry: finding quadratures and fixing tangents to curves. Finding quadratures means finding areas under curves, while fixing tangents means ordering lines to curves so that the line touches the curve at one and only one point. By applying algebraic operations to geometrical magnitudes, as Vièta did, it is possible to grasp that areas are the result of multiplying lines together. Lines, on the other hand, are derived by finding the roots of areas; in other words, the areas that are put together by multiplying lines can be taken apart by dividing the areas back into lines. Multiplying and dividing are reversible operations, and the key to systematic thinking is to be able to operate in reversible ways. But Vièta's thinking and his modes of expressions were too closely tied to his geometrical imagination to grasp that, just as numbers can be multiplied and divided, so too geometrical quantities can be multiplied and divided. Descartes grasped that it did not make any difference whether the quantities were numerical or geometrical; what did matter was the way one operated on these quantities. While Descartes certainly realized that multiplying and dividing numbers were reversible operations, he could not generalize that reversal so that it encompassed the field of geometry. Thus, neither Descartes nor Fermat was able to grasp that problems of finding tangents to curves was the reverse problem of finding areas under curves.

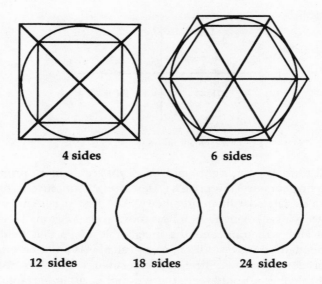

4 sides   **6 sides**

12 sides   **18 sides**   **24 sides**

Figure 2.5 Enclosed and enclosing regular polygons

Newton, who did recognize that these two problems and procedures were inversely related, was genuinely surprised that Pascal, who used the same diagrams he used, failed to grasp the reversible relations between fixing curves through tangents, and fixing the same curves through rectilinear areas.[10] The former procedure when generalized yields the basic notion of 'derivative,' and the latter when generalized yields the basic notion of 'integral'; derivatives and integrals are the basic unknowns in calculus. To put this problem in the form of a simple diagram, consider the way Archimedes posed the problem of calculus (Figure 2.5). In this diagram a square is inscribed in a circle and another square circumscribed about the same circle. By increasing the number of sides of the inner square, you a polygon is formed, which continues to enlarge until eventually the sides of the polygon tend to coincide with the circle as the areas of circle and polygon approach equality. The reverse procedure is continuously to increase the number of sides of the circumscribed square, thereby steadily decreasing its area until it tends to coincide with the circle. Such a diagram illustrates the basic problems in developing the branch of mathematics we call calculus.

First, we notice that the process of increasing and decreasing the areas are reversible operations; second, that the operations continue steadily, approaching the limit when the polygon will coincide with the circle;

and third, that as the operations continue, the magnitudes of the sides get smaller and smaller until they become infinitely small. It is easy enough to imagine that if the sides become infinitely small, they will eventually transform into infinitely tiny points, and so the points of the three figures will tend to be the same. But this is a mistake. We cannot imagine the infinitely small or large; what we can do is imagine finitely small lines and assume that they are infinitely small.[11] Here we have a simplified version of the basic problem in calculus, namely, the problem of a series of changes that continue in an orderly way toward a limit. The number of the inscribed polygon sides steadily increases as the area of the inscribed polygon approaches a limit where it will be equal to the area of the circle. And we have the reverse series of increasing sides that steadily diminish the area of the circumscribed polygon as it approaches the limit where the area of the circumscribed polygon will equal the area of the circle.

It would seem that geometric ideas such as these, which were common among the Greeks, would have readily led to the development of calculus. In fact, so difficult are the ideas involved in calculus that neither Newton nor Leibniz, who discovered and developed the procedures of calculus, was able adequately to define the basic concepts such as derivative, integral, limit, function, and number. These concepts were not rigorously defined until the middle of the nineteenth century, which meant that scientists were able to 'do' calculus long before they were able to state and define just what calculus was.

Thanks to Carl Boyer's brilliant and detailed study, *The History of Calculus and Its Conceptual Development*, we have a remarkable account of the scientists who made significant contributions to the study of calculus, including its inventors, Newton and Leibniz. Yet, as Boyer points out, all of these scientists failed in their attempts to define the basic concepts of calculus because they were unable to free themselves from their own geometrical imagination, and so continued to try to picture intelligibilities that were non-imaginable yet fully understandable. The critical step in solving this problem was to move away from geometrical terms and relations and develop a more arithmetical type of thinking. This is why Vièta's break with ordinary language as he attempted to develop a symbolic algebra was such an important first step. Vièta's move from the Greek method of geometrical algebra, and especially his ability to classify equations in terms of the powers of the operation involved in the equations, began to shift attention away from the terms and toward the operations ordering the pattern of relations among these changing terms. The significant step was to treat the terms as variables. Descartes did this when, in attempting to solve certain geometrical problems that had baffled the ancients, he discovered that his method yielded not one solution, but a series of solutions. And the series was grounded in a set of operations that could generate both numbers and/or geometrical magnitudes. The problem was how to limit this series of continuously changing numerical or geometrical ratios. To do this was to move from analytic geometry to calculus. Descartes was unable to make this move, but he set the stage for Newton's work.

Before leaving Descartes, it is important to note that he was also on the verge of the notion of function since his equations included two unknowns as variables that could be coordinated to one another. At the heart of calculus are the notions of function and limit. Functions are operations that order two or more series of changing quantities to one another. This means that the two series of changing quantities can therefore be correlated and grasped as one series. How the single series proceeds depends on the way we coordinate the two series of changing terms or variables. Thus, in a simple linear equation like $x = y$, we have a series of x and a series of y variables that change continuously, but they do so in an unchanging way, namely, the value of x will always equal the value of y. Geometrically, we can imagine the change as in Figure 2.6. If x is three units long, then y is three units long. If x is 2.3 units long, then y is the same length. We say that y varies as x, or x varies as y, or the varying values of x and y keep changing in an unchanging way. Or, geometrically, we could say that the set of points that form the diagonal of the square keeps moving in a continuous straight line whose successive positions, sizes, and shapes are a function of the position, size, and shape of the two series of points that form the changing sides of the square. This notion of a function as an unchanging correlation among changing quantities becomes the central meaning of the new notion of scientific law that emerges in the Renaissance. But before we come to this topic, I wish to draw attention to the problem of the limit, the other key idea in calculus.

With the development of coordinate geometry and the new notion of a variable, there emerged the idea of generating a series of terms as a series of sums or products, a series that can be interpreted either numerically or geometrically. This opened up the problem of how to fix the limit of such series. Newton himself was not able to resolve this problem, but he was able to grasp that the form of such numbers was a serial form. Numbers follow one another, but the way they follow depends on the way the successive terms are ordered or united. Numbers flow or proceed continuously, but the 'flow' is irrelevant and can be put aside because the relevant point is the way the flow or continuum is ordered or formed. What was missing in Newton's discovery of serial forms was an answer to the question about the limit of the series which leads to the possibility of different species of series.

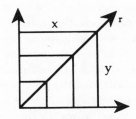

Figure 2.6 Directed posi-
tioning radius vector
(x, y, r)

1b Nineteenth-Century Mathematics

The problem for nineteenth-century mathematicians was to specify different numbers by the operations that produced the form of the series, which
in turn made the numbers what they were. Thus, the series of natural numbers 1, 2, 3, 4, 5, 6, 7, 8, 9, 10, 11, etc., is made by adding one to each number generated. Placing 'etc.' after 11, you are indicating that the series can
go on in the same way as long as you please. Or you are saying that the
operation of adding is capable of fixing a series of natural numbers by
repeating the act of adding the basic unit '1' to every successive compound
unit that we generate. Finally, if you ask, Why is the number 4 what it is?,
the answer is that 4 is a sum, and it is so because of the way you generated it
by adding 1 to 3. The 'form' of the number 4 was given to it by the operation of adding.

Once you have distinguished the form of the number from the act of
adding, you can proceed to ask, How many different forms of numbers are
there? And the answer is that it depends on how many different ways you
can actualize the forms of possible numbers. Or you may ask, What are the
properties of the operations that make this or that form or species of numbers the way they are? This is why the discovery of algebra in the Renaissance was so crucial in the development of mathematics. By stating $a + b = b$
$+ a$, you indicate that the a and b are not your concern because they can
vary. This allows you to ask, What is adding? Or, What am I doing when I
am adding? This is a new level of abstraction since you are abstracting from
the content, a and b, and focusing on the way the operation of adding
forms numbers into sums. You discover that adding is an operation that
combines numbers into a series of sums in such a way that the ordering of
the numbers added or multiplied does not make a difference, but in subtracting or dividing the order does make a difference. This can lead to the
critical discovery that adding and subtracting are reversible operations.

These four operations, two reversible pairs, form a system of operations by which you can make and remake all kinds of numbers – sums, products, quotients, and remainders. This points to the further discovery in the nineteenth century that it is possible to shift from one system of number species to a higher system that includes and transcends the lower system because the higher system exploits potentialities in numbers that the lower forms did not develop. Thus, the previous example of $a + b = b + a$ shows that adding can form numbers in different ways. One simple sequence 1, 2, 3, 4, etc., reveals that numbers can be formed into a unified series of sums by adding, but numbers can also be added non-sequentially into a final sum: $1 + 2 + 3 + 4 = 10$, or $4 + 2 + 1 + 3 = 10$. This means that the sum 10 can be produced through a sequential serial order, but numbers can also be combined non-sequentially into the same sum. We count serially with numbers so frequently that we forget that numbers can also be thought of as a collection or aggregate that is not serialized. This is, of course, the foundational distinction between ordinal and cardinal numbers, but it was only by generating new species of numbers that Cantor showed the foundational importance of this distinction.

To clarify this point, let us consider how molecular arrangements can be reordered into a series of different plant species. New species of plants reveal new ways of transforming underlying molecular processes into different series of biochemical forms. Similarly, new species of numbers reveal that, for the higher system, the lower species of numbers can be considered as coincidental aggregates or potencies which are transformable into new and higher species. For the Greeks, $\sqrt{2}$ is not related to the natural numbers. But for Dedkind, who formulated a more general class of real numbers, the irrational numbers are simply a subspecies of this larger class. The irrational numbers also provided a way of limiting the class of natural numbers and at the same time they opened up the possibility of a new class of numbers. Together with the natural numbers, these new classes of numbers form the more comprehensive class of real numbers. To understand how this sort of transformation operates, it is important to recall that for the Greeks the $\sqrt{2}$ posed a limit to their mathematical thinking. However, as we saw in the first chapter, a limit can be understood in two different ways. First, a limit is a barrier that prevents you from moving on. But, in a second sense, a barrier can also be an opportunity: it reveals the fact that your previous thinking was limited, and it provokes you to transcend the limit. As a limit, it is unknown; as an opportunity, it becomes a known-unknown. And so you can think of $\sqrt{2}$ as both a limit to the rational numbers and an opening to a new species of numbers.

With all the new species of numbers being generated in the nineteenth century, the old Greek problem of the infinite emerged again as a central issue in mathematics.[12] The problem of the infinite made it possible for mathematicians to discover a mistake not only that mathematicians make, but that all human knowers keep making. It is that we do not know the infinite even though we keep imagining the infinite, and mistaking our presumed images of the infinite for an understanding of the infinite. To understand 'infinitely' is to understand everything about everything. Let us take the example of the ordinary number series, 1, 2, 3, 4, etc. Since the series can continue indefinitely, you may assume that 'infinity' is a number that belongs to this series. But the form of such a series is a series of terms generated by adding to any number the unit one $(n + 1)$. This is a very limited form of operating. What is endless or infinite is the matter or numerical possibilities that can be extended continuously by the operation of adding. Further, this indefinite potency is only actualized through the single form of adding, and so the form of this series is in fact a very limited form. The problem is your imagination. You mistakenly assume that your image is endless. How and why your imagination misleads you into thinking you know the infinite is a central theme of this whole study, and I will return to it throughout the succeeding chapters.

Two results of these developments in nineteenth-century mathematics should be noted. First, the foundation of mathematics became an important question in a quite new way. Second, the notion of a group became a central category in mathematics and, as assimilated by Piaget and other structuralists in our present century, it has become a basic conceptual tool in many non-mathematical disciplines. I would like to finish this brief history of mathematics with a few comments on both discoveries, beginning with the role of higher viewpoints or systems.

The hierarchical relation of systems can be seen if you consider the way we think of adding and subtracting whole numbers, fractions, powers and roots, integrals and derivatives. To test your own understanding of the different meanings of multiplying and dividing, ask yourself, Why is it that, when dividing one fraction by another fraction, you invert the divisor and multiply? We all know that the rules for multiplying and dividing fractions are different than those for whole numbers. The same is true for powers and roots. New rules have to be learned for multiplying and dividing whole numbers and whole numbers with exponents. Why are the 'laws of exponents' what they are? Or, moving on to signed numbers, Why is it that when you multiply a negative number by a negative number, you get a positive number? Why do the rules say what they do?

Unless you grasp how prior ways of operating on whole numbers can be adapted and extended to fractions by a more comprehensive understanding of what you are doing when adding, subtracting, multiplying, and dividing, you will not understand how the system that can construct (add, multiply) and deconstruct (divide, subtract) both whole numbers and fractions is a more flexible, comprehensive system. The same is true as you ascend to the system that can construct and deconstruct powers and roots (algebraic systems), derivatives, and integrals (calculus). At each level the new system moves to a higher and more comprehensive range of operations by reverting to lower numbers and magnitudes and discovering new possibilities or variabilities that the lower systems are not exploiting.

Moreover, the higher system of algebra does not negate or reverse the lower system of arithmetic, but leaves it free and autonomous to operate on its own level of meanings. In other words, you can do arithmetic or you can do algebra, but when you are doing algebra, you are also doing arithmetic because you transform the numbers into variables, letting yourself forget about them, in order to concentrate on the operations that control these variables. If we examine the hierarchical theory that is evolving in contemporary biological research, we find the same sort of thinking exemplified in the way that molecular processes become the variables that fall under the operational control of cells. Again, the key is the assumption that the lower variables, which may seem predetermined on the lower level, can be transformed and reorganized at the higher level.

2   History of Modern Physics

2a From Copernicus to Newton

Renaissance physics begins with Copernicus's decentering and recentering of the universe, moving from an earth-centered perspective to a sun-centered horizon.[13] Commentators have pointed out that a comparison of the patterning of the planets by Copernicus and Ptolemy do not seem to differ in any dramatic fashion. However, the implications and consequences of Copernicus's theory were far-reaching, especially in the context of Aristotle's basic distinction between things as they are related to us and things as they are in themselves, that is, in their relations to one another.

Things are related to you primarily through your sensory-motor system which continuously receives sensations both from the world around you and from inwardly-felt corporeal experiences. In contrast to these immediately inward and outward sensible experiences, there is the immediate, conscious experience of an unknown world that is present to you through your wondering and questioning. Both the sensible and the unknown worlds are immediate and become mediated through language. However, the immediate sensible, inner and outer world is a vector-world, and these vectors are consciously felt as up-down, right-left, front-back; these directed feelings are centered within your own sensory-motor system. In other words, you have a sensory-motor or skeletal-muscular coordinate system of felt vectors that orients your conscious, corporeal self to the world around you.

As Piaget pointed out, this sensory-motor system of consciously felt vectors is developed and mastered during the first two years of your life. In the next stage, you learn how to mediate this immediate sensible world through language as a linguistic up-down mediates your immediately felt up-down. You also learn to decenter yourself from your own sensory-motor coordinate system and recenter your corporeal frame of feelings with respect to other persons' up-down, left-right, front-back. But such recentering and shifting of perspectives is done within the familiar and consciously felt earth-centered world. Copernicus, on the other hand, proposed to recenter the universe in a way that radically altered the center of the universe and, in doing so, he raised fundamental questions, not only about the cosmological order, but more significantly about the very foundations of the ways we know.

Copernicus's new system of the heavens made slow progress until it was taken up by Galileo over one hundred years later. While some of Copernicus's ideas challenged Aristotle's theories of the universe, Copernicus left intact the fundamental distinction between the perfect, incorruptible order of the celestial spheres and the imperfect, corruptible order of terrestrial living things. Galileo's telescope changed that when he discovered that the moon showed evidence of being made out of the same 'stuff' as the earth, and also that the moons of Jupiter went around their own planet and not around the sun. While the sun centered the planets, the planets centered their respective moons. Galileo's astronomical discoveries were dramatic and controversial, but much more significant was his contribution to terrestrial mechanics.

What is significant for our discussion is, not the content of Galileo's discoveries, but the cognitional implications of his thinking. Just as Copernicus had advanced Aristotle's distinction between descriptive knowing of things in relation to our sensory-motor system and things as related to one another in an explanatory context, so Galileo advanced the same distinction. If you judge the speed of falling bodies by your skeletal-muscular sensations of heavy and light, then you would expect heavy objects to fall faster than light objects, as, of course, they do. But if you suspect that the weight of objects does not explain the why of falling bodies, then you can suggest that an observer should abstract from the way things fall and pay attention to the distance through which the body falls and the time it takes to traverse those distances. How did Galileo come to suspect that weight was not the cause or the why of falling bodies? The suggestion was not new. There was a long history of objections about Aristotle's explanation of falling bodies. Galileo's major achievement was to do for the science of motion what Euclid had done for the science of geometry. In Galileo's *Two New Sciences*, there is the second 'new' science, what today is called 'kinematics' (a study of motion without considering force and mass). Many of the theorems in Galileo's systematic treatment had been worked out by his predecessors, but nobody had ever assembled them into a systematic treatise, using the same form as Euclid had used in constructing his systematic treatise on geometry.

Galileo begins by defining uniform motion, or what we call constant velocity. He proceeds to a definition of acceleration which is derived from his earlier definition of velocity. While velocity is defined in terms of durations and distances, acceleration is defined in terms of changing velocities, or the rate at which the velocity is changing. Two things need to be noted about these definitions. First, Aristotle had defined velocity in terms of the forces that were exerted on the object; thus, a greater force would produce a proportionately greater velocity. Galileo, in contrast, abstracted from force. Second, Aristotle defined the velocity as directly proportionate to the force and inversely proportionate to the resistance ($V = F/R$). Galileo, on the other hand, abstracted from resistance. Why does Aristotle include force, weight, and resistance when explaining the cause or the why of motion, while Galileo excluded them? As we noted in chapter 1, scientists exclude or abstract from certain factors because they realize that these factors are not essential in understanding the causes of motion. Both Aristotle and Galileo understood the cause of motion to be a proportion (a form), but they differed in what the contents of that proportion would be. An important clue to Galileo's understanding is the fact that he distinguished very carefully between velocity and acceleration; Aristotle did not. This does not mean that Aristotle was wrong; it means that Galileo was more abstract, that is, more comprehensive. Furthermore, acceleration cannot be observed, as Galileo defined it; it is not possible to see continuously changing velocities. When trying to observe a stone fall at steadily increasing speeds, you can see things speed up and slow down, but you cannot observe a continuously increasing velocity. Finally, Galileo's paradigm for studying motion was the pendulum. He observed that pendulums of different weights but of the same lengths took the same time to complete a full swing which suggested that weight may not be the significant variable. Also, pendulums traveling through shorter or longer arcs completed their swings in the same times, and so the distance of the drop of the pendulum, and not the distance of the arc, proved to be a critical variable (Figure 2.7). These observations provided clues for conjecturing that bodies of different weights would fall at identical rates, if we abstracted from the resistances of the media through which they fall. Thus, Galileo, moved into a new field of intelligibilities.

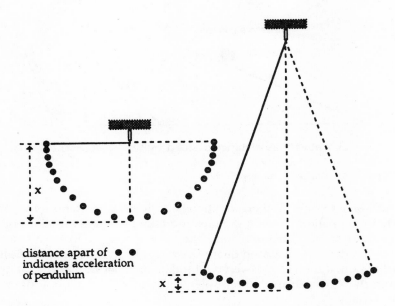

distance apart of ● ●
indicates acceleration
of pendulum

Figure 2.7 Depth of arc (x), the critical variable in timing the swing of the pendulum

Although most of the theorems Galileo proposed and demonstrated were to a large extent already known, two aspects were original. He set up an organized science that analyzed different species of free-falling bodies, and he did what the earlier Scholastics had never done: he set up experiments to test his arguments and conclusions.

The medieval Scholastics had worked out the mean speed rule, which states that the average velocity of a free fall was one-half of the sum of the initial and final speeds. But no one had ever thought it was necessary to test this rule. Why, then, did Galileo decide to move in the direction of an experiment? Galileo was arguing in a fundamentally different framework since he was assuming the Copernican context, which meant that the earth was moving around the sun. Further, while any number of scholastics had distinguished uniform velocity and uniform acceleration, no one had actually measured what the precise ratio was at which uniform acceleration occurred. Finally, to test for acceleration was to test for something that could not be observed, and so required a further, remarkable insight to figure out how to set up an experiment that would verify such a hypothesis. Galileo's insight was to slow down the fall, letting balls roll down a very smooth channel sixteen feet long. Then he compared the times it took to roll down shorter channels at the same height, and found the times were

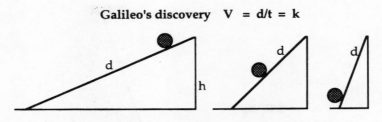

velocity as distance divided by time is constant

Figure 2.8 Galileo's discovery $V = d/t = k$

proportional to one another, which meant the measurements were different but the relation between the measured distances and durations of the
longer and shorter channels were the same (Figure 2.8). As we would
phrase it today, the measured quantities varied in an invariant way. Galileo
concluded that he had discovered a fundamental law of nature that operated in the same way in different places and times, discounting the resistance variable.

However, it is on the 'fourth day' of Galileo's dialogue in his *Two New Sciences* that his genius shines the brightest. As Galileo noted, people had previously observed that projectiles when fired follow a curved path. But no
one however had been able to analyze the curve and demonstrate that it
was a parabola.[14] In analyzing the curve of projectiles and showing the
parabola, Galileo was able to carry abstract thinking into a whole new area
of understanding. Apollonius, in his *Treatise on Conic Sections*, had shown
how the conic curves could be constructed by cutting a cone with a large
plane (Figure 2.9). Just as he had extended Euclid's analysis, so Galileo
assimilated and accommodated Apollonius's analysis into problems of
physics. Galileo deconstructed a single curvilinear motion into two
continuously changing rectilinear motions. Let us consider the case of a
projectile fired from the muzzle of a gun. The projectile, once fired, is sub-
jected to two forces: the vertical, downward force of gravity and the forward, horizontal, inertial force. These two forces combine to produce a
downward curving path. The shape of the path depends on the muzzle
velocity of the gun (assuming gravity stays the same). Galileo knew from
Apollonius how to construct various curves, and he knew from the medieval Scholastics how to plot two different changing geometrical quantities
as a series of changing physical quantities. It sounds easy once the insights
have occurred and have been conceived, but without the original insights,
the problem is not even a problem.

What is especially interesting is the way Newton assimilated and accom-

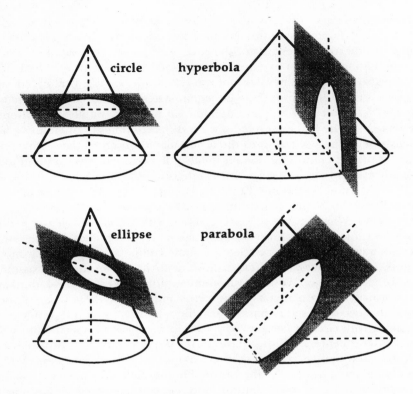

Figure 2.9 Apollonius' conic sections

modated Galileo's geometrizing of the problem of projectiles and used it as the foundation for constructing a new ordering of the entire universe. But before Newton, there were four other significant figures: Kepler, Brahe, Descartes, and Christian Huygens. Together they set the stage for Newton's new cosmological order. While Galileo was working out a new science of terrestrial motions, Kepler was constructing a new patterning of celestial motions.

It is not certain that Galileo had ever read Kepler's publications of his new planetary laws but, if he did, he dismissed them. This is especially ironic because Kepler, like Galileo, was trying to advance the Copernican solar-centered framework. Like Galileo, he was convinced that nature was uniform, and that a simpler and more systematic account of the planetary system could be discovered by a more careful geometrizing of the problem. However, Kepler was working in a very different context than Galileo because he had inherited an extraordinary accumulation of observational data on planetary positions. Kepler was the assistant to Tycho Brahe, one of the most famous astronomers in Europe and the first astronomer to keep careful nightly records of the successive planetary positions. Besides accumulating the most extensive and detailed observations of the planets, Brahe also put forth a new cosmology. Like Copernicus's, Brahe's cosmology was a transformation of the Ptolemaic system, but unlike Copernicus's, Brahe's cosmology was geocentered. In his first publication, Kepler recorded that he had attempted seventy different times to fit either Copernicus's or Brahe's system into the accumulated observed data. Only after these repeated failures did Kepler finally put aside what was common to all the ancient and modern cosmological theories: the circle.

Plato, Aristotle, Ptolemy, Copernicus, and Tycho Brahe were all convinced that the planetary movements had to be circular, either simple or compound. Why were they so preoccupied with the circle? Heavenly bodies were thought to be more perfect than terrestrial bodies, and the most perfect way to move is in a circle or in some combination of circular movements, such as epicycles. Circular movements had been the basic assumption of all the major Western astronomers since the early Greek thinkers. To discard circular planetary movements and replace them with elliptical motions was Kepler's remarkable achievement. A second problem in breaking with circular celestial paths was losing the center of the universe. Circles have centers. Ellipses have, not a single center, but two foci. For Aristotle and Galileo, natural motion was motion toward the center. While, for Galileo, weight was not the cause of bodies falling to the earth, falling toward the center was the natural movement of terrestrial bodies, just as moving circularly was natural for celestial bodies. It is interesting to note that Kepler's second law not only was understood and formulated before his first law, but was conceived on the assumption of circular, not elliptical, movements. Kepler corrected this mistake when he finally abstracted from circular orbits and began to consider other types of curved orbits.

There was another fundamental difference between Galileo's law of terrestrial motion and Kepler's law of celestial motion. Galileo had abstracted from weight and other forces as he was able to conceive an idealized mathematical motion. In this context, Galileo formulated a science of kinematics (without notions of force and mass), and not a science of dynamics. Kepler, on the other hand, attempted to construct a celestial dynamics by proposing that the planets were held in their orbits by a force emanating from the sun. Kepler even suggested that such a force emanating from the moon might explain the changing tides on earth. But what was the nature of this mysterious solar force that governed the planets and directed them along their elliptical paths? It was questions like this one that made the whole of Kepler's system highly dubious, and so Kepler's three laws remained at the periphery of the new cosmological context that began to emerge during the first part of the seventeenth century.

The next key figure in establishing this new scientific context was Descartes. Living as we do in the late twentieth century, long after nature has been stripped of mythical and occult powers, it is difficult to appreciate just why this mythical view was such a long and troublesome problem, and also why Descartes, along with most of the scientists of his day, insisted on a mechanical philosophy of nature that made no appeal to hidden, mysterious, and occult causes.[15] What these thinkers wanted was a mechanical explanation of how the universe operated, and the first systematic attempt to provide such an explanation was given by Descartes. Descartes's problem was, first, to transform Galileo's kinematics into a mechanics and, second, to correct Kepler's celestial mechanics and, finally, to join them together into a general science of mechanics that would explain both terrestrial and celestial motions. Descartes failed to solve the first two problems, but in trying to construct a new world system, he set forth a basic premise that became the fundamental axiom in Newton's new world order, namely, the principle of inertia.

The principle of inertia is another example of an inverse insight that dramatically changes, not the contents of science, but the way that scientists wonder. For Galileo, circular motion was not a problem, but it was for Descartes because, in his view, bodies naturally tended to move in straight lines, not circles. So if the planets were moving in circular paths, then scientists had a problem. What caused these planets to change from their natural straight line motion and follow a curved motion? According to Descartes, bodies naturally tended to travel with a uniform velocity; if bodies were accelerating, as Galileo's law states, then what was causing them to accelerate? Descartes's explanation was that they were forced to behave that way by pressures created by whirlpools of fluids composed of tiny, invisible particles which filled the universe. This was Descartes's famous theory of the vortices, which had wide appeal at the time primarily because it provided a mechanical explanation of the impact that swirling fluids had on larger bodies: swirling fluids transmitted their motion to larger bodies. At the core of this theory of vortices was the problem of what happens when one body strikes another body. Here was a problem that needed the sort of mathematical idealization that Galileo had given to falling bodies and projectiles. Descartes never attempted such an analysis, but his disciple Christian Huygens did.

This problem is more complicated than Galileo's falling bodies because it involves two bodies and, therefore, the problem of shifting from one perspective to the other. For Descartes, moving and resting were relative terms, but when Huygens attempted to analyze the way an object, either at rest or in motion, impacts another object, either at rest or in motion, he found a contradiction in Descartes's explanation of the way one body can move another body without any loss of motion.[16] Huygens proceeded to work out the kinematics of impacting bodies in the same way that Galileo had solved the problem of falling bodies. He discovered that it was not a set quantity of motion that was being conserved, as Descartes thought, but a different quantity: momentum (mv).

Huygens next turned to the problem of circular motion, again following Descartes's basic principle of inertia: all bodies tend to move in a straight line away from the center at a uniform velocity. Huygens's experimental model was the sling which was used to restrain a whirling stone. It was in this experimental context that weight as a force re-entered the emerging theoretical context. If you swing a stone in a circle, you can feel the weight of the stone as a force pulling the string, as the stone 'tries' to escape and fly off in a straight line. Weight, in this context, becomes a center-fleeing force and a force that will increase as you increase the speed of the mass that orbits around and around. This means that the force required to hold the stone in its moving circular path is proportional to increases in the escape velocity of the stone, which implies that the force is proportional, not to velocity, but to changing velocities or acceleration. Huygens worked out the exact mathematical proportion ($F = mv^2/r$), and employed these new mathematical meanings to interpret the dynamics of pendulum motions. Thus, we have for the first time a correlation between weight and acceleration and, what is even more significant, a mathematical analysis of circular motions.

Let us look closely at what Huygens achieved. Galileo had put aside weight, force, and resistance as 'causes' of motion, but the enriching side of his abstraction was to discover an 'invisible' but intelligible and measurable cause of motion, namely, acceleration (I say 'invisible' because continuous acceleration cannot be observed). Galileo's abstraction introduced into science the concepts of velocity and acceleration, precisely defined and experimentally verified. Huygens followed the same method: precise mathematical analysis coupled with experimental verification of highly abstract concepts. Huygens provided science with two of the causes of motion which had been put aside by Galileo. These causes were mathematically verified correlations of force, mass, and velocity. Today we know that weight is defined as mass times acceleration (ma) and that this is a force. In fact, $F = ma$ is Newton's second law.

What was going forward in Renaissance physics was a double movement. On the one hand, the sensible world of familiar things was being transcended by powerful abstractions that provided scientists with universal or comprehensive correlations among continuously moving masses; on the other hand, carefully conceived experimentations were being employed to verify these abstract, comprehensive correlations. The result was a new type of law, which we call the 'classical law.'

In the second paragraph of his first book on physics, Aristotle stated: 'the natural way to proceed is from what is more known and clearer to us to what is by nature clearer and more known.' I have referred to this distinction as the difference between descriptive and explanatory knowing. Scientists begin by describing things, but eventually they break with the descriptive or sensibly observable properties of things and begin to correlate the measurable properties of things to one another. Galileo made this break. It was a momentous one because it moved science in one small area into a strictly explanatory context. He did so by powerful mathematical abstractions that dramatically extended the universality of scientific understanding. Equally important, Galileo learned how to transform mathematical concepts into physically measurable concepts. Thus, science was advancing in two different ways, from the top down via mathematical developments and from the bottom up via the generation of experimental data. Christian Huygens was a key player in this advance, along with a number of other important figures who together set the stage for Newton's new ordering of the universe.

2b Newton's New World-Order

There are a number of ways of summarizing Newton's contributions. One way is this: Galileo worked out a terrestrial kinematics while Kepler proposed a celestial dynamics, and Newton's task was to combine the two into a new science of mechanics or dynamics. Galileo's terrestrial kinematics had to be transformed into a terrestrial dynamics and Kepler's attempt at a celestial dynamics had to be refined and corrected. A second way: Galileo's laws specified how terrestrial bodies moved, but did not explain why they moved with a continuous acceleration. Kepler's laws stated what the shapes, sizes, and periods of planetary motions are, but he did not explain why the planetary orbits have these shapes, sizes, and periods. A third way of approaching Newton's contributions is to see that Newton took Galileo's basic terms and relations – distance, time, velocity, and acceleration – added to these mass and force, and then proceeded to combine these terms in various ways to demonstrate how Galileo's and Kepler's laws could be derived as special cases of his more general law. In other words, Newton had to transform the planetary laws of motion and the law of falling bodies into specific examples of a single universal law. But to do this, he needed the basic assumption of his own first law, and new definitions of force and mass, which he worked out in his second and third laws.

Inverse insights reorient the way scientists wonder, but they also presume a major advance in understanding that sets the stage for realizing that the prior way of putting the question was misleading. Just how Descartes and Newton arrived at the principle of inertia would require a more careful analysis than is possible here, but certainly their respective discoveries in mathematics must have played a significant role. In discussing the history of mathematics, we saw that Descartes, unlike the Greeks, could multiply a line by a line and get a line. He could think of a line as a series of numerical products which could be extended indefinitely, and he could also think of a curve as a series of intersecting straight lines. To break with circular inertia and move to rectilinear inertia was certainly related to his own ability to abstract from images and think instead in different species of intelligible but unimaginable series. Likewise, the fact that Newton was probably the first person to think in terms of reversible series of quadratures and tangents was certainly critical to his ability to conceive of planetary orbits as compound vectors that could be deconstructed into centrifugal and centripetal rectilinear vectors. Moreover, if we examine Newton's three basic laws, we can grasp why he was able to take advantage of the principle of inertia in a way that Descartes could not.

The law of inertia, Newton's first law, states that a body will remain in a state of rest or in a state of motion unless it is acted upon by an unbalanced force. This law covers resting and moving masses as two different but related states. This can be clarified if we state the second law algebraically, as it is familiarly given: If $F = ma$, then $F - ma = 0$, and so zero acceleration is a limit case of Newton's second law. How this limit case applies to the first law can be seen if we notice that the first law is not about the way bodies change, but about their ability to resist changes, namely, if a body is in a balanced state, it is in an unchanging state. It makes no difference whether the balanced state is zero miles per hour, or a hundred miles per hour. The first law, then, introduces a definition of inertia, or that property of a body by which it can resist changes and preserve its present state of resting or moving.

The second law ($F = ma$) is concerned with the way a body changes its state or form of motion by means of a force. Force is defined as that which effects a change in the velocity (i.e., acceleration), but it is also defined as giving direction to that change. Force, therefore, is defined as a vector quantity which, when impressed upon a body, will direct changes in the velocity of that body in the direction toward which the force is applied. If the body is moving horizontally and the force is impressed vertically, then the force will effect an acceleration not in the horizontal, but in the vertical direction (Figure 2.10). What Newton had in mind here is probably Galileo's deconstructing of a projectile's motion into a horizontal velocity

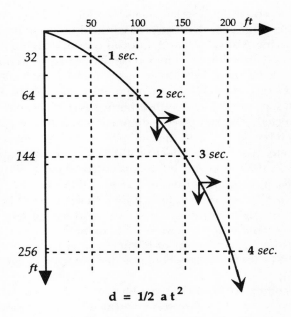

Figure 2.10 Galileo's deconstruction of projectile motion
into two rectilinear forces

and into a downward vertical acceleration. Or, more generally, a body can
be receiving accelerating forces from many different directions, and the
actual accelerating path of the body will be the resultant combination
reached by adding up all the vectors. (However, such vector addition is a
nineteenth-century invention.) The familiar algebraic statement of the second law is $F = ma$. It is easy to grasp in the formula that the second law is a
definition of force as an acceleration, but it also includes a definition of
mass that comes from the first law. This law can be phrased algebraically as
follows: if $F = ma$, then $F - ma = 0$. The '$-ma$' refers to the ability of a mass to
resist change and remain inert, so the '$-ma = I$' (inertia). $F + I = 0$ would,
therefore, be a restatement of the second law in terms of the first law. And
so the second law gives us our first definition of mass as inertial mass. This
is important because, if we shift to the third law, we have a further definition of mass as gravitational mass.

The third law states that when one body exerts a force on a second body,
the second body exerts a force of equal magnitude but opposite in direction and along the same line of action. It is important to notice how this
law relates to the first law: the first law specifies the way bodies resist being
changed, but the third law specifies the way bodies attract one another. It

should also be noted that the law states that forces always act in pairs, or that they operate reciprocally. The law is difficult to grasp because you can imagine A forcing B or B forcing A, but you cannot imagine A and B operating in opposed directions simultaneously. The third law is not only a relation of A to B, but a correlation of A to B and B to A. Moreover, the correlation is a directed correlation, and so it is a coordination. A attracts B in a directed way and B attracts A in the opposite direction. A and B are mutually directed. The sun gives a directed action to the earth, and the earth gives a directed action to the sun, but because the mass of the sun is so much greater, the earth's effect on the sun is negligible, though real. The earth pulls the moon and the moon pulls the earth. Trying to figure out the mutual attractions of the sun, earth, and moon, or any three planets gives us the 'three body problem' that Newton faced but could not solve. But having defined forces and masses and having recontextualized his predecessor's definitions, Newton could demonstrate that Kepler's and Galileo's laws were special cases of his new system of terms and relations (f, m, v, a, d, t) or that their laws could be derived from the general law $F = G\,(m_1 \cdot m_2)/r^2$.

This new context of meanings established by Newton posed a major problem. If every mass in the universe is attracted by, and resistant to, every other mass in the universe, how could a scientist ever select a coordinate system for ordering the masses of this universe to one another in any 'certain and necessary' way? Scientific measurements could not be the same everywhere because 'everywhere' is related to its local field of forces, and there seems to be no universal, homogeneous 'where' that would remain the same throughout the universe. Whatever physical body or place scientists use as the origin of the coordinating system, with which they intend to measure their data, will not be a fixed, unchanging body or place. According to the universal law of gravitation, there is no physical framework free of gravitational forces, and so any particular framework will be moving at a different accelerating speed, at a different time, and in a different direction than any other physical framework. The problem is, therefore, how can scientists make spatiotemporal measurements in one framework and transfer these measurements to other, differently moving frameworks? Or how can scientists make measurements that would be valid for all possible frameworks?

Newton was perhaps the first person to think within a four-quadrant coordinate system, capable of systematically transferring every point in Euclidean space into a position, and then correlating every position to every other by coordinating them all to the centering coordinate, zero, where all opposed directions could be both reversed and united. The problem was to find a physical center for uniting all the differently moving masses to one another. Our personal and public coordinate systems are not valid in every place and time, but only in very limited perspectives, and so it was necessary to abstract from these perspectives and ground the new order of the universe in an unlimited or absolute framework that would not vary from one year to the next or from one spatial center to another. The only option, Newton thought, would be an absolute, unlimited, spatiotemporal framework. To accomplish this, he centered his new universal world-order in an absolute infinite space and in an absolute unchanging time. This absolute infinite framework does not in fact exist, yet it took scientists two hundred years to reverse this foundational mistake.

2c From Newton to Contemporary Physics

Newton had assumed that a solar-centered framework was a motionless framework just like the so-called fixed stars. Yet, according to Newton's own first law, it was possible and even consistent to assume that the sun, as well as all the so-called fixed stars, were moving. This would mean, of course, that all physically centered frameworks were moving, and that there was no stationary or privileged center in our universe, nor would there be any privileged position from which to measure distances, durations, velocities, and accelerations. But if there was no privileged center, perhaps there was a privileged 'now,' present everywhere at the same time, which could provide a common standard for measuring all the temporal changes observed in the different frameworks. This was the assumption of scientists from the time of Galileo until Einstein.

Thus we come to the difficult question of time. For Aristotle, time was the numbering and measuring of local motions derived from successively traversed distances. Since there were many local motions, it follows that there were many different times, but these differences could be united if it is assumed that the outermost sphere of the heavens provided observers with a standard motion, to which all other motions can be referred. However, this basic standard was removed when Copernicus decentered and recentered the order of the universe. As a result, Newton proposed a mathematical time that was conceived as having the same properties as his absolute mathematical space. This absolute time, like absolute space, was perfectly homogeneous, infinitely continuous, and infinitely divisible into intervals that smoothly succeeded one another and flowed in a perfectly endless stream.

An important feature of this notion of time was that, while changes occurred in this time, the time itself remained perfectly the same everywhere. Thus, time is not affected by the changes that occur within it. While there is temporal succession, there is no beginning or end, no past or present, since this would mean that the first and last intervals would be different from the other intervals. Time does not become, but always was and always will be. Motion occurs in time, things exist in time, but time itself does not change: it is everlastingly the same. Time, like space, is empty, and so things exist and move in this infinitely empty space and time. However, Einstein proved that there was no such thing as infinite space and time.[17]

When Einstein was asked how his notion of space and time differed from Newton's, he responded that, if Newton's universe was emptied of everything in it, there would still be an infinite space and infinite time remaining, but if his universe was emptied, there would be no space and time left over. In other words, Einstein achieved a fundamental reversal of the basic limits of the Newtonian universe. And he did it by following the method of science, which includes not only the indirect verification or correction of prior scientific conclusions, but also a correction of the basic pattern of terms and relations (i.e., d, t, v, a, m, f).

Strange as it may seem, scientists do not trust either Newton's or Einstein's theory; rather, they trust their own minds and their ability to operate in accord with the mind's own normative procedures for advancing, correcting, and even reversing the basic discoveries of earlier scientists. The most dramatic instance of this is an inverse insight, which is what Einstein achieved.

Einstein eliminated the hidden assumption of absolute space and time which no scientist had ever verified. He did so because the scientific method includes as one of its normative procedures a complete explanation of the physical universe. Galileo, Newton, and others assumed, but did not verify, absolute space and time, and it was this false assumption that led them to overlook the need to explain why space and time are the way they are. For Newton, the gravitational equations explained why things move in space and time the way they do; for Einstein, it is the reverse – space and time are the way they are because accelerating gravitational fields make them behave the way they do. In Aristotelian terms, space and time are the matter, while gravity is the form. It is a fundamental mistake to think that matter explains form; it is the form that causes the matter to be the way it is.

Obviously, Einstein did not explain his theory of relativity in this way, but there are certain key points in Einstein's own context that allow for this kind of interpretation. Einstein set down two basic assumptions. First, the laws of physics are the same for all scientists who observe and measure physical processes in inertial (non-accelerating) frameworks. The second postulate limits just how fast these inertial frames can move, namely, the speed of light. There are similarities between Newton's postulate of inertia and these two postulates, but there are also important modifications. The most obvious is that there is no set limit to velocities in Newton's proposed universe, whereas there is a definite 'speed-limit' in Einstein's universe. Also, Newton is dealing with the science of dynamics, but Einstein is generalizing Newton's postulate to include all known physical laws, including the optical laws of electromagnetic radiation. Further, for Newton there is no explicit reference to scientific observers and their respective measuring frames, whereas Einstein is drawing attention to the process of scientific measuring and is making a basic distinction between the values or contents of measurements and the pattern of relations among these measurements. This last point is critical. In Galileo's and Newton's time, scientists did not express laws in precise mathematical form as they do today. Thus, the kind of mathematical law discovered by Galileo can be stated in the algebraic form: $v = d/t$ or $d = v/t$. If we define a scientific law such as $v = d/t$ as a normative, unchanging pattern of relations among changing variables, then the variables are d, v, and t, but the way these variables vary is determined by the operations implied in the expression $v = d/t$, that is, velocity is a quotient determined by dividing the distances traversed by the durations which elapsed in traveling those distances. Einstein's first postulate distinguishes the variations of v, d, and t from the invariant way they are related. The velocities, distances, and times keep changing but the way they change is unchanging.

This is an Aristotelian form/matter distinction: the form is the invariant pattern of the relations and the matter is the changing variables. Einstein is not saying that physical measurements will be the same in different, inertial frames; he is saying that there is an invariant pattern within the changing measurements. The variable values, namely, the measurements, can be different in the two frames, but the pattern of relations, or the function, will be the same. But how is this different from what Einstein's fellow scientists were saying at the turn of the century?

While most scientists would not have been able to distinguish the invariant from the variable contents in the explicit way that Einstein did, it was certainly implicit in their thinking. Moreover, in shifting from one frame to another, scientists had already worked out how the actual measurements of lengths could contract in shifting from one inertial frame at a lower constant velocity to a second inertial frame at a higher constant speed, and how temporal measurements could dilate in the same type of transformation. In working out these transformations, the scientists clung to an infinite or absolute frame; they did not realize the radical and foundational consequences of those transformations. The consequences of such transformations emerge when 'the absolute unchanging frame' is eliminated, which thereby eliminates infinite or absolute time and space. The further consequence is that not only are all times and spaces and velocities limited, but they are also intrinsically related to, and dependent on, one another. Thus, there are not temporal durations succeeding one another in an endless continuum that are independent of space, and vice versa. There is no endless space that is perfectly at rest and unchanging, and so there is no absolute or unconditional motion.

In the classical world of physics, motion was measured as a change in position taking place in time. Time, being the independent variable, was not considered to be dependent on changes in place. But Einstein made time a dependent variable. This meant that temporal measurements varied with spatial measurements and vice versa. But if velocity is measured through distances and times, then velocity is also a dependent variable. All three – d, v, and t – are mutually related and intrinsically determined by one another. In the equation $v = d/t$, the three variables are intrinsically determining one another.

This 'intrinsic dependence' of distance and durations can be noted in the way Einstein began by defining what he meant by ordering one 'now' to another 'now,' that is, by simultaneity. If we assume that all 'nows' are absolutely the same, then we can have any number of successions that can be related to one another by relating all of them to an absolute, eternal, unconditional 'now.' For Einstein there is no unlimited 'now'; he defines two events as simultaneous to one observer if a light flash observed at position x and at time t and a second flash at position x_1 and time t_1 arrive at a geometrically measured midpoint at the same time. It should be note that the time is co-ordered to a position and position co-ordered to time.[18] Einstein places this coordinate or reference system with an observer on a train moving at an unchanging speed (i.e., an inertial frame) in a straight line, and he places another spatiotemporal coordinate system with a stationary observer on the bank of the railroad. In this situation what is simultaneous for the moving observer on the train will not be simultaneous for the stationary observer; it will be successive. If we have an absolute unlimited framework to which these two limited frameworks are related, then we do not have to explain the fact that they will record two different versions of the same temporal order of the events. Einstein, however, explained these differences by insisting that they are real but irrelevant.

Scientists do not have to pay attention to such differences because the same law or normative pattern of correlations can be used in both frameworks, even though the spatiotemporal measurements are actually different. To grasp this invariance, however, we must transform one set of measurements into the other, not by the traditionally Galilean transformation that assumed an absolute, unlimited frame, but by the Lorentz transformation that allows for spatial contractions and temporal dilations in different inertial frames. This means that, if one person is moving steadily at one-third the speed of light while the other person moves steadily at one-half the speed of light, their measurements of an object will be different. According to Einstein, they are both correct because temporal successions and spatial intervals can actually shrink or expand. Nobody spontaneously thinks that this will happen, but Einstein says it does, because he has understood that classical laws have an invariant as well as a variable property and the measured variables do not make the invariant pattern the way it is; rather, it is just the opposite.

Einstein's mind was able to fix two incarnate observing scientists, in two differently moving frameworks, and then distinguish the difference in their measurements from the laws directing those measurements. In other words, Einstein distinguished the way scientists work within spatiotemporal frameworks, even though they may transcend the limits of their frameworks, by distinguishing the invariant pattern of relations from the variable terms of the pattern.

A look at the notion of mass as it was understood before and after Einstein will reveal just how foundational his postulates were. Mass was defined by Newton as a quantity of matter, and by its ability to resist changes in its state of motion. In the atomic theory of matter the two key characteristics of mass were its ability to occupy space and the fact that it was indestructible. Such atomic masses were so hard that they resisted all divisions or, as Lavoisier put it, they could not be broken down or deconstructed into more fundamental units. Dalton presented the first account of this mechanical notion of solid, indestructible atomic masses. Dalton's theory of the atomic mass was a chemist's theory, but during the twentieth century with developments in the study of electricity and magnetism, the emphasis shifted to the subatomic structure of the atom; discoveries by Faraday and Maxwell led to an electromagnetic theory of mass and force, which was comparable to Newton's gravitational theory of mass and force.

Between Newton and Einstein, two different traditions in mechanics had developed – Newtonian mechanics and Lagrange-Euler mechanics. For Newton, space, time, mass, and force were the basic terms but in Lagrange-Euler's system, they were space, time, mass, and energy. The two traditions were brought together mathematically by Hamilton, and this new synthesis was significantly generalized by James Joule.[19] In the 1840s, Joule provided experimental proof that work and heat were convertible. A precise amount of work yielded a precise amount of heat. That heat and work were interchangeable at a fixed rate suggested to scientists that the different forces in the universe might be related and capable of being converted or transformed from one form of force into another. Further study and experimentation led to the realization that it was not force that was being

converted and conserved, but energy. The way nature worked was to convert different forms of energy – heat, light, electricity, magnetism – from
one mode of being into another while conserving the total quantity of
energy which was itself indestructible.

All these advances were in the context of what was called the ether frame
but, as further research in electromagnetic fields revealed, the mass of
electrons actually increased with increases in their velocity; the notion of
the ether was called upon to explain such phenomena. Eventually, after
experimental failures, the notion of the ether became suspect, and Einstein's postulates eliminated ether altogether, thereby forcing scientists to
reformulate Newton's notion of mass. The result was Einstein's famous formulation of the equivalence of mass and energy, $E = mc^2$. This meant that
just as space determines time and time determines space, so velocity determines mass and mass determines velocity. Einstein's second postulate that
fixed the limit of all velocities to the speed of light meant that all four
terms – space, time, velocity, and mass – were interrelated and intrinsically
dependent on one another.

With these observations, we can begin to grasp what Einstein meant
when he said that if everything was taken out of his universe there would
be no space and time left over. The reason is that atoms, through their
gravitational and electromagnetic patterns of behavior, made space and
time the way they are. By removing Newton's absolute frame of reference,
Einstein showed that space and time are not unlimited, empty realities, but
gravitational and electromagnetic forms of energy.

If we take the two basic laws of gravity and electricity in classical physics,
Newton's F (gravity) $= G\ (m_1 \cdot m_2)/r^2$ and Coulomb's F (electric) $= K\ (q_1 \cdot$
$q_2)/r^2$, we can see how Einstein recontextualized them. In the classical context, we might say that Newton's laws explain how any two masses behave
gravitationally in space and time, while Coulomb's law explains how two
masses behave electrically in space and time. But in Einstein's context,
these laws explain space and time. Space and time are no longer unlimited
containers. Space and time are intelligible, and their intelligibility is apprehended insofar as we understand the gravitational and electromagnetic
equations that express that intelligibility. Atomic masses interact with one
another gravitationally and electromagnetically, and in so interacting they
make spaces and times behave the way they do. But the way these atomic
masses interact is limited. What Einstein's assumption did was to bring out,
not only that space, time, mass, and energy are all intrinsically related to
one another, but also that they are also intrinsically limited.

Somewhat ironically, in a law like $F = G\ (m_1\,m_2)/r^2$ there is no reason why
the variables cannot vary in an unlimited way, but Einstein's theory does
place a limit on velocity and masses and Newton's laws apply only to cer-

tain, limited cases. In other words, Newton's laws were not universals but limited universals; he was simply unaware of the limits. Einstein did not eliminate Newton's discoveries, but he did recontextualize them and give them new and quite richer meanings.

In a final comparison of Einstein and Aristotle, it is interesting to note how energy functions in Einstein's context the way matter functions in Aristotle's physics. Matter for Aristotle is that which is capable of receiving form; similarly, energy is the potency or 'matter' that can be informed gravitationally, electromagnetically, or thermally. It is the form that makes the matter what it is and behave the way it does; and similarly, what energy is and how it functions depends on the forms it receives.

3   Statistical Science

There were serious limits to Einstein's own discoveries but, like Newton, he was unaware of them. Einstein refused to accept the implications of a second scientific method which emerged alongside the Galilean-Newtonian classical methods in the late nineteenth century, namely, statistical method. Method is a procedure for discovering what we do not know. And from the time of Socrates we have known that knowing what we do not know is remarkably difficult because this usually involves discovering that we were mistaken in what we thought we knew. In mathematics and physics, scientists thought that their ultimate goal was to geometrize physical processes in the context of Euclidean assumptions and Newtonian mechanics, and then discovered that these theories were neither universal nor necessary, but restricted to very specialized, limiting conditions. Such a discovery both corrects a prior misunderstanding and advances science on a new path of development, and this is what happened with the emergence of statistical science. The implications, however, were much richer and more foundational: statistical sciences eventually undermined most of the explicit but unverified assumptions about the mechanistic and deterministic character of the ordering of the universe.[20]

The major achievement of Galileo was to abstract from the sensible experiences of falling bodies (such as their weight and resistance) and focus instead on the strictly measurable aspects of certain properties of falling bodies (such as the distances and durations of the fall), but statisticians take a dramatically different approach. First, they do not abstract from the descriptive properties – of a falling penny in a coin toss, for example. They are interested in observing on which side the penny happens to land. They do not measure most aspects of the fall; rather, they count 'happenings' – how many times the penny happens to fall heads or tails. Statisticians are interested, not in the process of falling, but in actual concrete happenings, occurrences, or events – in the occurrence of heads or tails. As well, and more significantly, statisticians are examining discontinuous processes, whereas Galileo was examining a continuous process. Flipping coins produces a head, then a tail, or two tails and one head, or a run of heads, etc. The point is that statistical scientists expect that these happenings will be discontinuous. Even more startling for Galileo would be the statistical assumption that it is possible to discover a scientific law in such discontinuous happenings.

This assumption would also have startled Aristotle. Aristotle was quite aware of 'happenings or occurrences' and that such happenings were discontinuous, but he never would have forseen a science of 'accidental happenings,' nor would have Galileo and Newton. Yet that is what happened in the nineteenth century as scientists developed the new sciences of thermodynamics and the kinetic theory of gases and, in this century, quantum theory. I will return to these discoveries in the fourth chapter, but here my focus is on the new type of 'statistical insight' discovered by statisticians.

Classical insights involve the discovery of a function, an unchanging correlation of two or more changing, measurable variations. This also seems to be what statistical scientists are expecting to find, namely, a correlation between possible occurrences of heads or tails. But there is a noticeable difference between these two types of scientific correlations, and we can classify the difference by focusing on the two different ways that classical and statistical scientists abstract from data in order to formulate their respective insights into laws. Again, it is the shift from the descriptive pattern of sensible correlations to reach strictly intelligible correlations that provides a clue. Classical scientists abstract from particular happenings because they assume that such singular occurrences or events are not relevant. What is relevant is the 'unchanging correlation' that fixes the series of happenings by ordering the 'flow' of events through a 'serial form.' What classical scientists do not expect is that the discontinuous and unexpected events which interrupt the serial flow will reveal anything that they do not already know, or could know, by their classical method. But this is precisely what the statistical scientist does expect. When tossing coins if we get a steady flow of heads and no tails, then the statistical scientist knows we are cheating. Or if we get an unending series of one head, followed by one tail, followed by one head, followed by one tail, etc., then the statistical scientist will tell us that this is a systematic process, not a discontinuous statistical process. The difference between classical and statistical insights may be further clarified if we shift our attention to the way that classical and statistical scientists formulate their insights.

Today we are not surprised when scientists speak of a 'law' of probability. But for scientists like Galileo and Newton, and even Einstein, the notion of a law, and the notion of science itself, is one that goes back to Aristotle's *Posterior Analytics*. Science was a search for certain, necessary causes, and so a law was a formulation of such a certain, necessary cause. The discovery of functions, or of 'unchanging correlations,' did not seem to challenge either the classical notion of science or the classical notion of a law, even though the function is abstracted from concrete, descriptive correlations and particular happenings. However, to state that we can have a 'law' that is a probability is a direct challenge to the basic notions of what science is and what a law is. Yet that is what statistical science has done. In the case of coin tossing, the law is that we have a fifty-fifty chance of throwing a head or a tail. The law, however, is not about what will happen in a particular case, nor about what will happen in a small number of cases. Rather, the law states what will happen over a long period of time and in a large series of cases. Further, the longer we throw the coin, the more evident will be the effect of the law.

Statisticians study and count particular happenings or events, but they do so to discover a general law. A frequency or probability is a correlation of possible events to actual events. This means that in formulating a frequency or probability, we conceive an ideal norm or law that tells us what probably will happen in a population, but not what actually will happen in any individual case. It is a determinate law in the sense that it determines or predicts what probably will happen. The most interesting and remarkable aspect of a law of probability lies in its expectancy. Statistical thinkers expect exceptions. While the odds or frequencies of getting heads or tails are fifty-fifty, that frequency does not exclude a run of ten heads. Ordinarily, we will not get ten heads in a row, but the statistical scientist does not exclude this possibility because the law includes the possibility of an unusual course of events. What is excluded by the law? This question pinpoints the most surprising feature of statistical thinking because the answer is another instance of that strange and rare type of insight we have named inverse insight.

A probability is an ideal frequency which expects exceptions but does not expect 'systematic' exceptions. If we keep throwing heads one after the other, the statistician knows we have a 'loaded coin.' When a series of throws begins to look like a continuous flow of events without any discontinuities or interruptions, then we have a systematic series of events, not a probable one. In other words, statistical scientists expect a certain type of exception, namely, a nonsystematic exception. What the ordinary person calls luck or a most unusual run of events, a statistical thinker understands as a 'non-systematic divergence from an ideal frequency.' The reason why the statistician is not concerned about such unusual sequences is because statistical laws are about the long run and, in the long run, a short run of exceptional events, or good luck, will be canceled out by an opposite run of tosses or by bad luck. As wise gamblers know, 'the house' wins in the long run.

I will return to statistical laws in chapter 4 and discuss how they complement classical laws, but now a few observations about the way statistical thinkers wonder or question. Aristotle's remarkable achievement in advancing systematic thinking was to focus on the way we wonder about ourselves and the world around us by carefully analyzing the sort of questions that we ask. I have already stressed the significance of the what and why questions and the way the latter orients us toward discovering an 'unknown form or proportion' that patterns the sensible data to be the way they are. Forms or proportions are intelligibilities, so are functions or correlations which also provide us with the whys or intelligibilities.

With statistical laws of probability, we have a quite different type of intelligibility or unknown that we also wish to know, namely, frequencies or probabilities. And such insights are answers to quite different questions. Frequencies are insights that respond to such questions as How often? and How many? Newton would have been very surprised to be asked, How often has the sun risen? As we shall see, statistical insights also answer such questions as Where? When? and How long? How these different questions can be integrated will be discussed later, but let me finish this chapter by drawing attention to a common feature of both classical and statistical laws. Classical laws do not deal with particular concrete cases; rather, they seek a universal, comprehensive understanding and explanation of how things behave and interact with one another. Statistical scientists count concrete actual cases, and they do so in order to discover ideal frequencies from which concrete actual cases may diverge in nonsystematic ways. There is, however, a method for dealing with concrete particular cases precisely as particular and concrete. It is to the study of this common-sense method of knowing that we now turn.

3

Common Sense

In chapter 1, you were invited through various examples to appropriate yourself as a questioner and understander who has insights and who attempts to define them. The examples offered were taken primarily from mathematics and science. In the second chapter, readers were encouraged to assimilate how such insights accumulate and can become the basis for systematic and statistical understanding of the physical universe. In the formation of these scientific systems, the special role of inverse insight was stressed, as well as the historical significance of the shift from descriptive to explanatory contexts of knowing. Finally, in the shift from classical to statistical laws, you began to appreciate that the problem of concrete knowing is much more complex than is ordinarily assumed.

It was the remarkable historical success of mathematical and scientific knowing that made the more familiar and ordinary way of knowing much more difficult to appreciate and appropriate. In addition, in the development of scientific knowing there has been not only a prejudice against common-sense knowing, but also a major attempt to discredit and invalidate it. Before dealing with these prejudices, I will briefly set forth certain major characteristics of common-sense knowing as it contrasts with scientific knowing.[1]

1   Common-Sense Knowing

Historians of science have frequently pointed out that scientific knowledge of the physical universe existed long before the Greeks; yet there was a significant difference between the sort of science found among Egyptians and Babylonians and science as it came to be practiced by the Greeks. Before the Greeks, scientific knowledge tended to be pursued primarily for practical and religious purposes. Thus, the study of celestial patterns was undertaken for such reasons as fixing calendars for ritualistic events and for planting crops. With the Greeks, new interests and patterns of thought purged of practical desires and purposes gradually emerged, as knowing for the sake of knowing made its appearance on the stage of human history.

Common-sense knowers are interested in knowing, not for its own sake, but for purposes of developing more intelligent and successful ways of living. Living is not something we do abstractly; it is concrete and particular, and its concreteness and particularity stand in a certain tension with the methods and goals of natural science. For, while scientists have to verify their theories in concrete particular givens, they are primarily interested not in these particular cases, but in a universal explanation of all particular cases. In other words, the emergence of theoretical knowing did not do away with the need for common-sense knowing. While it provided a critical perspective for reflecting on common-sense knowing, it did not, and cannot, replace practical patterns of knowing. When scientists leave their labs to go home, they do not use scientific knowing to drive; they use the practical skills they have acquired to perform that specific task. Knowing how to drive is not just knowing how to think and judge correctly; it is knowing how to do something. We can learn mathematics by studying books, but we cannot learn how to play the piano simply by reading books about playing the piano.

Common sense is a way of knowing that is specialized and oriented to concrete particular tasks. It is a way of knowing that is as old as human history. People have always had to learn how to live, and to do so intelligently is a matter of raising questions and getting insights. What orients the flow of such questions and insights is the desire to know how to solve certain practical problems.[2] Whether it is a question of hunting or fishing, farming or building homes, the problem is solved not simply by knowing, but by knowing how to organize and execute a course of actions, and to do so intelligently and efficiently. Common-sense knowers are not especially interested in knowing why fish and birds are what they are, but they are interested in knowing how to catch and cook them. To wonder why stones or trees are what they are involves a remarkably different type of questioning, which flows from a very different orienting desire. And, as Socrates discovered, people of common sense can become quite suspicious and even hostile when questioned, not about how to live, but about how to choose the best possible way of living.

A further characteristic of common-sense knowing is that it is not interested in moving out of the descriptive, subject-centered context of knowing. It knows things in their descriptive appearances, but it is not interested in understanding and judging these things in the general and special relations they may have to one another. For the same reason, common sense is not interested in, nor does it have any need for, a technical language. Scientists and mathematicians develop technical languages in order to pin down precisely just what they mean when they use words such as 'triangle' and 'circle,' as Euclid did, or 'mass' and 'force,' as Newton did; they formulate a technical language because they do not want the meaning of the terms changing with each successive theorem. However, if you are trying to solve problems of daily living, then you have no interest in universal solutions because problems change, if not everyday, then every other day, or week, or year: what worked last week may not work this week. Situations change and people's attitudes are continuously shifting, and since people of common sense know this, they keep a watchful eye and try to adapt to such changes as they occur. This does not mean that common-sense knowledge does not accumulate; certainly people learn by their mistakes and correct them. Further, because common sense deals with particular cases, it always remains an incomplete set of insights that can be adapted to changes only by further insights into the concrete particular case at hand.

This same character of common-sense knowing can be seen in the contrast between a proverb and a law. A law, like Newton's universal law of gravitation, $F = G(m_1 \cdot m_2)/r^2$, is conceived in abstraction from concrete, particular cases in order to provide a universal explanation for all cases; a proverb, on the other hand, may or may not apply to this or that particular situation. Only an insight or set of insights into the particular situation at hand will inform you whether the proverb applies in this situation. For this reason you sometimes find two proverbs that seem contradictory: 'Look before you leap' is directly opposed to 'He who hesitates is lost.' Which proverb is appropriate in any given situation depends on acquiring an additional insight into the concrete particular circumstances of the situation. Similarly, the advice you give a person depends on who the person is, and how you communicate with that person also depends on the temperament of the person being addressed. Newton was not interested in addressing a particular person, nor a particular group of people, nor even a national group. Science transcends cultural barriers.

Characteristics of common sense can be formulated considering the various differentiations of common sense. Socrates was impressed by the knowledge of various craftsmen, such as navigators, cobblers, carpenters, and other followers of a trade. Each group knew how to perform specific tasks, but did not 'know' in the way Socrates wanted to know. However, since Socrates himself did not have a theory of common-sense knowing, he did not realize that such knowledge was necessarily specialized and limited.

Knowing how to navigate a ship will not help you in trying to mend a shoe, and knowing how to bake a cake will not teach you how to cultivate orchids. Each task requires specific knowledge and skills in order to achieve a particular goal. It also requires a certain singlemindedness, a specialization of knowledge that directs the attention of the knower to particular concrete aspects of experience while putting aside other aspects. To develop the skillful knowledge of the baker or butcher requires time, effort, and an alert apprentice who learns by watching, listening, and testing the insights acquired.[3] Such learning accumulates, and gradually the novice becomes a specialized knower, able to perform a set of specialized tasks with ease and efficiency. Common-sense knowing, then, involves the development of skills to perform specific tasks within a social community.

Common-sense knowing also presents a paradox. Bakers make their cakes for customers, but in the process of learning how to bake they are also making themselves into bakers. Just as physicists make themselves into scientific knowers, they also make themselves into teachers, gradually acquiring the practical skills required to perform that task. In making themselves into teachers, they may also make themselves into members of the educational community. Similarly the butcher and baker both make themselves into a certain type of practical knower so that they can cooperate with other skilled workers in bringing about a common ordering of different, specialized, economic tasks. Certain personal habits are simultaneously social habits since they are acquired in order to interact with other workers. The paradox is that the subjective world of the butcher and baker is simultaneously the intersubjective world of an economic exchange community. When the baker goes to the store to sell bread and the customer goes to the same store to buy bread, they are enacting an exchange; the social scientist understands their behavior as functioning within an economic institution based on a set of cooperative agreements. The bakers and their customers, however, do not know the economic institution they are making in the process of their buying and selling. Each person knows only her or his own particular, repeating patterns of coming and going within the business market, not the repeating collective cycles in which she or he participates and which she or he constitutes through her or his interpersonal, cyclical behavior. Behind the simple exchange of the baker's agreement to sell and the customer's decision to buy is a web of assumptions that are, for the most part, unknown to the buyer and the seller who perform these transactions, which are part of a particular market system. What are the motives that make such a market system move in these repeating cycles if the parties to the exchange system do not know the economic institutions in which they are performing their respective roles and tasks? To answer this question we need to identify a third form of knowing.

they don't know that they are part of a larger system

theoretical
common sense
symbolic knowing

2   Symbolic Patterns of Knowing

So far in our discussion you, the reader, have been invited to appropriate yourself as a theoretical knower (scientific and mathematical) and as a common-sense knower, but there is a third pattern of knowing that is as natural and primordial as practical knowing, namely, symbolic knowing.[4] Just as common-sense knowing was denigrated and devalued by the blossoming of theoretical knowing in the seventeenth century, so also was symbolic knowing. It is only in the twentieth century that any sustained effort has been made to appropriate what we are doing when we are symbolizing. Contemporary scholars have taught us to think of ourselves as symbolic animals. Such a definition provides us with a more concrete, comprehensive way to think about ourselves. The persuasive significance of this pattern of knowing will become especially apparent when we analyze ourselves as choosers in chapter 7 and as lovers in chapter 8.

The pedagogical advantage in beginning the appropriation of yourself as an understander with examples from mathematics and science becomes apparent as we turn to common sense. It is much more difficult to specify the activity of insight or understanding in common-sense patterns of knowing because such knowing does not specialize in understanding for the sake of understanding. The same is even more true of symbolic knowing because it is even more spontaneous and concrete than the other patterns that you have attempted to appropriate and assimilate. For example, while driving a car requires practical intelligence, smiling seems to be nothing more than a spontaneous reflex. Clearly, the meaning expressed and recognized in a smile is not the sort of knowing that grasps the why of a circle or of acceleration, nor even knowing how to tie a shoelace, but there is a meaning in a smile and it is symbolic meaning.

smile symbolizes happiness

To grasp what is meant by symbolic meaning, let us consider the context in which you smile. You may do mathematics or mow the lawn by yourself but ordinarily you do not smile when alone. Smiling usually assumes an intersubjective situation and intends to communicate your attitude toward another person and to effect in that other person a similar attitude toward you. Such meaning is, moreover, obvious and immediate. The person you smile at grasps the meaning spontaneously and responds with a similar expression, thereby creating a temporary bond. Further, a smile is not an expression of your mind as found in Euclid's *Elements*. It is an expression of one person to another; it is expressive of the whole person – body and soul. Finally, the smile is not a verbal expression, it is preverbal. You learn to smile long before you learn to speak, which means that symbolic meanings are more elemental and primordial forms of meaning than linguistic meaning, just as common-sense pat-

terns of knowing and meaning are prior to, and more universal than theoretical patterns of knowing.

Symbols, then, are not expressive of the abstract concepts that ground
theories and lead to conclusions. Smiles are not the result of a reflective
process, nor are they expressions of practical ideas. They are concrete com-
munications expressed by one person and recognized by another which
create an intersubjective situation of shared feelings. But just what are
these feelings that are expressed? And, if they are not ideas or concepts or
judgments, then why would we speak of them as expressions of meaning
and not just expressions of feeling? If we go back to chapter 1, we find a
clue in the act of questioning which precedes and sets the conditions for
insights. The most remarkable character of questioning is the way it
transforms your sensible or imaginable experiences into 'wonderable
experiences.' Questioning transforms sensibly known experiences into
intelligibly unknown experiences. But such sensibly known and intelligibly
unknown experiences may be directed by your disinterested desire to know
or by your practical, interested desire to know. In the symbolic pattern of
experience, what is intended is a more primordial wondering that is oriented not to the instrumental intending of practical living, nor to the theoretical intending of scientific knowing, but to a more undifferentiated
wonder of simply being a living being in tune with other beings. Such symbolic intending or meaning is not abstract, but completely concrete and
foundational.

Before you come to know your own personal identity, you feel a spontaneous identity with whatever and whomever enters into your field of awareness. This primary undifferentiated field of awareness develops and
gradually differentiates into other persons and things, but still there
remains this basic and foundational pattern of shared human intending.
Thus, long before the Greeks began wondering why earth, air, fire, and
water were what they were, people had interpreted these four basic elements within various primordial patterns of symbolic meanings. Water was
an object of symbolic wonder long before it became the object of Thales's
philosophical wondering. And even though water became known as a
chemical compound, it still evokes a primordial awe and wonder that we
feel and express in a variety of symbolic ways. The problem is that, once
theoretical patterns emerged, a tendency to devalue symbolic knowing also
emerged, since this way of knowing seemed anything but reasonable, especially if the meaning of reasoning is limited to theoretical reasoning.
Today, thanks to theories of symbolism, we realize that we do reason with
symbols, but this way of reasoning is very different from conceptualist reasoning.

I shall examine symbolic patterns of reasoning in the last two chapters.

Here I wish to draw attention to symbols as our most spontaneous and primordial pattern of meaning which operates on all levels of being from unconscious, vital processes to higher realms of conscious knowing and choosing. Most importantly, symbols operate through images that evoke the feelings that supply the motivation for carrying out decisions. This means that there is a close relation between common-sense patterns and symbolic patterns of experience.

symbols cause us to feel a certain way, then act

3   Dramatic Pattern of Experience

Thusfar we have considered three different patterns of experience: theoretical; common-sense; and symbolic. Obviously, there are not three knowers, but one concrete conscious subject who has many different conscious interests and aspirations, and those interests aspire to quite different goals or objectives. It is imperative to clarify and distinguish these three different conscious patterns since the failure to do so has been a recurring source of philosophical differences and disputes. These three different patterns of experience can now combined into various structural wholes, and you can then begin appropriating the way you, as a concrete knower, actually operate and cooperate with other knowers. To fully appropriate yourself as a knower, it will be necessary to focus on yourself as reflecting and judging, but in proceeding methodically, we will not discuss this activity until chapter 5. Similarly, only after you have appropriated yourself as a knower will we proceed to analyze in detail activities of judging, deliberating, and deciding. Judging and deciding, however, are implicit in all the patterns we have discussed.

The dramatic pattern of experience combines the symbolic and practical patterns within the one concrete operating subject. Let us take as an example a family dinner. The family is satisfying a basic biological need for nourishment just as a flock of geese might gather to feed. However, unlike the animal meal, the human dinner requires a considerable amount of practical wisdom, most of which has been inherited by the family, but it also requires the skill of knowing how to cook and adapt recipes to a particular style of preparation. Finally, there is the symbolic meaning of a family dining together. The baby learns to eat almost spontaneously, but learning how to dine requires a number of years of mastering the ability to use a knife, fork, spoon, and all the other table manners that different cultures prescribe as accepted modes of behavior. In addition, tables are set in various ways, most of which are also cultural conventions that the family inherits along with the elaborate rules of etiquette and politeness that dictate how the members of the family are to behave when dining together. It is only when we stop and reflect on all the various particulars of such a simple and ordinary event that we realize how much of a ritualized ceremony dining together actually is. The same is true of all the other ordinary events that make up the daily living of any cultural community. Why is human dining so ritualistic and ceremonial? Clearly, it is not the desire for food and nourishment that leads people to establish such conventions and customs. The problem in articulating the meaning of any symbol or symbolic activity is that symbols express simultaneously a multitude of meanings. Moreover, these meanings will vary from one culture to another, and the meanings will change at different times and on different occasions. But, in general, we may say that the manners and mores of dining satisfying a desire for people in a family to come together and express how they care for and respect one another and to express that they are a domestic community founded on love and friendship. However, families are not always harmonious unions and if we think of a family dinner as a symbolic drama, it will provide us with a set of basic terms for analyzing in a more differentiated way both the broader cultural community and its history.

Dramas are about concrete tensions and struggles that emerge in human communities as different persons move toward their respective destinies. The traditional philosophical term for such struggles is 'dialectic,' which can be defined as 'an opposition among linked sources of change.'[5] Thus, in appropriating ourselves as understanders, we have been concerned with the tensions between questions that initiate change and the insights that resolve these tensions. In a drama, however, the tensions are twofold: there are the tensions within the individual characters and the tensions that develop among the characters. An internal dialectic develops within each of the characters and an external, interpersonal dialectic develops between the characters. There are, then, two dramas in every drama: the inner psychological drama that goes on between the subject and himself or herself and the outer social drama that goes on within the community. Frequently the external social drama is a function of the internal psychological drama. The familiar terms of 'role' and 'plot' refer to these different dialectical functions.

'Role' is an important term in analyzing ourselves because it provides an initial shift from a descriptive to an explanatory perspective: it relates one character in a play to the other characters. Thus, terms like 'father' or 'daughter' specify not only the way one person is related to another, but also their mutual relations or correlations. And, just as I stressed the significance in Renaissance physics of developing a coordinate system that could correlate and unite all the opposing directions of the masses to one another, so the term 'plot' can be employed as a way of coordinating all the roles of the characters to one another in an ongoing dialectical development that will eventually be resolved in a successful or tragic ending. A

me *
Ali

drama, therefore, can be defined as the dialectical unfolding of a plot among the characters as they motivate themselves and one another toward a final destiny of success or failure. Such a destiny seems to flow from their decisions and actions and, at the same time, seems to transcend their intentions.

In a symbolic drama the characters may also function as representative figures. In the classic Greek tragedy *Antigone*, Creon is the representative of the civic community, while Antigone is the symbol of the family community; the plot is the dialectical unfolding of the tensions between the broader demands of civic love and loyalty and the more apparently limited demands of family piety. Again, there are two dialectical unfoldings: the inner psychological drama of Creon with himself and Antigone with herself and the two symbolic roles of the family versus the state. The successive modification of the internal, emotional states of Creon and Antigone evoke, and are evoked by, the successive states of the outer drama as the characters move toward, and are drawn by, their respective destinies. Thus, we identify in such symbolic dramas a basic tension between the spontaneous intersubjective ordering of persons into a family and the attempt of different families, using their practical common sense, to design a social order which will unite families into a civic community that will win their personal commitments and command their common allegiance. This means that we have identified three different dialectics: the tension of the person within himself or herself; the tension of persons within the group; and the tension between one community and another. However, there is a fourth and even more significant dialectic – the human historical drama – the tensions between any one historical community its predecessors and successors.

Antigone expresses the tension between Creon's administering the laws of the city and Antigone's observing the pious customs of the family. But how does Creon know if the laws he is upholding and administering are just laws? To a large extent, the laws that leaders and judges employ are normative procedures for making decisions which have been inherited from prior norms and decisions, and these in turn depend on prior cultural communities. In other words, there is this fundamental question that any cultural authority may have to face: How reasonable and just are the inherited cultural norms that provide the standards for communal judgments and decisions? To answer this question, cultural authorities need a transcultural norm that is not dependent on any cultural context, but that grounds and orders each and every cultural context. Creon's case could be compared to Newton's when he thought he was thinking and measuring in a completely universal framework but was, in fact, operating in a quite limited framework. However, the limits of that framework were hidden from him. Creon, like any civic leader, experiences, understands, judges, and decides within a cultural horizon whose limits are hidden, unless he can shift from a limited cultural context and move into a transcultural or historical horizon. It is in making such a shift that the fourth fundamental dialectic between symbolic practical knowing and our theoretical historical knowing, or between our interested desire to know and our disinterested desire, comes to light.

Henry Ford is credited with saying, 'History is bunk!,' which implies that the disinterested study of your historical past is not going to help you make automobiles. However, without the historical progress in technology that Americans had inherited from past cultural achievements, Henry Ford would have been bunk. Without such an historical inheritance, Henry Ford would have had to spend his time inventing the wheel. In other words, you are living in a history whether you know it or not. The social, political, economic, educational, and religious institutions with their respective roles and goals have been, for the most part, inherited from prior generations and, whether these inherited schemes are the result of accumulated insights or the product of accumulated oversights, depends on the way these four cultural dialectics were operating in those past communities. In any individual knower four different dialectics are operating: first, the inner dialectic between the ego and the self; second, the dialectic between the subject and the groups within which he or she operates and cooperates; third, the concrete tensions between different groups within the same cultural community and with other living cultural communities; and fourth, the tension between present cultural communities and their past and future communities. How are we to relate these four dialectical tensions? We have seen that the inner dialectic of the self is functionally related to the social dialectic in terms of various roles that the subject plays. Thus, the social dialectic tends to condition the way personal dialectics unfold. But the basic dialectic is a historical one since it sets the directions and conditions the way the other three operate. This also means that, while every human person is a social being, even more basically, we are 'historical beings.' Let us examine these dialectical tensions in more detail.

Dialectic implies a tension of opposed orientations within one and the same subject. How does this dialectic operate within your conscious field? As we have seen in our brief analysis of symbolic knowing, each person operates on many different levels: an unconscious biological level; a conscious psychic level; an intellectual level (which we will subdivide in chapter 5 into a direct and reflexive level); and, finally, a deliberative level (which will be disclosed in detail in chapter 7). On all these different levels each person has to develop; just as organisms develop through biological processes, so animals develop through organic and psychic processes, while persons develop organically, psychically, and intellectually. Traditionally these different levels have been considered as a hierarchy with the lower levels providing potentialities for higher activities. In plants, chemical aggregates provide opportunities for higher biological processes, thereby revealing plants as biochemical operators. Animals exploit these same biological processes to develop even more elaborate and more highly specialized organs in order to develop higher, conscious psychic schemes. This means that animals operate psychically through various organic nervous systems that distinguish the lower and higher animals. At the human level, these lower psychic patterns of sensing, remembering, and imagining provide the potential for insights that transform these lower psychic flows into the higher intellectual schemes that give rise to the different patterns of knowing.

In plants, animals, and people, then, there are tensions or needs operating simultaneously on different levels and between levels. For example, sexual tensions emerge from the unconscious organic level and rise to the conscious psychic, intellectual, or symbolic level when we wonder and ask: What is the meaning of these feelings that are orienting me toward sexual satisfaction on the psychic level and, at the same time, orienting me toward unknown meanings on the intellectual and/or symbolic levels? Such feelings direct us, but their objective is realized on different levels. To harmonize these multiple tensions, not once but throughout a lifetime of changing desires and fears, sets the human problem.

The difficulty of this problem can be underscored by noting that in these tensions we also find oppositions. There may emerge a basic opposition between sensing and understanding, just as there may arise a basic opposition between eating and intelligible eating, between sexual satisfaction and intelligible sexual satisfaction. Such tensions and oppositions are conscious and consciously experienced by every person. The problem emerges when the opposition turns into a conflict and these opposed tendencies begin to operate at cross-purposes. Tensions, which otherwise could be constructive, begin to produce disorders leading to various types of biases and eventually to decline and breakdown. The problem is the familiar moral problem, but at this point of our study I wish to treat such disorders and biases as primarily intellectual problems and delay any explicit moral considerations until chapter 7.

4   Biases

We have seen that there are four conscious dialectical tensions operating in each person: the person with self; self with society; present groupings within society or of societies with one another; any present social grouping with human history. Now I want to show how these four different but related dialectics unfold and thereby set the conditions for four different ways by which knowers may prevent insights from emerging. Besides the desire to understand there is also the fear of understanding. Just how such fears can block and repress insights now needs to be analyzed.

4a Dramatic Bias

As we have just seen, each of us is engaged in two different dramas. There is the familiar drama between people played out on artistic stages or on actual historical stages which is concerned with alternative courses of action within people's lives. There is also the newly discovered drama that takes place within the field of our own conscious selves. It is 'new' in the sense that, since the turn of this century, we have the theoretical tools to analyze it.[6] Thanks especially to scholars who initiated the study of symbols and the way they function in human knowing and choosing, we can now explain our interior conscious lives in new ways. The analytic tools of Freud and Jung, in particular, have proved to be especially important.

In Freud's analysis of our inner drama of self with self, there is a dialectical interplay of the conscious 'ego' with the lower 'id,' but this dialectical tension takes place under the influence, or domination, of our social conscience or 'superego.' Jung, on the other hand, would have the conscious ego in conflict with our preconscious or unconscious 'shadow,' while our interpersonal self tends to find itself in conflict with our conscious 'anima.'[7] For both there is the interplay of lower and higher levels, conscious and unconscious.

We began the appropriation of ourselves with the higher level of questioning as it operates on our lower conscious contents. Now we are in position to note that this questioning takes place in the context of higher and lower activities. We are all familiar with stories about absent-minded professors who become so absorbed in the intellectual pattern of experience that they forget to eat or, like Thales, tumble into the well. There is also the case of the mother who can hear her child crying in another room when no one else notices the sound. The point is that our attentive wondering operates in different patterns, and these patterns may engage the whole person on different levels both inwardly and outwardly. Wondering for the mother may be worrying, an anxious concern for her child that totally absorbs her whole being. It is in such contexts that we can discern the significance of Freud's term 'censor.'

Besides the desire to know manifesting itself in attentive questioning, there are the fears that may block or divert this questioning. Just as your questioning reaches from the intelligible level down into the sensible level and prepares the data of your internal or external consciousness for insights, so your anxieties and fears can direct questioning away from certain conscious data. You do not wish to understand certain data because you are fearful of making discoveries; you 'censor' such revelations and thus prevent them from emerging. How does such censoring operate? The explanation is to be found in your ability to control or direct or evoke feelings through images. Questioning deals primarily with images, and images are associated with feelings, memories, and expectations. Some of these activities are more spontaneous than others, which means that they are less under your control. While such levels of control differ widely according to different stages of a person's learning, there are important differences between your sensible and imaginative experiences. You cannot see and hear whatever you wish, but you can, within limited ranges, form visual and auditory images as you wish. Images pivot between your sensible and intelligible worlds, and since these images may be more or less controlled, you can use such images to direct your feelings. Feelings, then, may arise quite spontaneously from lower-level sensible activities, and such feelings may make you anxious, resentful, aggressive, or any other of a host of disturbing passions. How you interpret such feelings depends to a large extent on the way you question them. The questions are, in turn, provoked by images, and how you attend to and interpret your feelings can be indirectly controlled by choosing the images that you select to question.

Freud's 'censor' can be described as how you avoid getting insights about yourself that would reveal you to yourself in ways you fear, disapprove or even detest. Thus in Freud's classic Oedipus case where a boy has sexual feelings toward his mother, the feelings are not under his direct conscious control, but the way he admits these feelings into self-awareness will depend on the images he engenders or remembers, and the way he understands himself in relation to these feelings that are evoked by these images.

Freud focused on two types of feelings – sexual and self-preserving. His preoccupation with sexual desires and fears is especially instructive. Sexual desires are conditioned by unconscious, organic, and psychic changes, and at any stage of your development there are continual psychosomatic changes taking place which have to be assimilated into the emotional context of your developing self. The notion of development will be explored later, but the point to note here is that Freud's preoccupation with sexual feelings was justified since such feelings at different stages in your life require frequent adjustment and reinterpretation. If you do not successfully integrate these neurophysiological changes into your higher conscious, psychic, and intellectual schemes, but suppress them instead, the result may be a variety of abnormal patterns of behaviors. Such abnormal-ities may remain within the field of your own inner consciousness, resulting in a split between the outer persona you disclose to others in playing social roles and the inner ego that behaves in quite different ways on the private stage of your own awareness.

4b Individual Bias

While the discoveries of Freud and Jung opened up a whole new field for analyzing our relations to ourselves and others, there is the older and more familiar bias of selfishness or egoism. The dialectical tension at work in selfishness goes against the spontaneous tendency that people feel of belonging to one another, a spontaneous intersubjectivity. Before the 'we' that each of us develops by being part of a family, a neighborhood, a polity, or church, there is the more primordial 'we' that is present and spontaneously operating within every person. Such spontaneous feelings of belonging have more recently been articulated in terms of 'compassion' by Rousseau[8] and, in a more recent and differentiated way, by Scheler in terms of 'community feeling' and 'fellow feeling.'[9]

Opposed to such spontaneous intersubjectivity, there is our common-sense or practical intelligence which leads to the formation of social, economic, political, and religious organizations or institutions. The members of one intersubjective group must learn how to cooperate with members of other groups in seeking a recurring flow of the different types of goods and services that the community as a whole desires. The challenge that each individual faces is to learn how to cooperate in ways that are fair to others or, as the golden rule puts it, to do unto others as you would have them do unto you. To violate this rule is to go against your own spontaneous intersubjectivity, but to do so you have to be intelligent enough to figure out how the common institutional schemes you wish to exploit actually operate.[10]

Paradoxically, then, selfishness requires that you must be intelligent enough to discover how to design and implement a self-serving course of action, yet not intelligent enough to recognize and acknowledge yourself as exploiting the members of your own community. In repressing those further relevant questions that would bring to light the self-indulgent egotism of your present course of action, you are actually making yourself unlovable both to yourself and to your friends. How does the egotist prevent the emergence of the further significant questions which would lead to an understanding of the self as a shrewd but self-regarding self? The egotist does so by suppressing fellow feelings, by imagining others to be inferior and unworthy of his or her concern. In addition, the egotist has available a range of false images that will trigger a range of false insights, which we traditionally categorize as excuses and rationalizations. If the egotist does not want to wonder about the fuller implications of his or her mode of cooperation within the community, he or she must restrict the free play of images to prevent repressed feelings from emerging, since they could provide motivation for considering alternative courses of cooperating. In other words, the same basic mechanisms that you use to rationalize your relations to yourself can also be employed to falsify your ways of relating to the members of your own community.

4c Group Bias

A third and more subtle form of deception is the bias that develops between different socioeconomic groups within the same community.[11] Before turning to this issue, we need to consider why there are different communities or classes within a social order and why there are more classes today than in previous eras. We have so many different classes in our contemporary social orderings because we have so many different tasks to be performed, and we have so many different tasks because our practical intelligence is so inventive in generating and implementing new ways of living and working together. But why not have a classless society? Because it is reasonable and intelligent to divide up different tasks and set up cooperative schemes that will provide for basic and surplus needs within our social, religious, political, academic, and economic communities. Common-sense knowing, or practical intelligence, generates successive social orders with their ever increasing need for new and more specialized tasks of common-sense knowing and doing.

Besides the smooth evolution of different classes, cooperating in increasingly complex and concretely intelligent ways of life, there are also class conflicts, the dialectical tensions that emerge between different groups. For example, in the economic community, as Jane Jacobs points out, it was not the people who made carriages for horses who invented automobiles, nor did the group who made iceboxes invent refrigerators.[12] The people who were producing the iceboxes would quickly grasp that the introduction of refrigerators into the economic order would eventually put them out of business. And if the icebox community had the ability to prevent the manufacture of refrigerators, it would probably do so to preserve its own economic cooperative scheme for making a living. Any number of rationalizations could be proposed, such as the invention was impractical or would disrupt the social order. In this case, the rationalization would appeal primarily to those whose living depended on making and selling iceboxes. The result would be the division of the social order into two groups: the small, new 'creative minority' that desired a new way of making a living and the older and once creative community that has now become the 'dominant minority' – a progressive community versus a reactionary one.

The case I have described is a simple illustration of why the ordinary cycle of new ideas followed by new courses of actions does not result in continuously expanding and increasingly intelligent schemes of cooperating communities. In the first place, most new ideas are not practical and do not solve the concrete problems at hand. In the second place, ideas that are practical and meet the issues squarely will become operative only if they can overcome the passive resistance to change that operates in personal or collective habits. Personal and social habits take time to form, but once established, they generate their own momentum or inertia. Besides passive resistance, there is also the active resistance that a group can exercise if it has the power to render inoperative new and intelligible courses of action that would work to its own disadvantage. Such power plays can call upon group loyalties to repress and sidetrack relevant questions that would generate understanding and new attitudes for pursuing more reasonable courses of action. The self-regarding community is especially successful in elaborating excuses and rationalization for the collective disorder and injustices that it inflicts on other groups within the community. Whereas individual egotists have to protect themselves against 'the slings and arrows' of the members of the group they are exploiting, group egotism can generate a socially supported ideology, or system of ideas, that defends and justifies the status quo as well as their own self-serving way of life. Even further, group bias can establish a market for similar distorted opinions and doctrines which will support and further rationalize such social implications.

It was Freud who pioneered research into modes of individual self-deception, and it was Rousseau, Hegel, and Marx who drew attention to various forms of group biases and the false consciences that they generate, practice, and disseminate.[13] But there is a deeper and more foundational dialectic that needs to be understood.

4d General Bias

We have been moving toward the appropriation and identification of our selves as knowers. In the course of history and in our own biographies, intelligence has played a significant role, but what has been the purpose and the pattern of that knowing? Common-sense intelligence that specializes in concrete practical tasks is as old as the human race, so also are symbolic patterns of knowing, and both patterns have been operative in our own biographies from early childhood. But to develop a disinterested desire in knowing, to want to know for the sake of knowing, did not emerge in human history until the time of the Greeks.

In your own particular history, it takes considerable training and purging of other desires before you begin to feel comfortable in a purely intellectual pattern of knowing. Even after you have acquired a taste for purely intellectual issues, you are still a long way from making such a disinterested desire to know the central orienting desire of your living. The reason is, of course, that purely intellectual patterns emerge in a person who already has a different orienting set of personal and collective habits. So in the Hellenic culture the rise of theoretical patterns took place in communities already oriented by their symbolic and practical patterns of knowing.

Since common-sense patterns of knowing specialize in solving concrete particular problems and since theory is concerned with complex long-term issues, it would seem that theoretical and common-sense patterns of knowing should complement one another. The dialectical tension between your interested and disinterested desire to know should bring about long-term progress. The dialectical tensions that stem from oppositions, however, all too easily turn into contradictions and gradually generate biases that steadily lead to decline and from decline to disorder and eventual breakdown. The ruins of great civilizations stand as grim reminders and a mockery of the enthusiastic heralds of human progress. While personal and group biases stem from a failure in the unfolding of common-sense knowing, general bias is primarily a failure on the part of practical knowers to accept the fact that common-sense knowing is a limited, specialized form of knowing. Rather than accept such a limitation, practical knowers pretend to be omniscient knowers who tend to spurn and depreciate theoretical knowers as impractical idealists lost in their abstractions. Thus, we have the familiar conflict between egg-head intellectualists and hard-boiled pragmatists, which is more of a group conflict stemming from group biases. General bias, on the other hand, tends to underlie and operate in both groups without their even suspecting it.

The source of the problem of general bias is the tension between interested and disinterested knowing. The solution is not to disparage either pattern of knowing but to legitimate both patterns, and to understand precisely how they may actually complement one another. Put in its broadest context, common-sense knowers have to become long-term historical knowers if they are to understand how and why their own social order is operating the way it is. Common-sense knowers are not historical knowers; they are concerned with short-term problems, while historical knowers are trying to understand how a long series of past common-sense knowers and their respective communities have made history and handed it on in its present form.

5   Long Cycle of Decline

It is important to distinguish in any social situation those disorders that arise from particular groups in society and those that result from the general neglect by all communities. There is a significant difference between short-term disorders that result from class or group biases and the long-term disorders that stem from the general bias.[14] This distinction between short-term and long-term cycles of disorders needs some clarification. We are all familiar with ideas about progress and growth, but explanations of decline and contracting horizons are less familiar. Let us consider first the problem of correcting class conflicts. In the examples of iceboxes and refrigerators or horse carriages and automobiles, we find advances in technology which result in, among other things, material comfort. Such advances, though they may go against the vested interests of certain economic groups, are very difficult to block, even in the short run. However, if we examine attempted reforms or improvements in religious, political, and other social groups, we find it is much more difficult to correct group biases. What usually happens is that the social order divides into a reform group and a reactionary group. The reform group may turn rebellious and break away, or it may become revolutionary and end up using force to accomplish its goals. Unfortunately, this course of events has two negative results. The reform group becomes the new dominant group and will develop symbolic stories, rituals, slogans, and songs to celebrate and justify its own wisdom and righteousness while denouncing the follies and injustices of the vanquished. The defeated group, on the other hand, has its own hatreds and resentful memories which it will hand on to future generations to motivate and promote revenge whenever opportunities for retribution emerge. In this scenario a group bias is overcome, but in such a way that two new group biases have been generated in correcting the older bias.

If this scenario is repeated over several centuries, the results will bring to light how the general bias interacts with group bias to generate a long cycle of decline, which leads to a series of lower viewpoints or constricting social and cultural horizons. To grasp the results of this long cycle of decline, let us recall that the basic dialectic is between the interested, practical knowing of common sense and the disinterested desire of theoretical knowing. While there is a tension and opposition between these two concrete conscious poles, there could be harmonious complementarity. But for such complementarity to emerge, people who are working out day- to-day solutions to the problems of practical living must realize that common sense is a specialized pattern of knowing that is limited to particular problems and particular solutions. It cannot deal adequately with problems inherited from past generations that are blocking questions, insights, and ideas that could become operative if these inherited biases and disorienting cultural assumptions were recognized and removed. In other words, common-sense knowers must realize and acknowledge their own limitations and agree to cooperate with knowers whose insights and ideas have their source, not in short-term objectives and practices, but in long-term concerns and consequences. To people of common sense, this sounds like more foolishness; even worse, to some it may sound like the blind leading the blind. Such long-term interpretations and evaluations seem like mere idealism and folly because general bias has been so effective in establishing the attitudes and opinions that make these interpretations seem like wishful thinking. Just as common-sense insights accumulate to form a solid core of intelligent working assumptions that lead to progress, just as simple excuses and rationalizations accumulate and become permanent disorders in the social order, so too a historical series of social disorders can set up a longer cycle that form tensions between the hard-boiled pragmatists and the abstract, impractical theoreticians.

The hard-boiled pragmatists have to work out their day-to-day problems in a social order that is the result, not only of past intelligent policies, but also of various forms of institutionalized disorders. What works in such historical situations are not coherent and reasonable courses of action because the policies are not dealing with reasonable and coherent situations. What will work is some form of compromise that does not challenge the actual source of the disorders, but effects a plausible adaptation to these present disorders. This means that the cycles of daily living can keep moving in some combination of reasonable and unreasonable practices. The result is that the common-sense desire to know will itself become distorted. But what is much more serious is that the same sort of distortion can spread to the theoretical sphere. Theoreticians grow up in the same concrete social order and disorders as practical knowers, and so theory can be subject to similar pressures and disorientations which may gradually compromise the different long-term objectives and disinterested desires that initiate and sustain their passion for learning. Gradually the goal of disinterested knowing is no longer an open-ended inquiry and critical reflection, but some truncated version of it which, in the limit, surrenders its own norms and objectives. In such a limit case, instead of the disinterested desire providing norms for judging the situations, the reverse occurs, as the facts of the socially disordered situations become the basis and provide the norms for an empirical science of human behavior. Thus the dramatic warning by Machiavelli:

For imagination has created many principalities and republics that have never been seen or known to have any real existence, for how we live is so different from how we ought to live that he who studies what ought to be done rather than what is done will learn the way to his downfall rather than to his preservation. A man striving in every way to be good will meet his ruin among the great number who are not good. Hence it is necessary for a prince, if he wishes to remain in power, to learn how not to be good and to use his knowledge or refrain from using it as he may need.[15]

Norms for questioning and understanding, therefore, are to be subordinated to the concrete disordered performances of different communities. The general bias, which has its origin in the dialectic between the interested and disinterested desire to know, eventually inhibits the progress toward more highly intelligent policies and courses of action in the short term, but also in the long run, it tends to distort the unfolding of the disinterested desire to know. What is needed to reverse this general bias is a new and higher viewpoint that will attack the problem at its source. What is needed is a method that can interpret the historical sequence of cultures in a critically normative way. The purpose of such a critique would be, not just to understand human history, but to understand it in a way that human communities can become more responsible for the history they have inherited and for the history they are making and transmitting to further generations.

It is too early in our study to examine how such new ways of becoming responsible are to be developed, but we may sketch several important steps that have to be taken. First, a critical study of history begins with an understanding of the notion of a dialectic as a correlation of concretely opposed activities that modify one another as they unfold. Second, these concretely opposed patterns of understanding may operate positively or negatively, thereby generating the cumulative results we know as progress or decline. Third, there are four different dialectics operating in any individual, but the basic dialectic is between the interested and disinterested desire to know. Fourth, the disinterested desire to know is preoccupied with long-term cumulative results while the interested desire to know attends to short-term problems of daily living and their solutions. There is a fundamental distinction to be made, therefore, between short-term and long-term progress and decline. Fifth, in order to overcome long-term decline it is critical that a distinction be made between group bias, and general bias since the short-term interests of common-sense knowers can recognize social disorders that arise from the various forms of group biases such as class conflicts, vested interests, and dominant minorities.

The much more serious problem is that the usual common-sense strategy for eliminating operative group biases is through the use of force and violence. This, in turn, sets the conditions for two new group biases, and if this sequence is repeated the much longer cycle of decline sets in, bringing with it various degrees of despair about appealing to a people's desire to know, since such appeals sound like pious platitudes or utopian proposals. Finally, it is critically important to grasp that, just as in the dialectic with yourself, you set up screening memories for censoring past events that you refuse to deal with, so too cultural communities construct stories, songs, rituals, and other means of symbolic expressions to screen out their own histories of past communal deeds which they refuse to acknowledge. Later chapters will spell out in more detail how such a critical history can be developed. The first step in this direction will be to explain the present ordering of our universe based on the method of knowing we have considered. The fundamental premise for setting forth such a world-order is that our universe is intelligible or understandable. As Einstein put it. 'The most incomprehensible thing about our universe is that it is comprehensible.' But, as we already have discovered, there are different types of intelligibilities: classical and statistical intelligibilities, common sense and symbolic intelligibilities. To understand our universe we must be able to integrate the different ways in which we understand. This, in turn, means that we must be able to integrate the different methods that guide our knowing activities toward these different forms of intelligibilities. It is to such an integration that we shall turn in the next chapter.

6   Summary

Although the first three chapters invite you, the reader, to appropriate your own activity of understanding, there is a significant difference between the first two chapters and this third chapter. The examples of insight presented in the first two chapters were taken from theoretical patterns of knowing which are oriented by a disinterested and detached desire to know universal objectives, while the acts of understanding examined in this chapter are oriented by an interested desire to know limited, pragmatic objectives. While these pragmatic objectives are symbolically motivated, in this chapter our concern is, not primarily with personal motives for seeking such goals, but with the broader interests that orient this pattern of knowing, and the fact that these motives direct a person's understanding toward concrete particular courses of action requiring specific skills to achieve particular tasks.

Economists or social scientists are interested in more universal courses of human actions, whereas people using common-sense patterns of knowing operate in much narrower and more specialized modes of knowing since their concern is to know how to perform concrete particular tasks. If you are interested in getting along with your neighbor, you are interested not in neighbors generally, but in neighbors who live in a particular place and time, who have particular temperaments, traits, and characters. General advice is helpful, but to be concretely helpful that general knowledge will have to be particularized through insights into concrete situations. And if you move to a different neighborhood, the concrete differences of that new situation will have to be understood in their particularity. To know how to live intelligently in any concrete social situation, you must operate in the common-sense pattern of knowing. You may bring more universal knowledge to bear on that situation, but such general knowledge must be particularized through common-sense insights into the concrete, here-and-now human situations.

If the continually shifting common-sense patterns of knowing are so central to the history of concrete human living, why has this pattern of knowing been so neglected by scholars? There are three reasons.

First, it was the dramatic success of theoretical, explanatory knowing in the seventeenth century that precipitated the epistemological crisis and turned philosophers' attention to the problem of the objectivity of knowing. As we have seen, the key step in that revolution was the shift from knowing things in a descriptive context to knowing things in an explanatory pattern where things are no longer related to the knowing subject, but are related to one another in recurring patterns. There was a tendency then among scholars to denigrate any method of knowing that did not operate in the explanatory context. Thus, descriptive knowing that relates things to the subject was criticized and invalidated as subjective and limited to surface appearances, as opposed to the theoretical pattern of knowing that disclosed the real inner structures of things.

This mistake was followed by the second oversight of failing to recognize that while theoretical knowing, as practiced by classical scientists such as Galileo and Newton, was valid, it was nevertheless an abstract and universal pattern of knowing. Although the universal laws of mechanics were thought to be verified in concrete instances, they were not verified in every past, present, and future concrete instance. The basic error was to assume that all past and future concrete instances were given and would be given in the same continuous fashion that classical scientists had assumed but had not actually verified. Or, to put it negatively, classical scientists did not assume that the present planetary cycles were operating in a field of statistically given conditions. Unlike contemporary meteorologists, who assume that weather cycles operate under statistically given conditions, classical scientists assumed that the present given conditions would continue to remain the same. Common-sense knowers, on the other hand, realize that situations and people change, and they do so, if not all the time, then at least some of the time. And occasionally these changes can be quite significant and surprising. Common-sense knowledge, then, is always incomplete and can only be completed by paying attention to the concrete tasks and particular people with whom you are working at any given time. To scientists who are attempting to understand the universe in a completely comprehensive way, the common-sense mode of understanding may seem to be rather superficial knowledge, but it is the mode of knowledge that scientists themselves use in dealing with the practical affairs of their own day-to-day living. Moreover, there is no other way of knowing the concrete, particular aspects of things.

A further reason why common-sense modes of knowing have been overlooked or degraded is because knowing concrete particular persons, places, and times is assumed to require no more than ordinary attentive sensing. To know that water, steam, and ice are different modes of behavior of one and the same operating substance (H_2O) requires 'looking' underneath the surface of things in order to reveal their hidden structures, whereas common-sense knowers observe only the outward sensible appearances of things and know only the shadows and surfaces of these things. To know the real substance of things we must put on the geometer's or the chemist's glasses and 'see' the inner constituents of these things. Behind this type of assertion is a basic epistemological assumption about what constitutes real objective knowing. I will address this epistemological issue in the fifth chapter, but here I would like to stress the crucial role that insights or understandings play in any pattern of knowing, and especially in the ordinary, familiar, but unthematized mode of common-sense knowing.

Let us take as an example the problem of knowing how to read. Before children learn how to read they can see the written or printed letters but cannot see words, phrases, sentences, and paragraphs. Children have an immediate sensible awareness of the letters, but it will take them a year or more to mediate and transform those immediate sensible experiences into readable experiences of different types of meaning. We cannot see meanings. Children must learn to read the invisible meanings within the visible marks. People who know how to read are so used to interpreting letters as words and phrases that they forget that such words and phrases cannot be seen. Words, then, are not immediate experiences but mediated, interpreted experiences, and without such mediating insights, the visible marks will have no meaning.

Because it took Galileo so many years to learn how to interpret the trajectory of a cannonball as a parabolic path, he realized that only through many acts of geometrical understanding could a person gradually acquire

such knowledge. However, he forgot that it also took long years of common-sense learning to know that there were such things as guns and can-
nonballs. If Galileo had admitted that these two quite different modes of
knowing were oriented by different desires and were seeking different
objectives he would have had to face the problem of integrating two different yet valid ways of knowing. Instead, he insisted that there was only one
valid way of 'really' knowing things, and that was the theoretical or geometrical way of knowing.

What Galileo did not realize was that there were two quite different
meanings of the term 'concrete.' First, the term refers to the immediate,
actual, and particular aspects of things that come to be interpreted and
mediated through common-sense modes of knowing. Second, the meaning of 'concrete' refers not only to the actual and particular things as particular, but to everything about these particular actual things. In other
words, the 'concrete' is both particular and comprehensive. To know the
concrete is both to know all things in their particular actuality and to know
these same things in a completely comprehensive manner. To accomplish
this means integrating scientific knowing with common-sense knowing.
But to do this we must first know what knowing is, and that there are different patterns of knowing, and that they operate in and through the same
basic structure of knowing for quite different but potentially complementary goals.

To actualize this potential complimentarity between these different patterns of knowing requires that knowers must be able to reconcile the differences between their interested short-term desire to know and their
disinterested long-term desire to know. In addition, they must know the
four different ways that both desires to know may be disoriented and distorted through the various forms of biases that truncate and alienate us
from the identity of ourselves. Besides the traditional and familiar selfish,
egotistical bias, there is the dramatic bias by which we betray ourselves by
setting up, through various strategies of censorship and repression, the
multiple forms of deceptions that we now label as neuroses. Because
insights are dependent on images, because images orient our feelings, and
because knowing depends on the desire to know that emerges in wondering and questioning, we may prevent unwanted discoveries about our psychic selves by redirecting those feelings; we reorient such feeling because
they would evoke questions that would condition the probable insights
which, in turn, would lead to the disclosure of a personal identity that we
are anxious to keep underground and unappropriated. The same sort of
cover-up operates even more effectively in group hostilities and hatreds as
one part of the population develops manners and modes of living and
behaving that repeatedly reinforce, rationalize, and justify their aversions

and animosities toward another group within the various social, economic, political, or religious institutional orderings of a community. However, such personal and group distortions that disorder our desire to know are secondary to the more subtle and pervasive general bias, which permeates every person and every historical community.

Intellectual development in any individual is a long, slow, and difficult process. The same is true for the communal development of knowing as it unfolds from the earliest periods of human history. The desire to know in systematic and theoretical ways did not emerge until quite recently in human history, while common-sense methods of knowing have been practiced since the beginning of human history. This suggests that when the desire to know in a systematic way finally emerged on the historical stage in ancient Greek culture, it arrived, not as a friend and ally of practical wisdom, but as its antagonist and enemy.

Because practical common-sense knowers do not know their own knowing, they do not know that practical knowing yields only very special, not general, knowledge. The tendency, then, is for common-sense knowers to assume they already know in the only way that is worth knowing. In other words, they assume they are 'omnicompetent' and omniscient knowers rather than extremely limited knowers. The critical probing of Socratic questioning was not interpreted by the Athenian citizens as the opening up a new horizon of knowing; rather, it was seen as a threat and insult to their own accepted way of life. And the Athenians' way of removing this Socratic threat to their culturally assumed wisdom was to deal with Socrates in the way they dealt with their other enemies – by the use of force. In other words, the conventional way to solve such problems was, not to take Socrates' questions seriously, but to silence these disturbing questions and then justify the injustice through some form of symbolic cover-up. The result was to make the Athenian political and social order, not the product of developing insights, but the product of oversights and irrational policies.

The more serious problem, however, was not the execution of Socrates or similar unreasonable policies; rather, it was that such policies became embedded in a social order which was itself the historical product of prior irrational policies. The consequence is that this distortion of the desire to know in a disinterested way can combine with group and individual biases to generate a longer cycle of decline. Group biases account for certain short-term cycles of disorder and unreasonable patterns of cooperative living, but if we add to such disorders the continual refusal to deal with long-term issues and policies, we end up with the basic problem of human history: communities that repeatedly solve real problems by attempting to obliterate them through various practices that either encourage or force reasonable people to behave in unreasonable ways, thereby, handing on to their historical successors a social order that is the result, not of reasonable practices and valuable policies, but of unreasonable, disordered ways of behaving.

The first consequence of such cumulative disorders is that social situations will exhibit a combination of reasonable and unreasonable policies. Not only do such social situations set the conditions for personal and group biases, but such situations are also less apt to evoke the fresh insights that would disclose alternative courses of action. However, there is an even more serious consequence that can emerge when social scientists attempt to interpret and evaluate just what is going forward through a historical sequence of such social orders. If social scientists take the actual data of the social situation as the norm for critically judging the reality of the situation, they are abandoning the normative guide that is intrinsic to their own desire to know. In place of this normative desire to know, social scientists substitute the concrete data of the social order, but such data combine ordered and disordered elements without providing any norm by which scientists can discern the difference between a social order and social disorders. Thus, we have the situations that I illustrated by the quotation from *The Prince*, where Machiavelli rejects any normative standard for governing a people other than the use of force and fraud.

It is too early in this study to set forth normative standards for dealing with such consequences but the first step in this direction is to set forth an account of the general ordering of the universe based on our analysis of scientific and practical knowing.

4

The World-Order of Things

In chapter 2 we sketched the history of mathematics and physics in order to draw attention to the two different scientific methods, classical and statistical. In chapter 3 we discussed dialectical method. In this chapter we will introduce genetic method.[1] All four methods are heuristic and, taken together, can form an integral, heuristic structure by which a knower can anticipate knowing all that there is to be known. A fuller investigation of this integral, heuristic structure will be undertaken in the later chapters on metaphysics and ethics, but here I wish to explore some preliminary aspects of this integrating structure. To begin, let us explore the meaning and significance of the term 'heuristic.'

1 Heuristic Structures

Any method is heuristic in the sense that it assists you in discovering what you do not know. The basic heuristic is the question that guides you toward an insight by transforming inner or outer sensible experiences into potentially intelligible experiences, known unknowns. Questioning, then, is a spontaneous, a priori way of knowing your own not knowing, and of leading you toward an insight. Questioning is not itself an a priori understanding, but it does disclose that a questioned experience is an understandable experience.

Methodical questioning goes a step further and reveals the type of insight being sought and how it will be conceived and verified. Thus, as we saw in chapter 2, Vièta took a major step toward making mathematics methodical when he named the unknown he was trying to discover. The point in analyzing Vièta's achievement was, not to learn mathematics, but to appropriate the way mathematical minds ask questions and anticipate answers in a methodical way. We noted that the type of anticipated insight kept changing until the nineteenth century, when the object sought or the insight anticipated was an understanding, not of unknown variables nor of unknown functions, but of an unknown group of functions systematically ordered, whose operating range could be specified by a set of axioms. Similar developments can be found in physics.

2   Classical Heuristic Structures

In practicing physics, both the Greeks and Galileo anticipated discovering proportions, but the proportions that Galileo anticipated were to be formulated in abstraction from certain sensible correlates such as weight and resistance. In other words, the type of insights Galileo anticipated, the way he formulated those insights, and the way he verified his formulations differed remarkably from the insights and formulations of the Greeks.[2] More importantly, Galileo's new method led directly to Newton's new heuristic anticipation, not just of proportioned ratios, but of a system of such ratios or correlations. Also, with Newton the notion of a function emerged and, with it, the notion of science as a search for unknown functions, began. With the discovery of such functions a new meaning of what is meant by a scientific law likewise emerged. A function is an unchanging correlation among two or more changing variables and, because the function is unchanging or invariant, it can serve as a norm for measuring two or more changing quantities whose changes are mutually dependent on one another.

The abstractive procedures for this new classical method were impressive, but they also posed a complex problem for classical scientists trying to verify their formulated laws or normative correlations. How is an abstract correlation verified? To solve this problem Galileo set up an experiment embodying an *idealized* set of conditions by which he intended to measure the times of falling bodies and to correlate those times to the distances through which they fell. Galileo's law does not state what will happen in this or that concrete actual case; rather, the law states what will happen under strictly controlled conditions. The law is an ideal norm. It abstracts from concrete falling bodies and attempts to establish a limit or mean around which actual concrete cases will converge or oscillate.[3]

Newton's problem of experimental verification was even more difficult since, unlike Galileo, Newton needed observational data on the planetary system. Newton assumed that the way the earth and the moon interacted would serve as a typical case of planetary motions and that this case could therefore be generalized to cover any other two interacting masses. He realized, however, that to try to verify how three or more bodies interacted would be too complex to be analyzed and verified. The important point to notice is that such a systematic ordering of the planetary motions was an abstract system of idealized averages. What Newton verified was not the actual systematic cycling of the planets about the sun, or of moons about planets, but a concretely possible system of cycles. Furthermore, Newton did not ask how this planetary cycling originated, how long it had been operating, how long it would continue to cycle, or how many planetary systems there are, or how they are distributed, etc. These are all scientific questions, but they are not the kind of questions, insights, and formulations that a classical scientist like Newton would have wondered about. However, these are just the sort of questions, insights, formulations, and verifications that would intrigue a statistical scientist.

3   Statistical Heuristic Structures

The astronomers who provided the data for Newton were also guided in their research by the classical assumption that the universe was an intelligible universe and that it could be understood in the way that Newton had set forth. It would have seemed contradictory to them to assume that the universe operated in nonsystematic ways and that such nonsystematic processes could also be intelligible. A nonsystematic ordering would seem to suggest a non-intelligible order. The surprise is that nonsystematic processes are intelligible, although the questions, insights, formulations, verifications, and data-collecting procedures that they require are quite different from those that classical investigators like Galileo, Kepler, and Newton practiced.[4] A graduate student in astronomy might count the number of stars on a photographic plate, but this is not the sort of data collecting that would have engaged astronomers like Kepler, Tycho Brahe, and Edmund Halley. What has counting stars to do with explaining the intelligible order of the universe? What sort of understanding does one expect to emerge by gathering data on 'numbers' of things? It turns out that large numbers are, in fact, very significant in statistical thinking and in understanding the actual order of our universe.

As we noted in chapter 2, statistical investigators do not abstract from descriptive correlates as classical scientists do. Nor do they abstract from particular cases. They count the actual number of people who have died or who were born during the last twenty years, for example, but they do so not because they are interested in such particular cases as particular. Common-sense knowing specializes in questioning and understanding concrete actual cases as concrete and particular, but statistical investigators have quite different questions and are seeking quite different answers. Statistical scientists deal with concrete particular happenings, in order to discover certain statistical regularities or frequencies. As we noted, statistical regularities admit exceptions, and statistical scientists expect that such exceptions will occur nonsystematically. Thus, the statistical law provides science with a very different notion of what a law is.[5]

In general, a classical law is an unchanging correlation among changing quantities that supplies scientists with a standard for measuring and predicting how such changes have occurred, are occurring, and will recur. A statistical correlation, however, is a probability or frequency, and while it provides a norm, it carries a quite different meaning. A classical norm was assumed to be a universal necessary standard for judging all cases without exception; Galileo did not anticipate discovering exceptions to the law of falling bodies. Statistical laws do anticipate such exceptions to ideal frequencies within a certain range, and so a statistical standard is not a universal necessary standard. Every now and then exceptions may occur, in fact, are expected to occur. In the case of coin tossing, the statistical norm allows us to distinguish between what is identified as an 'ordinary run' of tosses and what is an 'exceptional run' of events. Twenty heads in a row is a most exceptional run of events, whereas two or three in a row is ordinary. And we know this because we know in advance what is considered to be an average or ordinary course of events.

A statistical norm also enables scientists to distinguish between a short and a long run of events. Such methodical procedures or heuristic structures would have astonished Aristotle since they establish a scientific approach to contingent or accidental occurrences and, for Aristotle, science was a search for necessary and certain causes, as it also was for Galileo and Newton. That there was a law that was neither universal nor necessary would have astonished Kant, who also held on to the notion of law as universal and necessary. Yet both the classical notion of science and classical laws and the statistical notion of science and statistical laws are based on questioning experiences, understanding those experiences, formulating an understanding of those experiences, and then verifying the formulations of this understanding of questioned experiences. The difference between these two notions of science and their respective heuristic procedures is that they ask different types of questions, which in turn anticipate different types of insights, different types of formulations, and verifications. Let us consider how these two heuristic methods complement one another.

Statistical laws focus on events or occurrences or happenings, while classical laws are concerned, not with events, but with the form or kind of events that have occurred. For example, one of the first significant uses of statistical laws in the natural sciences was in the kinetic theory of gases. In any liter of oxygen there will be an incredibly vast aggregate of oxygen atoms. Classical scientists might ask, What is the law that governs the behavior of each and every one of these oxygen atoms? But statistical scientists will shift their attention to the behavior of an average molecule in the total aggregate. They discover these averages by distributing a set of velocities into more or less probable speeds, which can then be graphed in the familiar bell curve. Classical laws deal with different kinds of functions and statistical laws deal with their frequencies, thus complementing one another since classical laws deal with functions and statistical laws deal with the ideal frequencies with which those functions behave. Both laws are 'forms,' if by 'form' we mean an intelligibility. But they are quite different and distinguishable types of intelligibilities or 'forms.'

There is an even more significant complementarity if we recall that not only does the classical method anticipate the formulation of laws but, more significantly, classical scientists anticipate the integration and unification of laws into systems of laws. Similarly, statistical laws, which are expressed as normative probabilities, may be combined to specify different 'states' of these systems. For example, the human physiological system is made up of different interrelated subsystems – digestive, pulmonary, circulatory, excretory, nervous, etc. Doctors know the ideal rates at which these systems operate, and by testing persons of certain age groups, they can observe and measure the actual operation of our sub-systems. After measuring all these different rates, the doctor can assess the present 'state' of a person's physiological system. Classical scientists analyze the ways that pulmonary or digestive systems function, while statistical scientists specify the normative or ideal frequencies with which these systems ought to be operating in different situations.

This complementarity can be seen even more clearly if we consider the way statistical scientists collect data. For example, statistical scientists counting the number of births during any particular year abstract, first, from who is being born, second, from the particular places and particular times of the births, and, third and most significantly, from what birth is. Such collections assembled by statistical scientists are called an aggregate, that is, a group of events or happenings of a particular kind that have occurred in a certain geographical area during a specific time frame. The only relations among these events is coincidental; they occurred during particular times in particular places. There is no specific order to the way the births are counted except that they fall within certain geographical boundaries during a particular period. It is the same as economists counting or totaling up the gross national product of a country's economic activities during some definite period. Statistical economists are interested in not who produced the goods and services, nor how or why they were produced; rather, they are interested in the total amount.

This is certainly not a traditional philosophical or scientific concern. Traditionally, philosophers wondered about what things were and why they were what they were. It would seem very strange to such philosophers to assume a statistical perspective, focusing instead on how many and how often. Classical scientists are oriented by a concern for unity, but statistical scientists are preoccupied with totals and frequencies. Rather than attempting to characterize a group of things as a species, statistical scientists want to know the number of the species (the total, not the whole) and how often the individuals do whatever it is that they do (reproduce, marry, die, produce goods and services, etc.).

Both groups of scientists are interested in the scientific goal of going beyond mere description in order to reach explanations. Statistical scientists intend to explain what probably will happen next year or in ten years by generalizing from what has happened during the last ten or twenty years. Such scientific procedures produced a revolution in scientific thinking; scientific laws were considered to be, not norms for what might happen, but a prediction about what necessarily will happen. What classical scientists failed to realize was that, in formulating their laws, they had abstracted from certain aspects of concrete observable experiences that provided the field for statistical inquiry.

Gradually, as statistical science advanced in the twentieth century, the notion of necessity as an intrinsic property of a law has faded, and in its place the complementarity of these two methods has emerged. To study this complementarity in still more detail, we will consider the technical notion of a scheme of recurrence.[6]

4   Schemes of Recurrence

At the center of Aristotle's ordering of nature is the notion of a cycle, which may be defined as a set of events related to one another in such a way that the last event in the sequence sets the conditions for the sequence of events to be repeated. This notion can be applied to different kinds of things, such as planetary motions, seasonal changes, plants, animals, and humans; we also speak of the cycles of birth and death, cycles of production and consumption, historical cycles, etc. Thus 'cycle' can provide a foundational term that can be applied to different genera of things and also to the way they interact with one another on the same or different levels of being, according to the grade or perfection of their nature. For Aristotle the higher, heavenly bodies move in perfect, circular cycles, while the nearer planets move in more complex, less perfect, circular modes according to their less perfect natures. This partly explains the ancient contrast between the incorruptible celestial beings and their modes of behavior and the more corruptible terrestrial beings and their modes of behavior.

The most significant property of this notion of a cycle is that the temporal sequence of events ends in such a way as to initiate the new cycle. For example, middle *C* on the piano ends a diatonic scale of *do, re mi, so, fa, la, ti, do* and, at the same time, initiates the next diatonic series; *do* is both the last and the first note. Thus, a linear series of musical tones may also be understood as a cyclical series. The same diatonic scale may be expanded into a chromatic scale and then into the much more complex harmonic circle of fifths. Within such cyclical contexts, endless variations of melodic and harmonic sequences can be constructed. However, there is a hidden assumption in such cyclical order, namely, that the conditions for the repeating cycle will be provided continuously, whereas the opposite assumption is at the basis of statistical laws. Since statistical laws are also intelligible forms, there is no a priori reason for excluding the possibility that the actual order of the universe may be based on the assumptions of statistical thinking, as well as on classical thinking.

We may ask whether we can combine the traditional notion of continuous cyclical processes with the contemporary scientific notion of statistical regularities which assumes discontinuities. Not only are the two compatible, but together they provide scientists with a much more flexible notion of design or world-order and, as we shall see, such a design opens up the possibility for dynamic evolutionary developments.

Let us take as an example the game of poker. The game begins by shuffling the pack of cards in order to break up any prior sequence and to create a random mixture of fifty-two cards. The challenge for the players is to play their cards in the wisest way possible. After each hand is played the cycle is repeated, starting again with a random mixture of the cards. On the assumption that each player receives five out of a possible fifty-two cards, statistical scientists have worked out the possible combinations that can be constructed out of the five cards which the players receive and the probabilities of these combinations occurring. An informed player has some understanding of these odds, namely, certain combinations of cards will occur and recur more or less frequently. In the long run, the person who plays according to these ideal probabilities will be able to set up a repeating cycle of winning. Here we have an example of a cycle of recurring events that takes place in a random assortment of cards. Most significantly, this cycle does not begin and end on the assumption of continuous conditions being provided. The conditions for the winning scheme are discontinuous and involve a wide flexibility of strategic decisions according to the random or discontinuous reception of various possible combinations that each player receives. The cycle can begin with any given set of five cards, but the wise player operating under those conditions will still win in the long run. Moreover, the longer the game goes on the more evident will be the winning cycle of the best players. When understood in this way, the game of chance is not a game of chance at all, but a game in which possible, probable, and actual schemes of events keep recurring. In each hand that is dealt, there are five actual cards out of a possible fifty-two. A player will keep certain combinations of the five and discard the others according to a strategy of probabilities of receiving certain final combinations that will actually be played. To speak of poker as a game of chance explains nothing. But to specify the game in terms of probability is to 'explain' the game. Probability, therefore, may be defined as the intelligibility of chance. Or probability is an intelligible correlation of possibilities ordered by expected, idealized frequencies.

An application of this game model can be seen if we consider Darwin's theory of evolution. Before Darwin's arrival at the Galapagos Islands, he travelled along the coast of South America studying the rich variety of plant and animal life.[7] He assumed that this rich diversity in fauna and flora was probably due to the observable differences in climate, soil, and other geological and environmental conditions. Arriving at the islands, he was surprised when he found a wide range of plant and animal life all emerging and surviving within the very same environmental conditions. Later he returned to England wondering how there could be such a variety of plant and animal life existing and operating under such similar, environmental conditions. Eventually he answered this question by making two assumptions: first, that there are continuous variations in the naturally occurring species of plants, animals, and people as well as in the physical environment; second, that there is a continuous struggle for survival among these different species so that those species that are the best-adapted competitors will tend to survive the longest. If we examine Darwin's question in terms of our contemporary scientific knowledge and apply our model of a card game, we will see that the notion of a scheme of recurrence will provide a general heuristic notion for answering Darwin's question.

Today we know that earth, air, heat, water, and the other physical and chemical conditions of the Galapagos Islands form a solid, liquid, and gaseous aggregate of chemical atoms and compounds within which are innumerable biological possibilities that could be combined into recurring biological schemes. Further, just as in the card game of fifty-two possibilities there are the probabilities of different winning combinations, so too in the chemical aggregates of a given geographical area there are biological possibilities and probabilities for the actual emergence of different species of biochemical organisms operating in series of different and quite flexible schemes. There is some probability on the chemical level, then, that the compounds will come together in just the right combination for higher biological cycles to emerge. Just as the combinations of cards a player receives depends on certain combinations of fifty-two possibilities, so too various plant species in a geographical area are dealt a variety of chemical combinations of earth, air, water, light, etc. What these different organisms of the various species will do with these chemical processes depends on the range of biological schemes of intussusception, reproduction, and survival that these organisms can initiate and sustain. The wise card-player deals with different combinations in different ways, so plants deal with different chemical conditions in different ways. Any given plant is just one of an endless range of possible solutions to the problem of emergence and survival within a physical and chemical environment. Implied in this argument is the notion of a higher viewpoint or two-level thinking.

In doing algebra we are also doing arithmetic, but we are performing it in a new context of meanings. Just as insights transform possible intelligible experiences into actual intelligible experiences, so too the arithmetical rules dealing with numbers can be transformed by discovering new possibilities in numbers and operations that are not exploited on the level of arithmetic. In this way, numbers become variables (possibles) which may be interpreted either as numbers or as geometrical magnitudes. In other words, algebra can be developed into an analytic geometry where we can do arithmetic and geometry at the same time, but on a higher level. Similarly for plants, chemicals become variables that can be transformed into biochemical processes, and these biochemical processes can, in turn, be transformed by animals into psychological processes. The combination of the notion of a scheme of recurrence, which is itself an integration of classical and statistical procedures, can be combined with the notion of a higher viewpoint to provide us with a third heuristic structure – genetic heuristic structure.

5   Genetic Heuristic Structures

The first two methods – classical and statistical – were identified by a particular type of question that orients a knower toward an unknown intelligibility to be discovered through a specific type of understanding. The new question is about 'development' in knowing. We have seen how questions orient and direct knowers, first toward understanding and then to verification of that understanding, which in turn leads to new and further questions. The pursuit of such questions earlier in our history led the Greeks to the discovery of the pursuit of knowing for its own sake and then to the emergence of the ideal of systematic knowing.

Once systematic knowing had emerged, it eventually generated questionable experiences which could not be answered within the range of the known system, and so the need for a new and higher system emerged which would require an understanding, not only of prior questions and answers, but also of understandings that would deal with newly emerging questions. Gradually, after a lengthy period of trial and error, the new higher system emerged, but it did so, not in contradiction to the prior system, but by transforming the lower system, leaving it free to operate as it had previously done. For example, the new rules for operating in algebra do not contradict or put to an end the procedures of arithmetic; rather, they leave arithmetic free to operate according to its own rules. The emergence of a new system from a prior one, however, is not a logical emergence in the sense that the new rules are deducible from the old ones; it is a development in understanding that both understands the prior procedures and develops new and more universal ways of operating. This means that there are two quite different meanings of the way understanding develops. There is the development that takes place in the accumulation of insights, which lead to clustering that eventually coalesces to form a system. But systematic understanders may advance in such a way as to destabilize themselves as they generate questions and problems that cannot be solved within the present range of their horizon of questions and answers. Systematic understanders, therefore, may transcend the limits of their present intelligible horizons, raising questions that set up discontinuities and tensions within their present experiences and summoning them to further development. The longer the trial and error period proceeds, the more probable is the emergence of insights that go beyond the present level of understanding and move toward the formation of a new higher system.

What is development?[8] Development is not a deduction. Any system of thought involves a set of basic terms and relations and basic modes of operating procedures that can be formulated logically. From such a logical foundation the basic axioms for consistency can be tested, and then further possible deductions that can be generated within the system can be worked out. Such logical procedures are necessary for clarifying and defining the limits of your present systematic thinking, but the need for a new higher system cannot be deduced from your present system since it emerges in the form of questions that pose problems that cannot be resolved within the limits of your present operating systems. Such questions thereby orient you to an unknown. This new unknown that you have generated is the possibility of a new higher system that will emerge by meeting the demand you have set up by your own unanswered questions. Development, then, is an emergence of a new and higher integration that will include the prior integration but, more importantly, will provide you with a more complete and differentiated understanding than existed on the prior lower level.

Development can be further clarified if we relate it more precisely to classical and statistical method. Classical method leads to the discovery of functions or normative correlations among changing variables and then to ways of systematizing such correlates. Statistical thinking aims at characterizing the actual performance of these systems through frequencies that specify different operating states of the system at different times and places. This means that statistical frequencies can change while the classical correlations remain invariant. Genetic method, however, studies developments or sequences of changing classical correlates or sequences of systems of changing correlates. Just as classical method involves a notion of law in terms of functions, just as statistical method evolves a different type of law of frequencies, so genetic method evolves into a quite different type of law or normative intelligibility. A genetic law or a law of development is a law about changing systematic relations.

It may seem somewhat paradoxical to claim that there is a law of changing laws, but let us take the example of a tree. The oak tree evolves from a small acorn, and so we say that the acorn develops into an oak tree. But does the tree develop according to a law? We certainly speak of regularity in biological growth, but we also speak of the regularity in the planetary cycle. There are, then, two meanings of regularity: classical regularity and genetic or developmental regularity. There are regular biochemical processes going on in the acorn, but they are not the same biochemical processes going on in the oak tree. The planetary system undergoes regular changes, but they are not developmental changes. Ponds change from solid to liquid to gaseous states, but these 'changes of state' are not developmental changes. Acorns change from an immature, undifferentiated, embryonic state to a mature, highly differentiated, adult state, and they do so by going through a sequence of states that are related to one another as 'stages' or higher integrations in a developmental process.

There are, therefore, three types of laws or regularities or normative orderings, and they are based on three different forms of questions of three different types of insights and formulations. Finally, these three different types of questions, insights, formulations, and verifications form three different, but related, methods of scientific knowing. Classical method anticipates discovering laws that can be combined into various abstract schemes or patterns. Statistical method characterizes how often such abstract, possible schemes may emerge and survive, and statistical thinkers also anticipate that there will be nonsystematic occurrences diverging from these systematic occurrences. Genetic method anticipates that there will be a sequence of such systems that can be correlated developmentally. Beside these three heuristic structures, there is the fourth method we touched upon in the last chapter, the dialectical method.

6   Dialectical Heuristic Structures

In the history of science we noted the rare but significant form of insight called inverse insight. Such insights involve, not grasping direct intelligibilities, but realizing that the question being asked, in anticipation of an understanding, is simply the wrong question. What we grasp, then, in an inverse insight is a new way of anticipating questions that also corrects and reorients our basic assumptions which previously were hidden. In discussing common-sense patterns of knowing, we observed that our desire to know may be disoriented and mislead us into a false series of questions, and that common-sense schemes of operating and cooperating can also become biased and distorted, leading not to the discovery of new ways of cooperative living, but to the very opposite, namely, to new cycles of decline, breakdown, and eventual disintegration.

This means that the successive stages in such cycles of decline and breakdown of the cooperating schemes will not be intelligibly related. For example, to ask why a civilization moves from a failure to cooperate to hostility among its classes, to bitterness, hatred, violence, and eventually to breakdown is to seek an intelligible correlation among stages in decline where, in fact, there is no correlation and nothing to understand. Rather, as we saw, the correct approach is to wonder how reasonable people are able to effectively block out understanding and, thereby, act in unintelligible ways and encourage others to cooperate in these unreasonable schemes. Dialectical method, then, anticipates discovering, not light and reason, but darkness and unreasonableness. The dialectician realizes that the only way to correct such radical disorientations and distortions is to attempt to reorient the way people wonder through a basic reversal of the desires and fears that govern their knowings and doings.

Thus, these four methods – classical, statistical, genetic, and dialectic – can complement one another, and together they form an integral, heuristic structure through which we can anticipate a complete understanding of the physical, chemical, biological, and human historical universes. It is critical to note that these methods are not derived from scientific theories about the intelligibility of the physical universe or of historical communities, but are appropriations of the different ways that scientific knowing and common-sense knowing actually operate to produce their respective intelligibilities. We undertook a study of the history of the sciences not to learn physics, chemistry, and biology, but to understand the various ways that scientists question, understand, formulate, and verify scientific theories. The purpose was to know the capacities and functions of our own minds.

Putting this same issue another way, scientists themselves do not primarily trust in their scientific theories; rather, they trust the methods by which they developed these theories, the same methods by which they correct and verify their theories, and that method is their own inquiring, critical, and verifying mind. This may sound strange to scientists because they do not study their own minds and the normative procedures of human knowing. They are concerned with the cognitional contents that become known in the exercise of their own cognitional operations in accord with their own specialized methods. Philosophers, on the other hand, are interested in knowing their own knowing and in knowing the various methods by which knowers proceed to know what they know, and also why they do such knowing. This second question, namely, why we desire to know, will be taken up in chapter 5. Here I want to examine the possibilities of a world-order that is implied in knowing these first three methods of knowing – classical, statistical, and genetic. I will add the dialectical method in the later chapters.

7   World-Order

A heuristic structure anticipates a type of unknown that is to be known, and an integrated heuristic structure unites different types of unknowns into an organized whole through which a knower may anticipate knowing all that there is to be known, both in the differences and in the unifying relations. As I have stressed, heuristic structures are based not on the cognitional contents of scientific knowing, but on the cognitional activities of scientific knowers. Such cognitional activities do not determine a priori the specific contents of the various scientific fields, but they can and do determine a priori or heuristically the generic structure of those contents and the generic ordering of the universe that is to be known through those structured acts of knowing. In other words, just as classical scientists anticipate discovering functions without specifying what those functions are, just as statistical scientists anticipate discovering probabilities or frequencies without determining their specific content, so too the philosopher can combine these two different anticipations of scientific understanding into recurrent schemes without specifying the contents of those schemes. Further, the philosopher can anticipate that such schemes can be arranged into a world-order without determining what the specific schemes of this order will be. The contents have to be determined a posteriori.[9]

How are these heuristic schemes to be ordered? In addition to the type of insights anticipated in classical and statistical method, there is also the different type of understanding anticipated in genetic method, namely, an insight into development, the sort of understanding that can grasp a higher and lower system simultaneously. For example, it is the sort of understanding that grasps how, in doing analytic geometry, you are also doing algebra and simple geometry at a higher level, or how, plants are biochemical operators that can pattern chemical activities in biological ways. In other words, the way to order a series of recurring schemes is to order them as higher viewpoints in which the lower systems set the conditions for emergence and operation of higher systems. For example, lower algebraic schemes of knowing set the conditions for the emergence of higher schemes of analytic geometry which, in turn, set the conditions for the emergence of schemes of knowing calculus. Or atomic schemes set the conditions for forming chemical schemes which, in turn, set the conditions for biological schemes, etc. By combining classical, statistical, and genetic procedures for anticipating insights, you may set up a general heuristic structure that anticipates understanding the dynamic unfolding of the entire universe. The key notion for ordering this universe, then, is a 'conditioned series of schemes.' You can have a series of schemes where the first scheme in the series sets the conditions for the next set of schemes and these, in turn, set the conditions for succeeding sets of schemes. The paradigm for such a series is the way an insight emerges from a lower aggregate of sensible and imaginable experiences, and the way many insights coalesce into the theoretical whole we call a viewpoint or system.

Having an insight is not a necessary event. Insights may or may not occur, but you can make them more or less probable by changing the conditions under which they occur. Insights, then, are an 'emergent probability,' and the time of their emergence, while not necessary, follows a certain schedule of probabilities. In a coin toss, sooner or later you will get four heads in a row, or four of a kind, if you play the game long enough. Sooner or later the cure for cancer will emerge if present rate of research continues. In the very long run, probabilities approach certainty. A conditioned series of schemes, where the later schemes will probably emerge from the earlier schemes, provide us with a way of ordering a universe which, while not a necessary ordering, is nevertheless a remarkably intelligent and effective ordering. In such an ordered universe, nothing has to happen, but schemes of events will happen with more or less probability as the conditions change.

Before examining the characteristics of such a way of ordering a universe, let me give as an example of a conditioned series of schemes the planetary cycle investigated by Newton. Just how the planetary cycle emerged is not yet clear, but what is clear is that we could not have a hydro-logical scheme for circulating water over our planet earth if we did not first have a planetary scheme that was already recurring. The planetary scheme set the conditions that made the hydrological cycle of the planet earth pos-sible. We also know that certain planets do not have a recurring cycle of water falling from circulating clouds and forming rivers, streams, seas, and oceans, which sets conditions for solar energy to transform water back into mist, to recondense, form clouds, and repeat the cycle. The hydrological scheme, in turn, sets the conditions for the emergence of the nitrogen cycle which, in turn, sets conditions for emergence of the dietary schemes of plants and animals and people, etc. Thus, we see how later schemes in the series are conditioned by the earlier schemes, so that later schemes cannot emerge until earlier schemes have already emerged and are func-tioning in such a way as to make possible the probable emergence of a later schemes. While the later schemes are dependent on earlier schemes, they also assimilate, transform, and transcend the lower schemes so that there is an increasing complexity and control as we ascend from lower to higher schemes.

With this very general outline of a world-order composed of a 'condi-tioned series of recurrent schemes,' let us explore what certain major char-acteristics of such a world order would be by considering the following questions: Why is the universe so large? Why is the universe so old? Why are there so many hydrogen atoms and so few people? Why are there so many extinct animal species? The answer to these questions and similar ones can be stated quite briefly: the basic design or ordering of our uni-verse is a conditioned series of schemes that have emerged, are emerging, and will continue to emerge in accord with changing schedules of proba-bilities. This is a quite general answer and needs more clarifying details. Probabilities are idealized frequencies that correlate possibilities to actual, concrete frequencies. If the events in our universe are not necessary, but only probable, then, the total number of possible initial events becomes critically important in order to ensure that later schemes of events will emerge. The later a scheme occurs in a series, the less probable will be its occurrence, and so to guarantee its emergence, the total number of possi-ble occurrences becomes a key factor. This will be true whether one thinks of the origin of the universe in terms of a 'big bang,' or the even less likely hypotheses as 'continuous creation' or 'steady state.' Not all possibilities of those initial situations will be realized in the emergence of the first series of schemes. Similarly, in the next stage, not all possibilities will be realized, and so on through successive stages of the concrete realization of the initial number of possibilities. This means that the later a scheme emerges, the fewer number of places there will be where such schemes are functioning, and so the distribution of later schemes is less and less frequent. For example, there are fewer hydrological cycles than planetary schemes and fewer biological schemes than chemical ones. To counterbalance the successive lowering of probabilities of later schemes, it is important to have an extremely large universe. Yet increasing the size eventually runs into diminishing returns, and so time becomes a key variable. What will happen only once in a billion years will happen ten times in ten billion years, and so even extremely unlikely occurrences can be assured in a universe planned according to shifting probabilities.

However, it is important to remember that in such an ordered universe there is the problem of the 'probability of survival,' as well as probability of emergence. Once schemes have emerged and are functioning, they will continue to function only as long as the required conditions continue. But such conditions do not have to be given in the first place and, even when given they will only continue to persist according to a probability of survival. Furthermore, there is not only the possibility, but also the probability, of a breakdown and extinction of schemes. But just as the probability of survival can be low, so too it can also be very high. The mixture of high and low probabilities of emergence with high and low probabilities of survival can be combined to provide considerable flexibility. Thus, any scheme may have an origin of low probabilities and a survival of high probabilities, or just the opposite.

The point to such combinations is that a conditioned series of schemes emerging according to changing probabilities can be a very intelligible and effective way to order a universe. Even though nothing has to happen in a universe so ordered, results can be guaranteed because probabilities approach certainty in the long run. Such a design also allows for emergence of more and more complex systematic schemes, including those with very low probabilities. Such schemes can develop along many different routes since there are so many varieties of probable schemes that can emerge and survive, as we move through different times and in different places from one level to the next in a conditioned series. Such a comprehensive design or world-order is very stable, effective, and dynamic without having to be necessary and deterministic, as had been assumed in the deterministic and mechanistic world-order.

It is important to stress that this brief analysis of world-order is not dependent on the results of scientific discoveries and verifications; rather, it is dependent on the way scientists inquire into data, understand, conceive, correct, and verify their theoretical explanations of our universe. The world-order that I have just briefly sketched is a general understanding of the way our universe is structured. It is an order that is immanent in the world of our experience. It does not pretend to tell scientists what the contents of their various sciences will reveal. But it does insist that this universe is intelligible but not necessary; that there are different forms of intelligibilities; that these different forms of intelligibilities can be combined into a conditioned series of recurring schemes that are to be realized in accord with shifting probabilities; and that such a universe is open-ended but directed toward ever more complex and intelligible schemes. However, just what these schemes are, just what their numbers, distributions, concentrations, and times of emergence and survival are, are not determined. Such general and specific contents are to be determined a posteriori through methodical scientific research.

Further clarification of this generic world-order can be articulated by a brief contrast with Aristotle's world-order, and with that of mechanistic determinism which, in post-Renaissance thinking, replaced Aristotle's worldview.[10] Just as 'emergent probability' is based on the notion of science and law we developed in the earlier chapters, so the world-orders of both Aristotle and mechanistic determinism were based on quite different notions of science and law. In Aristotle's world-order, the fundamental contrast was between the necessary celestial movements of the sun, moon, and stars and the 'accidental' movements of terrestrial things. Further, Aristotle's notion of science as 'a search for certain knowledge of necessary causes' prevented him from developing a science of the contingent, although he did recognize the prevalence of accidental occurrences, or what we have named the 'nonsystematic divergence from idealized frequencies.' Aristotle attempted to order and control these terrestrial aggregates of accidental happenings by appealing to the seasonal and diurnal cycles of the sun and the eternal, necessary cycling of the stars and planets. Once classical laws were first discovered by Galileo and their abstract nature was understood, the possibility of statistical laws and schemes of recurrence became possible and a new world-order, in terms of a conditioned series of schemes unfolding according to changing probabilities of emergence and survival could be constructed. With this world-order Aristotle's eternal cycles disappear, and his notion of necessity can be replaced by the contemporary scientific notion of verified possibilities and probabilities. Mechanistic determinism as a world-order evolved from Galileo's discovery of what we have called classical laws. Such laws, when verified, explain what possibly will happen if conditions are continuously given according to classical assumptions. Classical laws assumed that other cases of the law are the same in all other places and at all other times. What was overlooked by classical scientists was that other cases were only possibly the same and not actually the same.

If we insist that classical laws are concrete, actual laws, we will certainly not expect to discover statistical laws, and much less genetic laws. Furthermore, if all the cases are actually the same, then there are no exceptions, and classical laws govern all cases with iron-clad certainty and necessity. In other words, classical laws govern the movements of the entire universe. Finally, the way that this completely deterministic world-order operates could be imagined as a gigantic machine whose parts were all interacting with one another in various mechanical ways. And so, while the universe was not a clock, it operated like a clock, and its movements were completely determined and universally predictable. However, it was the scientists themselves doing science who discovered statistical and genetic sciences which have completely marginalized such a mechanistic world-order.

8   Things

Up to this point in our study, you have been invited to appropriate yourself in terms of your own recurrent scheme of cognitional activities and the different ways that your desires and fears orient and pattern, or disorient and block, these cognitional activities. However, besides your recurring scheme of cognitional activities there is you, the subject, who performs these recurring schemes of knowing. Similarly, a distinction has been made between knowing things as they are related to self and knowing these same things in their relations to one another, but I have not focused attention on the things themselves which become known through these correlations. In the next chapter, I will analyze you, the subject, but in this chapter we will attend to the notion of a thing as it applies to conscious and to unconscious things.[11] This means that we must shift attention from the parts to the whole that grounds the parts. Let us take the example of a tree. We may point to a leaf or branch and ask, What part of the tree is this? Or we may point to the tree and ask, What is this unity or whole we call a tree? There are, then, two types of 'what' questions – one type attends to the whole, the other to the part. This seems obvious enough, but it is obvious because we are speaking in the familiar, descriptive pattern, of common-sense schemes of knowing. In this pattern we deal primarily with things as related to ourselves and not with things as they are related to one another. Furthermore, in this pattern of knowing we tend to limit our knowledge of things to their immediate sensible properties. Thus, trees are known by their colors, sizes, shapes, textures, sounds, odors, and so on.

Such descriptive knowing allows us to name and to talk about trees. Unfortunately, the descriptive, common-sense pattern of knowing has a tendency to think of itself as omniscient, assuming that it knows what things really are. Just what is meant by 'real' will be dealt with in the next chapter; here I wish to draw attention to the problem that arises when scientists shift from a descriptive to a fully explanatory context in which they know things, not in their relations to the knower, but in relation to one another. When this happens the notion of a thing becomes a much more complex problem. There is the well-known example of Sir Arthur Eddington's two tables: the common-sense table that is solid, brown, heavy, and standing still right there in front of you and the same table known by the physicist, which is composed of atoms, incredibly tiny masses that are colorless and moving at invisibly high speeds. Which is the real table? The one known in the familiar common-sense world of tables and chairs or the one known in the strictly explanatory context of scientific theory?

Such a striking contrast was made possible by Galileo's ability to put aside the descriptive properties of things and focus instead on the explanatory relations that things have to one another. However, Galileo failed to realize that the quantitative laws that he had discovered were abstract, and he further failed to realize that science deals, not primarily with things but with the relations between things. In order to understand things, attention must shift from the proportions or correlations of things to one another to the wholes or unities that are known in and through these schemes of recurring correlations. Galileo's discoveries and subsequent scientific explanations made possible a clarification between those things known in a descriptive common-sense context and those same things known in an explanatory context. This meant that it was possible to distinguish clearly between the unity of a thing as known through its sensible properties and the same unity as known through explanatory correlations. Scientists have always employed the notion of a thing, but they do not attend directly to this notion. To understand the thing, we have to shift from both the limited and specialized viewpoint of common sense and the remarkably different, abstract and limited perspective of science and consider things both in their descriptive and in their explanatory aspects, which means that we must consider them comprehensively and concretely. The term 'concrete' refers, not only to the particular and actual aspects of things, but also to their general and comprehensive characteristics. To know a thing concretely is to know that thing both comprehensively and singularly; it is to know a thing in the totality of its aspects. This suggests that there is a fundamental tension in the notion of thing between things as they are sensibly experienced and these same things as intelligibly experienced, between things known as sensible unities and those same things known as strictly intelligible unities. This tension is further exacerbated because we first know things in response to our biologically patterned needs which means that, underlying and conditioning the common-sense experience of things, there is the biological pattern of experience.

Babies are born with a need for nourishment, and those needs are conscious, dynamic drives that have an extroverted orientation: the inwardly experienced world of the baby is outwardly directed to satisfy its basic needs. This biological patterning of our inner and outer 'felt' world is one that human beings share with animals, which also experience inner needs that are outwardly directed to a world of sensible things which will satisfy their biological needs. In human beings, once biological needs are satisfied, other interests can assume 'felt' importance and direct attention to other patterns of knowing, such as the common-sense and theoretical patterns. However, the biological patterning of experience does not disappear. Since it is the first pattern to develop and it remains operative throughout our conscious living, it forms a permanent background to our inner and outer consciously 'felt' worlds. We assume this conscious, biological horizon without even calling attention to it.

It is, therefore, fundamentally important to distinguish between things as biologically experienced and things as known in the other patterns of experience in which we operate – common-sense, symbolic, and theoretical. Things as objects of biological desires are experienced as out-there, in front of us, right now. The test for the reality of these objects is their ability to satisfy our biological needs. Bees 'know' the difference between wax flowers and biologically satisfying flowers. Animals and humans can 'sense' the difference between objects that do and do not satisfy their needs. 'Real' bodies in the biological patterning of experience are ones that are out there, right now. Such things are sensed, directly and immediately. But sensing is not knowing; it is only a first step to knowing. Without insights that mediate and transcend the sensibly known unities, we cannot know the concrete, intelligible unities we mean by the term 'thing.' This does not invalidate the biological pattern of experience and biologically sensed bodies, but it does significantly limit that pattern. A body is not a thing.

The same sort of restriction applies to the common-sense pattern of knowing, and the world of things known through this pattern. Unlike the recurring biological patterning of our inner and outer sensible world, the common-sense pattern of knowing does involve insights through which things are made intelligible but only in a limited form of knowing, since in this pattern knowers are not especially interested in grasping the what and the why of things. They are interested instead in naming things and relating them to one another in terms of their sensible likenesses and differences. To know why things are what they are, and why they behave the way they do, we must move into an explanatory context in which things may be known, not only in their sensible relations to us, but also in their explanatory relations to one another. Things, then, may be experienced in many different patterns. In the biological pattern, things are experienced as bodies, directly and immediately, and such bodies are right out there now before us.[12] In the symbolic pattern, these same things may become strange, frightening, and quite mysterious. In the common-sense pattern, these same things are experienced as practical and useful for purposes of living. In the theoretical pattern, the same things tend to disappear as theoretical knowers abstract from their descriptive, sensible properties and move into a strictly intelligible world.

Ironically, scientific study also reveals how little we actually know about things and how far we are from a fully explanatory understanding of what different classes of things really are. If to know a thing concretely is to know that thing in the totality of its relations to other things, then to know the thing completely we must understand all the different ways that things can be known and be able to integrate these different patterns. To do this effectively requires nothing less than a metaphysical understanding of the complete being and behaving of things. I will turn to such considerations in chapter 6, but here I wish to indicate how the notion of a thing unites common-sense and scientific understanding. Let us return to the example of the two tables – the ordinary common-sense table and the explanatory table of contemporary science. There are not two tables, but one. Just as the solar-centered world of Copernicus and the geocentered world of common sense are not two worlds, so too there can be one and the same table known in two quite different contexts of knowing. In the example of the tree, there is the familiar common-sense tree with its observable attributes of leaves, stem, branches, bark, trunk, and roots. But there is also the tree that biologists know through their biochemical and biophysical theories. The common-sense knower recognizes this concrete particular object as a tree, but biologists abstract from particular trees and understand them in terms of a set of organic functions that are generally similar to those of any other tree. These same generic functions can be differentiated into a series of specifically different types of trees (i.e., different species). A statistical biologist can investigate the numbers and distributions that condition the emergence and survival rates of such trees, while the combination of classical, statistical, and genetic studies will reveal trees as dynamically unfolding systems of cellular schemes which recur with statistical regularity and which develop through a flexible series of higher organic integrations as they pass from an immature stage through a sequence of more mature stages until the adult stage is achieved.

Science, then, starts with particular trees but quickly moves to specific characteristics and eventually to more general characteristics. Thus the botanical classifying schemes of the Renaissance and earlier periods are primarily descriptive, but with the discovery of the cell and the study of cellular functions, biologists entered the more contemporary explanatory stage of Darwinian and post-Darwinian theories. In our own time, biomolecular studies are beginning to explain, not only what trees do, but why they do it, not only what trees look like, but why they have the shape, color, texture, leaves, branches, trunk, and roots that they have. In other words, present biological studies have begun to reverse the way biologists originally began to study trees. Earlier studies began from the external descriptive properties and raised questions about internal activities; contemporary scientists begin from biochemical and biophysical studies that are able in limited ways to explain why the external properties of biological things are the way they are. Thus the descriptive correlates are being mediated and generalized by explanatory correlates. The key to this reversal is the systematic understanding of the scientists which pivots between theoretical explanatory schemes and the descriptive context of concrete particular trees.

However, when scientists shift from their abstract, theoretical insights to this or that concrete, existing tree, there is implied in such a shift, not an abstractive insight, but a concretizing insight into the whole of this or that tree. Scientists do not deal explicitly with such 'wholes'; rather, they deal with the way that these 'wholes' are related to one another in their general and specialized ways of functioning. The person operating in the ordinary language world deals with wholes or things, but does so only in a descriptive way that correlates such wholes or things to herself or himself through observable properties (i.e., descriptive wholes characterized by descriptive parts). But scientists are beginning to mediate these descriptive or sensible correlates through ever more abstract and comprehensive correlates that explain why those descriptive wholes and parts are what they are and behave the way we see them behaving.

Now we can see the point of defining a thing as a concrete, individual existing unity considered in the totality of its parts or predicates.[13] The 'concrete' is particular and comprehensive; it is singular and universal. And the reason why the concrete is particular and general is because that is the way things are; any concrete, existing thing is 'one and many,' one in itself and many in its correlations with other things. To bridge this 'one and many' we need an insight into the whole (the thing) as one and many. Insight is that bridge or pivot, not as an abstractive insight, but as a concretizing insight that grasps the whole in the parts, the one in the many, the perduring identity in the differences, the unity in the relations. Putting this idea in more traditional language, we may say that the parts exist, not in themselves, but in and through the thing. The parts have an 'accidental existence,' not an 'essential existence.' The problem with this language is that it is too descriptive and may be misleading. For example, it is a mistake to think that we know the essences of trees; the essence is what we anticipate knowing when we know all that there is to be known about trees. Heuristic definitions and heuristic methods of science avoid this mistake. Translating this language into explanatory terms, we may say that trees exist in and through their present organic schemes of recurrence. These recurring schemes (parts) do not exist; they occur and recur according to a schedule of probabilities of emergence and survival. Things are the concrete, dynamic identities that perdure or subsist in these recurring schemes of changes.

The same subsistent unity or dynamic whole can be exemplified on the level of human things if we consider a novel such as Flaubert's Madame Bovary. The plot of this story may be understood as the flexible circle of recurring actions and interactions of the characters. The plot does not exist or subsist; rather, the characters, Emma and Charles, exist or subsist in and through their actions and interactions. Further, such characters do not exist and subsist all at once; they undergo developments which lead them toward their respective destinies. These characters subsist and conserve their identity through the successive scenes and episodes of the story. The 'wholes' of these characters are being realized in the cumulative changes that occur and recur in the different places, times, and circumstances of the pattern of schemes of their acting and interacting with one another that emerge as the novel is read. The whole or substantial form of any one of the characters, therefore, is an emerging whole, a dynamic unity and identity that is realized in accord with the series of successive changes or events as plotted by the author.

The story itself is also a whole in which concrete, individual, existing wholes – the characters and events – emerge in accord with the schedule of unfolding tensions that accumulate as these characters move toward a resolution that will bring about their final destiny. To consider the plot of the story, then, is to consider the ordering whole or narrative form of the story; it is to consider the story concretely; it is to grasp the subsisting identity, whole of the characters as presented to the readers by the author who has chosen a narrative form to order all the events of the story.

It takes time to tell a story and it takes time for characters to emerge. The characters do not happen all at once. Similarly, a tree is not given all at once. It takes time to be a tree. Trees are concrete, individual, dynamic wholes that emerge cumulatively in and through a sequence of biological schemes and in accord with a schedule of biological probabilities. Trees evolve in the lower aggregate of solid, liquid, and gaseous chemical molecules, which they assimilate and integrate into developing sequences of biochemical schemes of growing, reproducing, and defending their emerging unities. It also takes time to become water, although the temporal sequence in bonding atoms into molecules is a tiny fraction of the time it takes to accomplish cellular division and organic growth. Similarly, it takes time to form an atom or even an electron, although again the phase of formation is a mere fraction of what it takes to establish the rhythm of molecular bonding. Finally, it takes time to form a universe, if the plot of that universe is a conditioned series of higher things which emerge in lower aggregates of events, as these lower aggregates themselves are formed by lower things operating in schemes whose numbers, distributions, emergences, and survival are statistically determined.

The reason that this dynamic, unfolding universe of emerging things, existing and cooperating in their respective systems of schemes, is so difficult to grasp is because human beings, like animals and plants, exist and operate in lower schemes as transformed by higher schemes. This means that human beings, besides operating in cognitional schemes of knowing, also operate in psychic (animal), organic (molecular), and subatomic schemes. Animals do not live in and through practical schemes of knowing; they live in psychobiological schemes in which they operate and cooperate with other animal, plant, chemical, and atomic things. For animals these other things are consciously present as their ecological environment, and they are immediately present to them. Animals experience their environment of things sensibly and immediately, not mediately. And so animals do not know trees subsisting as things, since to know things requires a special type of insight. Animals do not understand trees; rather, they sense them, they smell them, they see, feel, touch, taste, and hear trees within their immediately present field of awareness.

This field may be differentiated into a subjective sensing pole and an objective sensed pole. The sensibly conscious animal feels itself attracted to, and directed by, the surrounding conscious field of objects. Both the subjective and objective poles are immediately conscious, and they are patterned according to the felt needs of the animals at particular times and within particular places. In other words, animals experience the world about them within their own conscious, spatiotemporal frames which are oriented according to their changing biological needs. Just as questions orient human knowers toward a field of intelligibly unknown objects, so too biological drives orient sensing animals toward a field of biologically satisfying objects. Animals are basically extroverts. They have specifically different ways of responding to their environments because they have different sensory-motor systems and different internally experienced drives, but these specifically different needs are all oriented to an outwardly experienced field of objects which will satisfy those needs. Animals do not have epistemological problems. They have a very successful 'sense' of reality, but they do not have an understanding of reality. Therefore, they do not mediate their immediate field of objects through questions and answers that cause human knowers to wonder if they have or have not correctly mediated the intelligibility of the sensible world. In other words, epistemological problems emerge only on the human level because human knowers operate in different schemes of knowing which frequently seem to be contradictory to one another.

Human beings are not animals, but they do operate in and through psychobiological schemes in which animals subsist. However, they also operate in practical, common-sense schemes of knowing, which place knowers within a world related to themselves and to others in and through descriptive patterns of experience.[14] To enter the world of theory, human knowers have to learn how to decenter themselves and recenter themselves within strictly explanatory patterns of knowing that correlate things to one another. Besides the subject-centered world known in and through practical schemes of operating and cooperating, and besides the theoretical world known through explanatory schemes, there are the lower psychobiological schemes of experiencing conditioning these higher schemes that human beings share with animals. Human knowers, then, live in the immediate world of sensible objects which they mediate symbolically, linguistically, pragmatically, and theoretically. The epistemological problem is to differentiate these patterns from one another and appropriate the various worlds of objects to which they orient us. It is to such problems we turn in the next chapter.

5

Self-Affirming Knower

Up to this point in our study the reader has been invited to appropriate those cognitive activities that are related to the central act of understanding called insight. In this chapter we move on to the second centering activity of knowing, namely, the indirect or reflective understanding that grounds your judging.[1] In the seventh chapter, we will consider the higher and more complex activity of choosing, and in the final chapter we shall focus on the self as a lover.

1   Knowing vs Meaning

Before considering the act of judging or reflective understanding, it is important to restate the basic procedures in self-appropriation. The primary problem has been to shift attention from what you know to your own activity of knowing. This does not mean that the objective contents of knowing will drop off and disappear as you shift your attention from what you are questioning to the activity of questioning, but it does mean that you will gradually learn how to expand your field of awareness to include both the activities of knowing and the intended terms of these activities. The emphasis, however, is on the activities, not on the terms or contents of the activities. The goal is to know the operating structure of your own knowing.

At this stage of our study it is important to draw attention to a problem of terminology. Since the middle of the nineteenth century, and especially during the twentieth century, philosophers have spoken and written more about problems in meaning than about knowing, and so it is important to provide an initial explanation of how knowing and meaning are related.

Meaning is a broader term than knowing, since meaning implies not only knowing, but also the expression of knowing in language or other media. Thus far I have avoided discussing language because, in appropriating yourself as a knower, language is a later and less important concern. Certainly language conditions the various patterns of your knowing, but it is the different activities of knowing that ultimately determine language. A statement as spoken or written is a linguistic expression, but it does not inform you of its meaning.[2] There is an important difference between what a person knows and the linguistic means that a person selects to communicate what he or she has understood and verified. Thus you may express what you know in Latin, Greek, French, English, or any other language you happen to know. This implies a basic distinction between what you know and the way you intend to communicate that knowing. To put the problem somewhat differently, if you are trying to interpret what an author or person means by what she or he says or writes, it is essential to understand, not just the words the author is using, but what he or she intended to mean by selecting those words and sentences. Behind the carriers of meaning is a 'meant,' and so if, for example, you want to know what Newton meant by the word 'mass,' then the question to consider is What was Newton's own understanding that he intended to express by the term 'mass'? Obviously Newton's words or symbols are important since it was through such words and symbols that his 'understood' or 'meant' was actually communicated. But an original thinker like Newton understood intelligibilities about this universe that had never been understood before, so while he may have used words that other authors also used, what he understood by those words was to some extent quite different. There is, then, an important distinction to be made between your thoughts or proposals and the sentences you select to express those thoughts or proposals. The foundational significance of this distinction between thoughts and sentences can be further clarified if we shift now to a discussion of judging.

2   Self as Judger

In studying the way insights occur, I stressed the significance of questioning as providing the normative orientation that leads you from not understanding toward understanding. Questioning places you in the paradoxical state of knowing your own not-knowing and simultaneously knowing your ability to understand this known-unknown. You realize that, in the act of understanding, you have the power of transforming problems into sudden solutions. Even more remarkable is the way insights, having been formulated into thoughts or ideas, can set the conditions for moving you up to a new and higher cognitional level by means of a quite different type of question.

The questions of what and why oriented you, as a knower, to seek, in the external, sensible data or in the internal data of your own consciousness, an unknown intelligibility. When the insight occurs it provides you with the ability to conceive that intelligibility according to the way you have understood it, which means including in your statements or definitions what you think is relevant to your understanding and excluding what is not. But such discoveries and formulations are simply definitions, ideas, opinions, or hypotheses about what may or may not be true. The cognitional process does not terminate with ideas, definitions, and propositions. Quite spontaneously you find yourself wondering, Is this idea correct?; Are these propositions really so? It is your own wondering that again supplies the motive and the direction that moves you towards a higher level of knowing. The same wondering that initiated your cognitional activities with the question of what or why now moves you beyond understanding, raising a further question about your insights and formulations and thereby opening up a third level of activities where you not only understand but begin to criticize and judge your prior understanding of your prior experiencing.

The question, Is it so?, which moves you beyond understanding to judging, does two things. First, when an idea, opinion, proposition, or scientific law is questioned in this way, it is transformed into a questionable idea. It becomes an idea or hypothesis that stands in need of verification. You may think you have a brilliant idea, but spontaneously you find yourself wondering, Is it so? Once this critical wondering begins, then your idea is transformed into a conditional idea that may or may not be true. Second the question, Is it so?, is a normative orienting that directs you toward a judgment that you have not yet judged. We already pointed out that a questioned experience is a known-unknown. Now we are identifying a second known-unknown, namely, a questioned idea that is known as a possibly intelligible idea, but unknown as an actually intelligible idea. Thus your desire to question spontaneously takes you, first, beyond sensible experiences into the field of intelligible experiences and, second, beyond possibly intelligible experiences into the field of actually intelligible experiences. Wondering does this spontaneously, normatively, and with a certain amount of nagging insistence. Once you ask the question, I wonder if my interpretation is true?, your wondering will linger on until you satisfy its demands and reach the goal toward which it is leading you, namely, Yes, it is so; No, it isn't; or It may be so. Unlike the question of what or why that directs you toward insights and ideas, the question, Is it so?, orients you to a yes, or no, or maybe.

Knowing is not a simple activity.[3] It is an activity composed of three different levels of activities, and these three levels are dynamically interrelated by your own wondering, which not only correlates these activities to one another, but also leads you to successive transformations of one level by the next until the final stage of knowing is achieved, namely, judging. The first level of outer or inner sensible experiences is, not knowing, but only a part of knowing. Similarly, the second level of understanding is, not knowing, but only a part. Only third-level judging completes the process of knowing, embracing all three levels, uniting them into the single structured activity that we name 'knowing.'

How do you answer the question, Is it so? What would your reasons be for stating that you are no longer thinking about an idea, but asserting it? Or, having reflected and thought about the idea, that you have come to the conclusion that this idea is correct? Exactly what causes this final judgment? Among the metaphors for making good judgments, the one of 'weighing the evidence' seems especially helpful in clarifying what causes judging. The judge and juror in a courtroom listen to the evidence and eventually must come to the conclusion of guilty or not guilty. In instructing jurors in a criminal case, the judge informs the jurors that they must find the defendant guilty if they are certain beyond a reasonable doubt. The jurors may have doubts about their prospective judgment, but are they reasonable doubts? And what does 'reasonable' refer to in this context? Reason refers to the reflective process that a person goes through in weighing the evidence to determine if it is sufficient to ground a judgment. If there is sufficient evidence to prove the defendant guilty, the jurors would be unreasonable if they did not proceed to judge the case.

What makes evidence sufficient depends on the context of your prior judgments. Just as direct insights cumulate into viewpoints, so prior judgments coalesce into the wider context or horizon of knowing within which you raise the question, Is it so? New judgments correct, complement, and extend the field of your past judgments. This means that you review and criticize prospective judgments in the context of your prior judgments. Because they are prior, they act as a heuristic structure within which you anticipate making further new judgments.[4] A key characteristic of insights is that they do not emerge and then disappear, but enter into the very texture of your mind. The same is true of past judgments or reflective understandings; they also provide a permanent background for future judgments. In traditional Scholastic philosophy such previously acquired judgments were defined as habits of the intellect that operate in certain circumstances spontaneously, guiding your questioning and bringing correctives into play as you reflect in preparation for making new judgments and broadening your field of expertise. Just as the carpenter's apprentice gradually acquires the mastery and familiarity of an experienced carpenter, so too a person gradually develops the reputation of being a wise and careful critic, capable of making reasonable, well-balanced judgments.

I wish to emphasize the central role that critical wondering plays in making good judgments. Just as the act of insight, on the second level of your cognitional activities, meets the demand of your inquisitive question of what or why, so reflective insights must meet the demand of your critical question, Is it really so? Answers to reflective wonder, however, do not emerge as sudden illuminations; rather, they are marked by slow, careful weighing of the evidence that you present to yourself. The 'sudden illumination' of an insight precedes and sets the conditions for your reflective understanding. Thus, in the case of being a juror, if you do not understand the evidence, then you cannot judge it. Reflective understanding assumes and builds upon direct understanding, as it transforms possibly correct understanding of evidence into actually correct knowing. When you ask yourself, 'Am I correct?,' 'Have I grasped the issue squarely?,' you set up within your own consciousness a demand for sufficient evidence. You must meet that demand and satisfy your own wondering before you can commit yourself to the judgment, Yes, it is so, or It may be so, but I am not certain. There are many different degrees of probability, but in the end the important point is that you must make the judgment. In other words, you cross-examine the adequacy and validity of your own understanding.

At the third level of judging, you find yourself acting with a qualitatively different feeling of freedom and responsibility than you were able to exercise on the second level of your understanding. This can be clearly demonstrated if we consider revealing aphorism of de la Rochefoucauld, 'Everyone complains about their memory but no one complains about their judgment.' This remark draws attention to the different levels of your knowing and the different kinds of awareness, that you experience at these different levels, as well as to the different degrees of responsibility. Thus, the aphorism draws attention to the kind of awareness you have of a first-level activity of remembering as contrasted with the third-level activity of judging. Let me explain. We have been using the term 'experiencing' to indicate the first-level cognitional activities, but 'experience' is a much broader term than this use of it implies. The first level of cognitional activities includes what has been traditionally named your internal and external sensory activities, such as the familiar external activities of seeing, hearing, smelling, tasting, touching, and such internal activities as feeling, imagining, and remembering. These activities occur, not singly, but in patterns and schemes. Also, since they involve unconscious, organic levels as well as conscious activities, I have referred to them as psychosomatic or psychobiological schemes of activities. The issue here is that you cannot direct and control these lower level activities to the degree that you can control your third-level activity of judging. What about your direction and control over second-level activities of questioning, understanding, and conceiving?

In raising a question about your sensible experiences, you set the conditions for the emergence of an insight, but questioning does not guarantee that the insight will occur. Insights are probable events and, while you may make them more or less probable, you cannot completely control their emergence. However, when you move on to the third level and ask the question, Is my insight correct?, your control of the cognitional process changes significantly. You can always judge, even when you do not understand, since you can say, I do not understand, which is itself a judgment. If you do understand, but do not have sufficient evidence to make a certain judgment, you can express this state of your mind and say, I am inclined to think or to doubt, etc. In other words, because you realize that you should not judge when the evidence is insufficient, you feel more responsible for your judging than you do for your understanding. Furthermore, you are more responsible for your second-level insights than for your first-level activities of remembering and hearing.

Your ability to control your activities, therefore, increases as you move from the first level of experiencing to the second level of questioning, understanding, and conceiving, and you have an even wider range of control as you move from the second to the third level. As we shall see in the seventh chapter, your control and responsibility reaches an even higher stage as you move on to the fourth level of evaluating and choosing a course of action. The 'I' that experiences is related to, but different from, the 'I' that questions and understands, and the 'I' that reflects and judges is also related to, but different than, the 'I' on the lower levels. Besides these three, there is more obviously one and the same 'I' that unites these three levels of activities into the single, unique identity. It is this unity that we shall consider in the next section.

Another way to emphasize the differences in your control over these three cognitional levels is to focus on the way that judging involves a personal commitment to what you judge or assert. People are very sensitive about their judgments because when they judge, for example, that a person is guilty, they are not saying that they merely think this person is guilty; rather, they have moved beyond thinking and taken the final cognitional step in which thinking becomes knowing. They do not think the person is guilty, they know it and assert it. So, if you question their judgment, you are questioning the personal commitment that they have made to the truth and accuracy of their judgment.

Paradoxically, then, judgments are both very personal and very public. A person is judged to be guilty, not because the juror said so, but because the juror judged that there was sufficient evidence to assert that this person did in fact commit the crime. In this way, judgments are very private and personal, but they are also impersonal and objectively public. The juror is asserting that any other knower who examines the evidence will also find in that evidence a sufficient reason for making the same judgment. This means that if you tell the truth, no matter how personal or private that truth may be, it has a public, shareable dimension that transcends any particular person and permits other knowers to participate in, and to make their own commitment to, this same truth. Thus many knowers can belong to and share in the same true judgments. And, while each judgment is personal and private, still correct judgments are also impersonal and public. There can be one truth that provides the ground for many knowers to commit themselves to belong to that truth. For example, Galileo's law of falling bodies and Newton's law of universal gravitation were discovered and verified by single knowers but they became the public property of a whole community of knowers. More surprising, Galileo and Newton have passed away but their judgments – insofar as they are correct – have perdured. What is this perduring public dimension of a correct judgment?

What perdures is not the conditions under which the judgment was made, but the intelligibility that was apprehended and affirmed. What gets judged when you judge is whether you have understood things correctly. What is common to knowers is not that they have had the same experiences, but that they have asked the same question about their insights and ideas, namely, Are they correct? What every knower shares is the demand that emerges consciously and spontaneously with the question, Is it so? It pervades every conscious knower, setting up a demand for sufficient evidence to ground our prospective judgment. Thus that critical question, Is it so?, motivates thinkers to become judgers. For example, the knower as a judger might say, This is an impressive idea, but is it so? Judging adds to your ideas the affirmation or negation, guilty or not guilty, true or false. However, the yes or no by itself does not make sense. Without the what or why of the second level, there is nothing to judge. Judging, then, borrows from the first two levels the contents for which it finds 'sufficient evidence,' and so asserts, Yes, it is so, or No, it is not so.

The simple yes or no may not seem significant, but it is important to notice what the judgment does to the synthesis of the first two levels. No longer is the synthesis a conditional synthesis, since it has been transformed through judging into an unconditional synthesis. The assertion, Yes, it is so, utters an absolute, and when you affirm unconditionally it is because you have grasped that the conditions have been given, as you have understood them to be given. This absolute is absolute only because the conditions are given. In other words, it is not a completely unconditioned absolute; rather, it is an absolute by virtue of its conditions having been given. It is a limited absolute. This discussion has treated the cognitional activity of judging in a general way. I would now like to consider two special forms of judging: common-sense judging and scientific judging.

2a Common-Sense Judgments

Common sense is a specialized pattern of knowing that is interested in solving our practical day-to-day problems of living in intelligent and reasonable ways. This pattern of cognitional activities develops to deal with concrete particular issues, which means that it is not prepared to deal with theoretical, comprehensive concerns. While common-sense knowers must learn how to cooperate with members of their family and neighborhood, while they must learn how to cooperate economically, politically, educationally, and religiously with other cooperating groups, common-sense knowers do not abstract from their own subject-centered, descriptive understandings and judgings of things. They do not seek the sort of comprehensive understanding of social, economic, and political structures that we find among human scientific knowers, such as sociologists and economists. But this does not mean that common-sense knowers do not or cannot judge correctly within the limits in which they operate.

The problem in making correct common-sense judgments is that these limits are very specialized, which means that the range of such judgments is always circumscribed and limited to a descriptive context of concrete, particular circumstances.[5] As an example there are the common-sense schemes that teachers acquire in learning how to communicate the subject matter of their discipline. Pedagogy is a skill or art that has to be learned; teachers observe, listen to advice, experiment and test different approaches, adjusting and correcting until they reach a certain mastery and feel comfortable in dealing with a range of different experiences in pragmatically successful ways. At this point teachers have acquired a context of judgments that permits them to prepare and organize their subject matter and to design effective means of communicating their material to a group of students. The level of mastery attained depends on the ease with which teachers are able to address different pedagogical problems and situations, correctly judging the receptivity of different types of students with respect to different materials. A teacher who has acquired such a set of practical judgments has a cluster of practical insights to which she or he adds, in every new situation or for every new object, the further insights for dealing successfully with this new situation. The teacher keeps generalizing or analogizing by grasping that every new situation can be dealt with as prior situations were judged. This is the way we reason, reflect, and judge in a common-sense pattern of knowing.

Common sense judging

It is natural for knowers to generalize, to argue from one particular case to successive similar cases. The problem, however, is not merely to analogize or generalize, but to do so accurately. In other words, the practically wise teacher knows how to size up a class and shift gears when he or she grasps that certain modifications in teaching are needed. Failure to make such modifications reveals how easy it is to generalize that the present situation and its problems can be solved in the same way as in prior situations when, in fact, there are differences in the 'givens' of this situation that demand to be attended to, understood, and judged in slightly different ways. As a result, the teacher blunders, and instead of understanding and correctly judging the situation, he or she misunderstands and misjudges.

To analyze and generalize from one situation and set of problems to the next, you need to check carefully and make certain that the situations are, in fact, actually similar. If you do make a mistake and misapprehend, then you may correct the mistake the next time by asking, Have I correctly understood this situation?; Have I reviewed and checked out this new situation carefully, allowing sufficient time for questioning to bring to light problematic differences that are sufficiently different from the prior sequence of situations to require new understandings and new procedures in order to achieve successful results?

How do you as judger know whether your critical questioning has been given sufficient time to bring to light problematic areas in your present practical situation? The norm for true judgments is sufficient evidence precisely as sufficient, and such evidence is sufficient when your insights meet the issues and problems precisely and correctly. The standard for correct insights, then, is correct questioning. Do your practical insights meet the demands of your critical wondering as it operates within the limits of common-sense interests? Such interests are limited, and so the problem is to establish the limits correctly. Thus in the case of learning a craft, we speak of skilled workers as persons who have learned their trade; they have reached a level of competence and mastery, which means they can judge correctly what the problems and situations are for a wide array of cases. The point is that skilled workers are able to make correct judgments in solving practical problems because they are operating in specialized, limited contexts in which they have already acquired the competence and skill to size up problematic situations correctly and to solve them easily and effectively. The wise worker, like Aristotle's wise person, knows 'the right thing to do, the right time, and the right way to do it.'

It is important to insist that such judgments are correct or true only within very limited contexts. They are limited to particular times and places, particular problems, and particular solutions. Quite a different type of judgment is needed if you wish to understand and judge correctly how the entire physical universe actually operates.

2b Scientific Judgments

If we shift from common-sense to scientific judgments, we can illustrate another specific type of the general form of reflective understanding. What, are scientists doing when they are making scientific judgments?[6] In chapter 2 we discussed the way that Galileo designed certain experimental procedures in order to test his hypothesis that all bodies fall with certain accelerating speeds. If a set of measurements of falling bodies are conditioned as Galileo hypothesized, then bodies will fall at the predicted speeds. But his set of measurements yielded the predicted proportion of distances to durations, and so he was correct in affirming his law of falling bodies. Such a scientific judgment, while it is generally like a common-sense judgment, is also specifically different.

In a common-sense judgment you do not decenter yourself from descriptive correlations and recenter yourself as an understander in a world of strictly intelligible correlations; rather, you remain within the world where the sun rises and sets and the earth does not rotate. There is a mistaken tendency to think that common-sense knowers do not mediate their immediate, sensible givens, but they do. As a common-sense knower, you mediate the world of things about you through ordinary linguistic patterns of meanings that make up your native language. You know what things are by learning that language, identifying certain objects in and through their appropriate attributes.

Galileo, however, was not patterning his immediate visual field since he had abstracted from descriptive correlates to focus on strictly explanatory correlates which, to be verified, required special experimental procedures. In verifying his hypothesis, Galileo reflected back on an observational field, but it was not an ordinary observational field. It was an experimentally mediated field and, more important, his intent was to reach an ultimate explanatory goal that would mediate, not only immediate experimental observables, but the entire universe of observables. Classical scientists like Galileo, Newton, and Einstein are not interested in mediating concrete, particular, descriptive relations; their interest lies in correctly mediating the explanatory relations that ground and explain why things behave and are seen and heard in the way they are. Thus scientists can explain why you see the sun rising and setting and why such judgments as the sun rises and sets are correct only within a very limited context. To understand and judge things concretely is to judge them comprehensively and completely in their relations to one another and in their particularity.

tougher for a universal explanation to be correct (handwritten annotation)

Common-sense judgments focus on concrete particularities, not on the concrete as universal and comprehensive. This explains why Galileo's laws and those of his contemporaries eventually led to the more comprehensive, systematic explanation of Newton, and from Newton to Einstein's even more comprehensive and more unified understanding and judging of the concrete orderings of things to one another in our physical universe. This also explains why common-sense judgments may be certainly correct while scientific judgments are only probable, although converging toward a fully comprehensive explanation.

Scientific judgments are cumulatively verified. Thus Galileo's laws of terrestrial motions and Kepler's laws of celestial motion are subsumed within Newton's systematic explanation of both terrestrial and celestial movements. In other words, just as practical knowing assimilates past advances, complementing, modifying, and correcting them, so scientists also correct, modify, and advance past scientific contexts. For example, if we were to trace the history of chemistry from the four-element theory of earth, air, fire, and water which developed in ancient Greek thought to the nineteenth-century ninety-two-element theory, we would have a marvelous example of scientific learning which proceeds, not deductively, but developmentally and discursively, as scientists assimilate, complement, correct, modify, eliminate, and cumulatively advance past, direct, and reflective theoretical understandings. Human learning, whether in practical day-to-day living or in scientific pursuits, proceeds by trial and error, advancing and declining in remarkably different but related ways.

To understand and judge this learning, you must know how insights accumulate into systematic unities and then generate further questions and insights that may demand corrections or, more important, a fundamental reversal through inverse insights. Knowing is a dynamic structure of three interrelated levels of cognitive activities that involves a much richer and more complex range of associative cyclings and recyclings of those levels than you could ever explicitly appropriate and formalize. In this interplay of functionally related levels of knowing, it is the second level of understanding that unites the third level of judging to the first level of experience by transforming your outer or inner conscious experiences from potentially intelligible experiences into actually intelligible experiences. For example, once you learn a language, you no longer simply experience familiar objects such as stones, trees, and water; rather, you experience them in truly intelligible ways if you can correctly name them in the familiar common-sense language world in which you live. Or you can experience the same objects in a scientifically probable way if you have acquired a chemical understanding of what stones and water are and why they behave the way that they do. The point is that not only do you verify your experiences of the world about you, but you also verify your intelligible experiences of the surrounding world. The sensible world about you and the felt world within you is mediated, transformed, and made luminous by your insights and judgments.

The fundamental problem in knowing yourself as a knower is that, like all of us, you have a spontaneous tendency to think that your immediate experience of your conscious activities is already a knowing of self, whereas it is only an experience of self. Experience of yourself performing these different activities of knowing is an unmediated experience that needs to be mediated by your own inquisitive and reflective wondering. There is a foundational difference, then, between experiencing knowing and knowing knowing. Further, and more important, there is a crucial distinction between experiencing yourself doing knowing and knowing yourself as a knower in and through your acts of knowing as they recur in the different patterns of knowing.

3   Self as Knower

you must understand the cognitive processes

Thus far I have been setting forth the clues that would provide you with conditions for appropriating your own cognitional activities. Having set down the meaning and conditions of knowing, you may now ask yourself, Am I a knower?; Do I experience, understand, and judge in the ways we have been discussing? You must answer these questions in terms of your own concrete, conscious activities. However, before the answer is made, it is necessary to clarify just what is meant by the term 'consciousness' or 'awareness.'[7]

3a Consciousness

The problem in self-appropriation is to develop some familiarity with the distinction between your own activities of knowing and the contents of those activities. Only in appropriating this distinction can you clarify the notion of consciousness. The basic mistake in analyzing the notion of consciousness or awareness is to confuse consciousness with attention or intention. This is the problem with Freud's distinction between consciousness and unconsciousness. Motives are thought to be unconscious because you are not paying attention to them, and so 'attending to' motives supposedly makes you conscious of them.

But contrary to this analysis, you can be conscious or aware without paying attention to that awareness. While you are sitting in a chair reading, you are aware of the pressure of your feet on the floor or of your back and buttocks on the chair, but you do not pay attention to this awareness or

F' Freud

experience unless some stimuli draws your attention or you deliberately shift your attention to that part of your conscious field. Attending, therefore, does not make you aware – you already are – but it does make you aware in a different way. For example, you may be lying on the beach, gazing absent-mindedly at the sky, when suddenly a sound attracts your attention and you wonder what it is. Wondering does not make you aware; it makes you intelligently aware, inquisitively conscious. Consciousness or awareness, then, is preliminary to attending, and sets the conditions for attending. If you were not already aware, you could not attend. Attending changes the way you are conscious, from being vaguely aware to being selectively and distinctly aware. However, besides the conscious act of attending, there is also you, the conscious subject, who is doing the attending. Consciousness is a characteristic not only of certain acts, but also of the subject's own mode of being.

Consciousness is not something that you can hold up for examination; rather, it is known indirectly through certain conscious acts you perform and through you, the subject, consciously acting. Not all of your acts are conscious. You cannot attend to the way your hair grows, or to the way you make red blood cells. You do these activities, but you do not do them consciously. Nor are all living things conscious. The major difference between a turtle and a tree is consciousness. Turtles are conscious, and certain of their acts are conscious. The tree is not conscious, nor are any of its acts conscious, that is, it does not operate consciously. Consciousness is a quality that is intrinsic to certain acts and to certain types of things. Could we say that consciousness is a way of knowing? Yes, but it is only a preliminary and very undifferentiated way. For this reason we can also consider that the word 'experience' shares the same meaning as 'consciousness.' To experience the world around you is to be aware or conscious of it, but this is a vague, undifferentiated, preliminary way of knowing. Is consciousness or experience an inward or outward awareness? It is both, since you only become aware of this distinction as you shift attention from outer to inner experiences, or the reverse. Through attentive or selective awareness, the distinction between inner and outer fields of awareness becomes differentiated, but before such selection the inner/outer distinction is not clear and distinct. Clarity and distinctness come from intellectual awareness, not from awareness. There are, therefore, different types of consciousness, awareness, or experience.

I defined consciousness as an awareness imminent in certain acts and in the subject of those acts. Just as there are three different levels of knowing, constituted through three different sets of activities, there are three different ways of being conscious: empirically, intelligently, and rationally or reflectively. Besides these different types of consciousness associated with the different levels of knowing, there is the more obvious unity or oneness of consciousness. I say 'more obvious' because you are more easily conscious of yourself in the undifferentiated unity of the self than you are of the three distinct levels of your consciousness. Only after a good deal of self-appropriation of the different levels of knowing are you able to distinguish these three different types of consciousness within the unity that is referred to as me or I. Besides the three different types of consciousness and the unity of the subject, there is a further and more complex aspect of consciousness: the problem of inner and outer awareness. This needs to be carefully scrutinized since it is the source of considerable confusion about the way we know. *internal + external*

When you are attending to the outer world through your sensory-motor activities, you have a double awareness of yourself. For example, in paying attention to your visual field, you are attentively aware of this outer field, but you are inattentively aware of your seeing and your self. You may shift your attention from the external, sensible data and start paying attention to your interior, conscious field, and when you do, you begin to experience your seeing and yourself as an object of attention. This means you are beginning to appropriate your own activity of seeing and yourself as a seer. When you do that you have a double awareness. You have an attentive awareness of your activity of seeing and of the subject who does the seeing, but the subject seeing is now objectively experienced, while the subject who is doing the attending is only subjectively experienced. In other words, every time you attend to and wonder about your own inner cognitional activities, you are attentively aware of yourself as an object being questioned, and inattentively aware of yourself as the subject who is doing the questioning. This means that in every act of self-appropriation, you generate a further experience or awareness of 'you,' the subject, which can subsequently be attended to and appropriated.

There is a difference, then, between knowing elephants and knowing your own subject. In both cases there is an object to be known, but in the case of self-knowing, the object is your own subject. However, while there is a difference between knowing self and knowing elephants, the difference is not in the acts of knowing, but in the fact that, in knowing self, you know yourself twice, first as a questioned object and simultaneously as experienced questioner. In knowing elephants, you know them as an object experienced, questioned, understood, conceived, reflected on, and judged, but at the same time, you are conscious of yourself, the subject, doing these acts of knowing. This latter awareness of self, however, is only an experience of your activities of knowing, and of you, the knower. The recurrent mistake in knowing self, then, is to assume that experience of self, which is an immediate awareness of self, is also a knowing of self. Experiencing of self is only a preliminary, vague, undifferentiated awareness of self that must be mediated by questions, insights, and judgments. Such mediation is what I have referred to as self-appropriation.

3b Self-Affirmation

With my analysis of consciousness in place, I now return to the question that I put to the reader, Are you a knower? The question may be expressed in the form of a syllogism: If you are a concrete, understandable unity that experiences, understands, and judges, then you are a knower. The conditioned is the statement: You are a knower, if you are a concrete, intelligible unity who experiences, understands, and judges. The field in which these conditions are to be verified is the data of your own consciousness. Are you conscious of yourself sensing, raising questions, getting insights, formulating them into ideas, questioning the ideas, and judging them? It is important to notice the question is not whether you know something. The question is about the performance of your own cognitional activities.[8] This is significant because we do not ordinarily think about knowing as 'doing.' Walking and working are examples of 'doing,' but knowing is assumed to be an internal, mental activity that is often contrasted with external exercise. However, it is important to think of knowing as something that you 'do' because in knowing what you 'do' is your self. Knowing is self-making.

There are several other important features of the question, Are you a knower? The question is not, Are you necessarily a knower? It is not, Were you always a knower? Nor is it, Will you always be a knower? Rather, the question asks you to make a concrete judgment of fact, here and now. Most surprising is the fact that you cannot escape the answer. You are, in fact, a knower. The reason is that the activities involved in knowing are not necessarily given; nevertheless, they are given, and given quite spontaneously. Like it or not, if your eyes are open and if you are conscious, then you will see. Spontaneously, questions arise and, while you may prevent certain insights from occurring, insights do occur and, just as naturally and inevitably, questions for judging emerge. You do not have to be a knower; you were not always a knower. But still the events of experiencing, understanding, and judging are given, given consciously, and given in your own presence. You may deny you are a knower, but that places you in a concrete contradiction with yourself, a contradiction between your own actual performance and your account of this performance. You have to use your own knowing in the very process of attempting to deny the fact that you are a knower. It is a fact, and facts are precise, public, and final. In this judgment of fact, you are affirming both your own cognitional activities and you, the

you are a knower no matter what

unity, who operates and exists in and through this recurring scheme of activities.

It is important to note that you cannot know yourself except in and through these activities. Your immediate awareness of yourself misleads you into thinking that you can know yourself directly and immediately. It is true that you can experience yourself or be aware of yourself directly and immediately, but being aware is not knowing; it is only a preliminary to knowing. Your experience of yourself has to be understood, and this understanding transforms your experienced self into an understood self. This mediation, however, stands in need of yet a further mediation by judging before you can reach a limited judgment about who you are. Thus, you actually use your own knowing to mediate your immediate conscious self. In so doing, you are both the subject 'doing' the knowing and the object who is being mediated and known. As a subject you are immediately experienced, but, as object, you are mediated and known. In self-appropriation or self-knowing, you are revealing your identity to yourself. This knowing of self, as a known object, provides the foundation for a science of epistemology and metaphysics.

My intention is not to prove to you that you are a knower. You do not 'prove' the act of playing tennis to someone; rather you invite them to play. My intention is to invite you to pay attention to your own experience and to discover that affirmation of yourself as a knower cannot be avoided. This procedure is somewhat similar to what Plato attempted to do in his Dialogues. The intent is not to prove that your opponent is wrong, but to bring your opponent to an awareness of the context of her assumptions, which she is presupposing without being aware that she is actually relying on these presuppositions as a basis for her arguments. A dialogue is not so much an argument or debate as it is an invitation for people to begin exploring the basis of reasoning itself. Self-appropriation, then, is a methodical procedure for inviting knowers to discover the irrefutable fact that, prior to any argument, prior to any categories or principles, you are a knower.

One reason why this judgment of self as a knower can become the foundation stone for a whole new method of philosophizing is because it is immutable. You cannot change the concrete fact that you are a knower. Such a judgment is not necessary, but it is a concrete judgment of fact, and as such it is a limited absolute, a limited invariant. Certainly you can expand and improve your knowledge of yourself. You can modify and correct your ideas and judgments, but to do so you will have to experience, question, understand, and judge. Any revision will have to be done by you, the reviser, using your own activities of knowing to carry out that revision.

Now that we have clarified that you are a knower, and what you do when you are 'doing' knowing, we can ask the second foundational question, Why do you do this activity of knowing? What is your objective in performing this recurring scheme of conscious activities?

4   Notion of Being

Once again the source for the answer is in the desire that raises, not only this question, but all the questions we have been considering up to this point. Why do we ask 'what' in the first place? Why do we ask 'why' about our answers to our 'what' questions? We ask 'what' because we are not satisfied with just hearing sounds and seeing shapes; we want to know what the sounds and shapes are. Questions reveal that there is more to knowing than sensing. Why do we insist on conceiving, defining, and formulating our insights? Because we want to know precisely what it is that we have understood. Why do we insist on questioning our definitions, formulations, and propositions? Because we want to know whether they are correct or incorrect. Why do we want to know if they are correct or incorrect? Because that is the final object of knowing. It is only through the mediation of correct propositions and verified theories that we come to know what actually is or is not. And such an absolute yes or no is what we are seeking. To know what actually is has been our objective right from the first question. It was the desire to know that initiated and sustained the process through the successive steps until the final term was achieved. Because what actually is cannot be known by sensing alone, nor by understanding alone, nor by judging alone, but only by and through the tripartite structure of correct knowing.

If the final term or objective of knowing is reached in a correct judgment, then why do the questions recur? They recur because any correct judgment is only a limited judgment, a limited absolute; and while correct judgments mediate your knowing what is real, such terminal objects will not wholly satisfy your desire to know, since that desire keeps initiating further inquiries, further formulations, further judgments. Besides any particular, terminal object, there also seems to be a further and final objective that needs to be analyzed and defined.

Let us recall the emphasis I have placed on the way that asking what or why governs and directs you toward a known-unknown that becomes known through an insight and how the question, Is it so?, orients you to a further known-unknown that becomes known through a judgment. Furthermore, questioning not only motivates you, but it does so normatively. Questioning sets the standards by which you measure your answers. Thus, your judgments must meet the criterion of your own questioning. You keep reflecting and wondering whether your prospective judgments really are so, and only when all the relevant questions are answered, do you then proceed to commit yourself to a yes or no. Not only does questioning direct you, but it also obliges you to follow the standard it sets, and it compels you to assent when and only when you have sufficient evidence. The normative orientation of wondering requires that you follow its direction. You cannot know what really is so unless you understand and correctly judge the reality in question. However, the reality in question is a limited reality, and the questioning is limited by the way your own interests and desires restrict your wondering to one of the patterns of knowing we have analyzed. Now we have shifted the wondering from a specific question or pattern and have begun to wonder about wondering itself, rather than about a specific form of that wondering.

We are trying to appropriate what is the nature of wondering itself. We are asking what we are doing when we are questioning, not in this or that pattern of knowing, but in any pattern of knowing. And because particular questioning in one or another pattern of knowing keeps initiating and sustaining further questioning, we can affirm that questioning leads us beyond these limited, terminal objects toward a final objective, which would be to know everything about everything. The traditional name for everything, and everything about everything, is 'being' or 'reality.'

5   Being as Unrestricted

As a knower you are always between the limited context of what you know and the potentially unlimited context of knowing everything about everything. This latter context is not only unlimited, it is also all-inclusive. If being includes everything and everything about everything, then nothing remains beyond it. More important, it has no beyond since it includes all. Such a final object is all-inclusive, without limits, restrictions, or conditions. This final object is not the limited absolute that you encounter in any correct judgment, but an unlimited, unconditional absolute.[9] A correct judgment is absolute only in virtue of the conditions having been given, as you have understood and judged them to be given. But there is nothing conditioned about the final objective since it is not 'virtually unconditioned,' but totally and completely unconditioned. However, since you have not understood and judged everything about everything, and since clarity and precision come from understanding and defining, how can you define what you have not understood?

You can know what you do not know by knowing the type of acts through which you will come to know what you do not now know. Thus, both on the second and third level of knowing, you can form anticipatory structures that heuristically define the unknown through those activities that will

have to know how you will come about knowing this stuff

make it known. This is the significance of implicit, heuristic, or second-order definitions. Rather than defining 'being,' which you do not understand and which you have not judged, you can define the acts and the totality of acts through which this unrestricted unknown will come to be known. 'Being' can be defined as that which you will know through the totality of correct judgments.

5a Notion of Being as Spontaneous

It is important to note that you cannot conceive of being until you have understood it, and you will not understand it until you have understood everything about everything, until you have had an unlimited understanding that understands everything concretely and completely. Therefore, this second-order definition of being is not a concept of being, but a 'notion' of being. A notion generally refers to a vague idea or hunch you have about something before you actually come to know or witness it. Notional knowing is a priori knowing, but the a priori in this case is the sort of notional knowing that emerges with wondering or questioning. Notional knowing, then, is knowing the way your own questioning guides you to acts of understanding, and then moves you beyond understanding to correct judging, and beyond correct judging to repeated questioning toward a final objective that has absolutely no limits. Being, then, is a notion defined in terms not of what it is, but of how it comes to be known and will actually be known. Such an account of being or reality seems rather complicated and abstract. Yet everyone spontaneously assumes that things really exist, without getting involved in any complicated, abstract reasoning process. It is important to distinguish between the spontaneously operative notion of being and a philosophical account of what this notion of being is.[10]

We do not have to teach children to question; they do so spontaneously and effortlessly. When children reach a certain age, we do not have to teach them to ask, Is that really so?, Are you just kidding?, Do you really mean it? Such critical questioning is spontaneous, immediate, and natural. Aristotle says the beginning of wisdom is wonder, but he also spoke of nature as 'the imminent principle of movement and rest.' What stirs up a knower is a question, and what quiets such a knower is a correct answer. Questioning and answering are natural to knowers, which means that the desire to know, and to know in an unrestricted way, is what human nature gives to human knowers.

It is natural for all people to want to know being or everything about everything. That is why the child spontaneously asks, What is this?, and eventually, Is it really so? A deliberate effort is needed to stop the question. No doubt the child will have to learn that there is a strategy to questioning and that some questions can be answered only after years of study, but to repress and cover over a question deliberately without sufficient reason goes against our nature. Obscurantism in any form is intolerable for the authentic human knower.

5b All-Pervasive Notion of Being

My emphasis in explaining the notion of being thus far has been on the questioning or intending, not on the object questioned and intended. It is important now to shift attention to the object, content, or term of the questioning and to appropriate the way the notion of being underlies, penetrates, and transcends every object questioned or intended. Questions move on three distinct, yet relatable levels, which means that the contents known on these different levels needs to be specified. The question, What is a tree?, transforms the sensibly experienced and named tree into a potentially intelligible experience, which permits us to wonder about its 'what.' Medieval Scholastics named this the 'quiddity' of the tree. The tree as sensed is sensibly known; the quiddity or 'whatness' is unknown, but desired to be known.

When the child learns the name of the thing, he or she has a nominal understanding of this sensible experience. Such nominal understanding focuses and illuminates this thing, and also makes it possible for knowers to analogize to other things having somewhat similar and somewhat different shapes, sizes, colors, textures, odors, etc. When a knower moves from a common-sense context of knowing the reality of trees and begins to wonder in a scientific context, the knower desires to know the reality of trees not only descriptively, but in abstraction from its descriptive characteristics; he or she begins to apprehend and judge it in its relations to other organic beings. Thus, the contemporary biologist knows that trees are biochemical and biophysical operators, and that trees are continuously integrating themselves in their environment through a flexible set of recurrent schemes, including such metabolic activities as meiosis and photosynthesis. Scientists tacitly know that, by forming such complex theories, they gradually come to know what trees really are and how they differ and relate to one another.

At the heart of such theoretical, cognitional processes is the guiding notion of being that moves scientists to wonder, not only inquisitively, but also critically. They challenge and cross-examine their own thinking because implicitly they know that thinking is not knowing, that thinking is transformed into knowing through judging or verifying. More importantly, they realize that any present verified theory is only a limited explanation of the actual reality of trees. The full and final reality is what biologists know

they do not know but want to know, and so their desire to know keeps leading them on to fresh inquiries that repeatedly transcend their present, pro-
visionally verified theories. Trees are assumed to be fully intelligible
realities, and biologists intend to know what those full and final intelligibilities actually are. However, while biologists are aware that they do not know
the final reality of trees, they do know something about trees, and what
they do know, insofar as it is correctly verified knowing, is what in fact trees
actually are. In other words, correct, explanatory knowing of things is not
extrinsic to the supposedly inner reality of things; rather, it is through correct knowing that the intrinsic reality of the trees is gradually being disclosed. Correct biological knowing reveals the intrinsic reality of biological
things.

There is not some further profound, inner reality within trees that philosophers or metaphysicians come to know. Biologists as biologists do not
seek to know everything, but they do seek to know what the actual reality
or being of trees is, and they are well on their way toward that specialized
goal. Being is what all knowers desire to know, and it is what they know in
some limited way whenever they know correctly. Being, therefore, is intrinsic to every individual being, but at the same time, it transcends and
grounds all that there is to be known. With this notion of being in hand,
we are now in a position to raise the epistemological question, namely, the
question about the objectivity of our knowing.

6   Notion of Objectivity

Epistemology is the science that deals with the validity or objectivity of
human knowing. I have argued that such a science depends on a prior cognitional theory that begins, not by asking about the validity of human
knowledge, but by asking about what you, as a concrete knowing subject,
are doing when you are 'doing' knowing. The answer is that you are doing
three different, but functionally relatable activities which you unite by your
own spontaneous wonder. This wonder manifests itself, first, as inquisitive
wonder, leading you from experiencing to understanding, and, then, as
critical wonder, directing you from understanding to judging.

After appropriating what you are doing when you are knowing, the question shifts from appropriating your own operations of knowing to the goal
intended in all the different patterns of knowing. This shift changes wondering from a cognitional concern to an epistemological concern. Instead
of asking, What am I doing when I am knowing?, you ask, Why do I do
knowing? The answer is given by appropriating the objective that is sought,
naturally and spontaneously, in every form of knowing, namely, some
aspect of the real or being. Being or reality is grasped in some limited way

by making a correct judgment, which limits you to what you have experienced, understood, and judged such a reality to be. But you want to know more than limited realities, and so your wondering spontaneously leads you beyond any limited, correct judgment toward an unlimited objective. The final comprehensive goal of knowing is to know everything about everything. Being or reality, then, is *why* knowing is what it is. Our knowing, therefore, becomes knowing whenever you know what is or is not so. That is your objective, and that is what makes you an objective, knowing subject. In other words, if you are faithful to your own desire to know, letting it unfold and direct your questioning, then that cognitive commitment to your desire to know will make your judgments objective. Paradoxically, being truly or authentically subjective is what makes you an objective knower.

No doubt for many readers this explanation will seem like an idealist or immanentist theory of objective knowing. The usual epistemological theory begins by assuming a separation of knowing subjects and known objects, and the epistemological problem is then posed by the question, How can I be sure that what I know within my mind corresponds to what is actually out there beyond my knowing mind? If we pose the epistemological problem this way, we are assuming a duality between knowing subjects and known objects. More importantly, we are silently assuming we already know what subjects and objects are because we are assuming that immediate experiencing or perceiving is knowing, and that it is already objective knowing.

We began this study not with you, the subject, but with your own performance of wondering. Only after you know your own knowing do you come to know yourself as a subject in and through your own knowing. You cannot know yourself directly and immediately, only indirectly and mediately. You can feel yourself directly and immediately, but feeling is an experience, an awareness, that may or may not become the object of your wondering, understanding, and judging. Only if and when your feelings are mediated by acts of understanding and correct judging will you know what these feelings actually are. Further, if these feelings are correctly understood, then the object correctly known is your own feelings. This means that your subjective feelings can become correctly known objects. Similarly, your own subject which is experienced in the act of knowing can become a correctly known object. Knowing is not a known subject confronting known objects; rather, correct knowing constitutes a limited identity between knowers and what they know. If you were an unlimited knower, then your knowing would be perfectly identical with your being, and you would be perfectly identical with yourself and all other beings, as Aristotle recognized.[11]

It may seem that knowing yourself is a special case of knowing, but this is not so. To know anything you must first have an experience, either of your sensible world or of your knowing self, then you must mediate that immediate awareness of yourself, or of your world, through acts of understanding and correct judging. In this sense, there is no difference between knowing self and knowing others. In knowing self, you are the conscious object being mediated, as well as the conscious subject doing the mediating, but as subject mediating, you are not known, but simply experienced. In every act of correct knowing of self, therefore, you provide yourself with further experiences of yourself, as a knower, that may in turn be mediated. In other words, while there is an identity between you, the knower, making yourself known, and you, the correctly known object, there is not a perfect identity. If there were, you would be creating yourself in the act of knowing yourself. Your being and your knowing would be the very same act.

The argument that knowing is by identity, and not by confrontation, is the key reason why we began by asking, What are you doing when you are 'doing' knowing?, before asking, What makes knowing objective knowing? Not only does this methodical approach avoid beginning with an assumed duality between knower and known, but it also explains why knowers tend to assume that there is such a duality present in objective knowing. There are, then, two major discoveries to be made in knowing your own knowing, which will explain why knowers assume that objective knowing is simply a matter of making certain that knowing subjects do not project their own subjectivity onto supposedly real objects. The first discovery is that knowing is not a simple activity, but three transcending and functionally united activities. The second is that knowers operate in different patterns, and one of those patterns correlates sensing subjects to sensed objects in the same way that animals 'know.' Animal knowing is, however, not a three-level knowing; rather, it is an immediate, directed experience toward an outer world of objects that will satisfy the animal's immediately felt, inner needs.

Human knowers also have inner and outer sensibly conscious poles of experiencing, and if they do not explicitly appropriate and mediate these sensory-motor vectors and recenter them within a strictly intelligibly mediated framework, then there is a recurring tendency to mistake the single-level objectivity of animal knowing with the three-level objectivity of human knowing. However, if you appropriate and mediate your own three levels of cognitive activities, you realize that objective knowing has three quite different, but relatable objectives that together make your knowing valid. In the· first place, there is the level of givenness. Zebras do not assume there are tigers when there are actually none given, and so zebras may be considered as objective knowers, if by objective knowing we mean not assuming that an object is empirically given when it really is not. Clearly, empirical givenness is one part of objective knowing, but it is only one part, and not the essential part. For human knowing, this empirical givenness is the least interesting property of knowing, since it never gets beyond correct sensing of things to the more interesting questions about what a thing is and why it is what it is. If you pursue these questions far enough, you will move from descriptive, extrinsic answers to the explanatory answers reached by scientists. But no matter how brilliant or fascinating such scientific explanations are, you will find yourself as a knower transcending such theoretical explanations and wondering, Are these apparently brilliant explanations actually verifiable?

Objective knowing not only requires an empirically given component and a second normative component (intelligibility), but also demands a third critical component. This critical component is the most important step since it transcends the prior two levels and transforms your thoughts and theories from plausible hypotheses about reality to critically verified explanations of what actually is, and is actually operating in and through various recurrent schemes. Judging gives objectivity its absoluteness, its factualness, its independence, its irrefutability. Judging commits you to a truth that is not only yours, but that may belong to every knower who wishes to know it.

There are, then, three different forms of objectivity in every correct judgment: empirical objectivity; normative objectivity; and absolute objectivity.[12] If a knower thinks that knowing is a simple one-level activity, that knower will have made the basic epistemological mistake of confusing the first-level immediate givenness of experience with the third-level critically mediated experience.

Where are these critically mediated facts if they are not out there independent of the knowing subject? The form of the question assumes that, if facts are truly real and objective, they must be contained by some form of space and time. But this is a second basic mistake. To correct this mistake requires the mediating insight of Einstein's inverse insight that eliminated and reversed Newton's assumptions that an absolute space and time actually existed. The 'absolute' that Newton was seeking in order to guarantee the objectivity of his knowing is to be found not in the concrete immediate givenness of this universe, but in correctly mediated judgments about that immediate givenness. Such judgments transform and transcend this immediate extrinsic given to commit you to an intrinsically intelligible universe of being, which ultimately contains and makes real every spatiotemporal limit. This means that correctly mediated facts are within the concrete intelligible universe of being, and not in space and time. Space and time are simply limits, limits that are the way they are and behave the way they do because of the gravitational and electromagnetic functions that form them. Put in traditional Aristotelian language, we may say that space and time are potencies or matters, and the reason why space and time act the way they do is because of the way they have been and are being formed in and through atomic schemes.

In the first two chapters, we noted that inverse insights do not correct your previous thoughts and judgments, except insofar as they correct the way you wonder about yourself or about the world. To correctly apprehend and judge the meaning of Einstein's inverse insight, you must redefine the way you wonder about what makes known objects objectively known. In other words, you need to reorganize the basic context of your assumptions regarding what is objective knowing and what makes it objective. All your judgments are within a context, which means that any epistemological theory about the validity of knowing assumes a context concerning the way knowing subjects are related to known objects. That is why I began by inviting you to know your own knowing before you make any judgment about what a subject is; what an object is; how subjects and objects are related and how they are distinguished.

The first section of this chapter clarified what you are doing when you are making correct judgments. The second section invited you to make the concrete judgment of the fact that you are a knower. The third section identified the object that all knowers intend whenever they know and in whatever patterns they know, namely, being itself. This fourth section has identified three functionally related properties of objectivity that are present in any correct judgments. Now we are in a position to establish a new basic context through which and from which you can develop an epistemological theory. The core of this new basic context consists in three distinct, but related judgments: (1) I am a knower; (2) there are existing objects if I know them through correct judgments, and such objects may be distinguished from one another, only if I know such distinctions through correct judgments; (3) I am not any one of these known objects that I have judged as real, existing objects. With and through these three judgments, we have a theory of objectivity because we can relate subjects to objects in and through this pattern or context of judgments.

Each of these three judgments – I am a knower; this is a desk; I am not a desk – is objective, which means that each has the three related properties of an objective judgment, namely, empirical, normative, and critical objectivity. Moreover, each judgment combines these three properties into a single, normative, and critically structured unity. It may seem strange to argue that you have to judge that you are not a desk. As a knower you seem to know that spontaneously. Not so. You may sense yourself and the desk as sensibly different, but sensing differences is not knowing differences. Scientists sensed that air was a single object for two thousand years before they discovered and judged that it was, in fact, made of many distinct gases. Differences as well as likenesses have to be understood and correctly judged before you can say that you know them. To know that you are not a desk is to make a judgment about a real distinction between yourself and an object that has an experiential, normative, and critical component that makes it true independently of your judgment.

With this pattern of judgments as a foundational premise for generalizing, you can go on to build a basic context that will ground the objectivity of judgments in the other specialized knowing contexts. In this context, for example, you can define a subject as an object who is a knower. In the field of objects you know, there are some objects that are also subjects, which means that they also are self-affirming knowers. What, then, is the core of this theory of objectivity? The core is that knowing is not one thing and reality another. Reality is known in and through experiencing it, understanding it, and correctly judging it. Reality is intrinsically intelligible, and the intelligible is what is real, provided that it is correctly verified. This principle attacks the basic assumptions that being subjective excludes being objective. But it is only by attending carefully to your own cognitional demands that you can become an objective judger. It is not the experience of reality that grounds your judgments, nor is it the intelligibility of reality that guarantees that your judgment will be objective, nor is it critical wondering that provides the motive for correct judging. Rather, all three components working together and united by you, the judger, provide the sufficient reason for committing yourself to the verified intelligibility of what you have judged really is so.

Correct explanatory knowing reveals the reality of things. Your knowing yourself is intrinsic to the reality that you are, and your knowing is also intrinsically related to any other reality you know correctly. The reality of living things, is what the biologists correctly judge them to be, and because they know their own minds are not satisfied with what they have already discovered and verified, they know at least tacitly that the final and full reality of life is unknown but essentially knowable. As we noted before, 'The most incomprehensible thing about this universe is that it is comprehensible.'

A further point to be noted in this theory of objectivity is that it permits us to distinguish between the limited objectivity achieved in the various patterns of knowing and the potential, unlimited objectivity that is based, not on limited interests and desires to know as we find in common-sense and scientific desires to know, but on the unlimited, disinterested desire to know all about all.

7   Summary

In the first section of this chapter, I distinguished between meaning and knowing for two reasons: first, to stress the difference between the terms or objects 'meant' as opposed to the activities which generate those terms or objects 'meant'; and second, to emphasize that, at this stage of self-knowing, our concern is not with language, but with the activities that generate, promote, and guide our use of language.

In the second section of this chapter, we moved from the second to the third level of cognitional activities, revealing that knowing is a tripartite structure of functionally related activities. In the third section, you were invited to identify and affirm yourself as a knower. At this stage, your own subject became the object to be known. Because you can make your own subject the object known, you can also specify or identify yourself and any other subject as, 'an object who is a knower.' This affirmation of self as a knower is the critical step in the whole process of self-knowing. The purpose of focusing on this affirmation of self is to emphasize and clarify precisely how as a knower you can make yourself known to yourself through your own tripartite structure of knowing. There is no other way of 'knowing' yourself, although knowers tend to assume that they can know themselves directly and immediately. While you can experience, or be conscious of, yourself directly and immediately, this immediate experience of self is not knowing self. Knowledge comes through the three interrelated acts of knowing that are required to mediate your immediate experience of yourself. Uncovering this mistaken assumption – that experiencing or perceiving self is knowing self – is an important step toward correcting a second mistaken assumption – that subjects and objects are already known through immediate awareness. This mistake confuses single-level sensible knowing and three-level sensible, intellectual, and rational knowing. Both of these mistakes assume a more primordial and pervasive mistake, which is to assume that subjects and objects are immediately known because reality is already known. And such reality is assumed to be known directly and immediately.

It is this third mistaken assumption that I have attempted to question in the section where I distinguished between a notion of being and a concept of being. Human knowers have, immediately and directly, a spontaneous and primordial wonder about being or reality, but they do not have a knowing of reality. Reality is not known and will not be known until every correct judgment that can be made has been made. We have an unrestricted potential to know, but we have not actualized that potential; quite simply, we do not know reality or being. What we do know is how we may come to know being, which is in and through our three-level set of activities of knowing.

Prior to knowing is wondering and that wondering is all-encompassing. Whenever you mediate your own immediate experience of yourself, you do so primarily within the conscious field of your own wondering, and not within the conscious field of sensing. The immediate conscious field of sensing is encompassed by, and included in, the all-inclusive, immediate awareness of unrestricted wonder. Once you grasp, first, that you must correctly mediate a knowledge of yourself within the immediate horizon set by wondering and, second, that you must mediate your immediate sensible world within the same all-encompassing horizon of wonder, then you are in a position to specify what it means to make an objectively valid judgment.

Managing to be objective in making judgments is usually posed as the problem of getting beyond an already known subject to an object that is affirmed to be known independently of the knowing subject. Such independence is assumed to be guaranteed if the known object is perceived to exist within reality, and not in some idealized sphere projected by the knower. My approach to the problem of objectivity has been just the opposite. I have assumed that neither you, the subject, nor objects, nor reality can be directly and immediately known. Instead I have identified the three-level structure of knowing, and through it I invited you to take yourself as the object to be understood and affirmed; your own subject becomes the to-be-known object. Second, I identified why we desire to know objects, whether these objects are self or anything else. The reason is that what you want to know is the reality of that object, and you do not know any object as real until you have correctly mediated that object within the immediate all-inclusive field of being. And even though you have already made a correct judgment of yourself or any other object, you do not know your own reality; rather, you have achieved only a very limited understanding of your reality. Your own reality will only be fully known when you have made the final correct judgment of who you actually are. The same goes for every other thing. Furthermore, you cannot define what you mean by making an objective judgment without first establishing a context or pattern of at least three judgments – a judgment of yourself as a knower; a judgment of some other object; and a judgment of the distinction between the knowing subject and the known object – because the notion of objectivity involves an understanding of the way subjects and objects are related and distinguished. All three judgments are posited within the spontaneous, immediate, and unlimited field of being or reality. This field is not the immediate sensible field that surrounds you; rather, it is the mysterious unknown field that is immediately present through your spontaneous wondering which encompasses and transcends the immediate sensible horizon. There is no question that this immediate sensible horizon is objectively given, but so is the much more important, transcending horizon that you 'experience' through wonder.

Having defined what knowing is, who you are, what being is, and what objectivity is, we can now proceed to set up a metaphysics based on this set of mutually defined terms.

6

Metaphysics

1 Traditional Metaphysics

For the early Greek thinkers, the primary problems were religious and moral, not metaphysical. This way of phrasing the problem is misleading since these early Greek thinkers did not differentiate between religious, moral, and metaphysical questions in the way we do. For these thinkers, the fundamental philosophical question tended to be, What is the best way to live?, rather than, What is the meaning of being? These two questions were certainly related, but with Aristotle the 'being question' and metaphysics took precedence over the moral question about the right way to live. Before proceeding, I need to explain what I mean by 'precedence.'

For Aristotle, metaphysics provided the basic context of meanings for the other sciences because metaphysics was concerned with the ultimate causes or constituents of the being of things, insofar as these things were beings.[1] Insofar as things move, they become objects for physicists; insofar as things live, they are objects for biologists; insofar as things sense and reason, they are objects for psychologists. But insofar as things are real things or beings, they are objects for metaphysicians. Thus, to study objects as metaphysical objects is to study them in the basic and most comprehensive way. In such a context, not only was metaphysics the most universal way to study objects, but it also provided the basic terms for studying the other, less universal sciences.

The approach to metaphysics that we have been proposing, however, is remarkably different. In the first place, we have begun, not with metaphysics, but with cognitional theory. More important, you the reader, have been invited to appropriate that cognitional theory in terms of your own cognitional operations, as distinguished from the contents that become known through these operations. Further, in focusing on the orienting wonder and questioning that precedes, directs, and coordinates these cognitional operations to one another, we have clarified and specified the ultimate objective that we seek whenever and in whatever pattern of knowing we are engaged. In the second place, this rather different method has led us to an epistemological theory in which the basic terms and relations of the theory are not derived from prior metaphysical terms and relations, as was the case in Aristotle's metaphysical theory of knowing. We have begun with your own actual performances of knowing. The intention was not only to discover the object you intended to know, but more significantly to know you the subject who operates in and through these activities, and who can be known 'objectively' only through your own cognitional activities. This means you can make your own subject the object of knowing, and having made yourself known as one more object within the horizon of all knowing – namely, 'being' – you can then proceed to correlate subjects to objects and to distinguish subjects from objects. To specify how subjects are related to, and distinguished from, objects is to set up a theory of objective knowing, an epistemology. In other words, we have derived a theory of objective knowing from a prior theory of knowing, and we are now about to derive a theory of metaphysics from these prior two theories. In doing so, we have reversed the traditional procedure of deriving the theory of objectivity and knowing from a prior metaphysical theory.

The reason for this reversal is methodological. As we saw in chapter 2, once the sciences broke loose from metaphysics and established their own methodical procedures with their own basic terms and relations, these sciences took off. Their remarkable success precipitated an epistemological crisis that set the conditions for Descartes's attempt to find a similar methodical approach to philosophy. With Descartes began the 'turn to the subject' and the beginning of the long process of discovering a new language for mediating, not only the subject, but also the 'operations' through which the subject acts and through which you, the subject, can make yourself known to yourself. The key to understanding this 'turn to the subject' is to appropriate the basic underlying and orienting wonder that directs your cognitional activities, and to appropriate the potentially unrestricted range and the objective of your wondering. To do this methodically, you must move from descriptive to explanatory patterns of knowing. The argument may be summarized this way: to 'explain' why your metaphysical theory operates the way it does, you must disclose how it derives from your epistemological theory; similarly, to 'explain' your epistemological theory, you must disclose how it depends on your own cognitional operations. In other words, to do philosophy methodically, we must start with the question, What are you doing when you are knowing? (cognitional theory), then shift to the question, Why is doing that knowing? (epistemological question), then shift to the question, What do you know when you know objectively? (metaphysical question).

2   Metaphysics: Terms and Relations

Traditionally, the fundamental concepts of metaphysics have been potency, form, and act, but a basic assumption in employing such categories was the philosopher's operative notion or definition of being. The recurring mistake of many philosophers has been to assume that we can form a concept of being, as Parmenides, Plato, and others did, whereas we have insisted on a 'notion' of being. What distinguishes a notion from a concept is that a notion is defined, not directly, but implicitly in terms of the cognitive acts through which being becomes known. More important, these cognitive acts through which being is defined arise from, and are sustained by, the underlying desire to know, as it initiates all our wondering and questioning, and also orients that questioning to an understanding that would grasp the intelligibility potentially present in all of our experiences. In addition, our intellects also apprehend other aspects of our experience that limit the intelligibilities we have apprehended, and because they limit that intelligibility, the knower abstracts from them, focusing instead on the intelligibilities as they pattern these experiences into some form of an intelligible unity. However, the desire to know, which initiates, sustains, and orients our questioning toward transforming unknown possible understandings into known possibilities, does not rest with knowing possible intelligibilities, but moves on to discover whether these possibilities are actual or not. But such correctly understood experiences explain only a small fraction of all the possible patterns of experiences that human beings have experienced and are experiencing. Our desire to know is all-inclusive; it will not be satisfied until every possible correct judgment has been made. In other words, just as the desire to know is unrestricted, so too the tripartite structure of our activities of knowing that mediates that desire is similarly oriented and specified. The term 'experience,' then, refers to all experiences; 'understanding' to all understandings; and 'judging' to all judgings. In this manner, we may extend our second-order, operational definition of being to the three activities by which and through which any being and all beings may be known. These three cognitional activities, provide us with a circle of terms and relations since understanding is what presupposes and complements experiencing, while judging presupposes and completes understanding. The three activities are related to one another in a mutually explanatory context that also mediates you, the knower, to yourself and, at the same time, correlates you to every other knower, since these related activities relate all knowers to the same objective, namely, being. It is being that explains why all knowers are engaged in knowing. Just as the acts of knowing are explanatorily related to one another, so too being and knowing are explanatorily related. Being is the objective of knowing, and knowing proceeds as it does in order to judge being.

Knowing, then, is not outside being; rather, the structure of knowing corresponds to, and is intrinsic to, the structure of being. To understand and affirm the intrinsic intelligibility of being, it is imperative to understand what it means to move from a descriptive to an explanatory context, and to make that move in such a way that does not discredit descriptive knowing, but that does criticize, recenter, and reorient such descriptive contexts. The metaphysics that we are proposing is an explanatory metaphysics, whose basic terms and relations are the knowers own tripartite, structured activities of knowing, as those structured acts of knowing are oriented by, and dynamically directed to, being.

Let us move on to define potency, form, and act. Potency is the structural component to be known in and through a complete intellectual patterning of all experience (the experience of all individuals, of all places and times, of all continuous processes, and of all random or nonsystematic divergencies from expected norms). Potency is to be known through a complete explanatory patterning of all experiences. Potency is not form, but it is functionally related to form. Form is defined as that structural component of being to be known through a complete explanatory account of all things as those things are related to one another. Act is the third structural component, the absolute final and unconditional element that completes and perfects the other two components. Act brings to a final realization and perfection the contribution of form and potency.[2] Taken together, these three structural components form a unity since what is experienced is what is understood and what is understood is what is judged. Furthermore, all three components are defined by the term 'form.' Experience presents rather than defines, and act affirms and denies rather than determines and specifies. It is form that specifies, determines, and defines what is presented by experience, while act is also defined by the same form. As well, form is specified as a full explanation of things in their relationships to other things. Thus, potency, form, and act share a common definition, and that definition is anticipatory, or heuristic and explanatory. Furthermore, all three are defined in terms of our own structure of knowing as oriented to an ultimate, unrestricted objective.

Thus, potency, form, and act constitute an integral, heuristic structure through which you and any other knower can anticipate knowing any and all beings in a fully explanatory way. Before we can apply this structure to the concrete universe of being, however, we must differentiate two general cases of potency, form, and act. Since potency, form, and act are defined through your own experiencing, understanding and judging as conditioned by your unrestricted desire to know, we can specify different cases of potency, form, and act because there are different ways of understanding, and judging experience. In the first four chapters, we specified two major types of understanding: understanding the way things are related to one another and understanding these same things as subsistent unities that perdure through successive changes. On the basis of these two different types of understanding, we can distinguish between the conjugate forms and the central form or unity that operates through these conjugate forms. Since these central forms exist in individual or limited ways, we can further identify central act as existence and central potency as the source that individualizes any existing central form. In addition, any individual existing unity or form operates through its own conjugate forms as they occur and recur in particular circumstances. Conjugate potency, then, refers to the particular limiting conditions under which things act, while conjugate act refers to the occurrence and recurrence of these conjugate forms. For example, a plant is an organic unity (central form) that exists (central act) in an individualized way (central potency). That same individual existing plant operates (conjugate act) reproductively (conjugate form) in certain particular ways (conjugate potency).

These six terms – central potency, form, act and conjugate potency, form, act – provide us with a set of basic terms and relations (1) for integrating the metaphysical structural constituents of single beings as they form a unity; (2) for relating and integrating single beings with other single beings of the same species; (3) for relating and integrating different species of being with other species of the same genera; (4) for relating and integrating any genera of being with any other genera within the dynamically developing universe of being. The rest of this chapter will attempt to spell out how these six terms and relations can be combined in these four ways to relate and systematically integrate all the different beings within the concrete universe of being. Having established the six basic terms and relations for developing a heuristic structure for integrating any and all things, first, in their own concrete existing unities and, second, in their various special and generic relations with one another, we can now specify how this integrating structure unifies the different departments of sciences and their respective fields of being.

The metaphysician's goal is to construct the integrating heuristic structure for the whole universe of being, while the scientist's concern is to develop specialized structures for understanding and judging the various limited domains of beings. While the metaphysician depends on the various sciences to provide the materials to be integrated, it is still the metaphysician who does the integrating since he or she knows the structure through which the scientist knows, and the metaphysician also knows that this structure corresponds to the intrinsic structure of beings insofar as those beings are known in verified, explanatory patterns. Moreover, metaphysicians who know their own knowing and the pattern within which they know can also integrate common-sense knowing with theoretical knowing, since they know that, while common-sense knowers operate in a descriptive context and are subject to a four fold set of biases in their pursuit of knowledge, their method of knowing is not only valid, but also the only way to know particular, concrete situations and how to operate intelligently and wisely within such a context. Metaphysicians are dependent on common-sense and scientific knowers to provide them with the data that they will transform, reorient, and unify into an ever expanding explanation of the entire universe of being.

3   Explanatory Genera and Species

In chapter 4, I sketched a world-order that united different things to one another horizontally through recurrent schemes and vertically through a conditioned series of things operating in their recurrent schemes. I also proposed that the emergence of these horizontally and vertically related levels of things operating in their recurrent schemes were being realized in accord with a changing schedule of probabilities. Such a world-order is not a necessary order operating under the sway of certain universal, necessary laws, nor is it a final and complete ordering; rather, it is an order that is still emerging. Although this order is only probable in its unfolding, such ordering can be quite stable and effective, without being necessary and deterministic, because emerging probabilities are very effective in the long run. Very large numbers of things, perduring through very long periods and distributed through vastly scattered situations, can bring about results in very effective and flexible ways.

This understanding of world-order through emergent probability was based on an analysis of cognitional activities and the ways insights accumulate into systematic viewpoints which can be combined into a range of recurring cycles of knowing. Such systems can set the conditions for the emergence of higher, more complex, and powerful systems, thereby generating a series of higher systems with each higher system emerging from the lower and, at the same time, modifying the materials of that lower system. We studied examples of such emerging, higher systems in the history of mathematics and physics. In this chapter, I have set forth the basic terms and relations for establishing a heuristic structure for explaining the actual operating order within the concrete universe of being. In other words, the world-order of chapter 4, which was based on cognitional analysis, now has to be recast in metaphysical terms. It will help to clarify our task if I briefly review the argument we have been following in the preceding five chapters.

The first step in chapter 1 was to focus on insights and the way they accumulate into higher viewpoints through more powerful methods of abstracting and defining theoretical terms and relations. The second step was to underscore the importance of heuristic procedures and the way theoretical knowers may anticipate knowing their unknown objectives. The third step was to appropriate the differences between the heuristic methods of theoretical and practical patterns of knowing and the four fold manner in which we may block insights. The fourth step was to combine the two different theoretical methods of anticipatory knowing – classical and statistical – within the explanatory notion of a 'recurrent scheme.' Combining the notion of recurrent schemes with higher viewpoints permitted us to explain the ordering of this universe in terms of emergent probability. Only at this point in the argument could we tackle the complex notion of 'thing' and contrast it to the familiar, descriptive notion of 'body,' which is usually mistaken as an 'out-there-now' real thing. The fifth step was to clarify precisely what constitutes a concrete judgment of fact and to invite you, the reader, to make the foundational and factual concrete judgment: I am a knower.

Only after having established what knowing is and the fact that each of us is a knower, did we proceed to focus on the question, Why is knowing what it is? The answer to that question established the unrestricted objective common to all knowers, namely, being. While that objective transcends all subjects and objects, it has also permeated, grounded, and directed every step in the entire course of our argument, as it also permeated and grounded the entire universe of objects at every level of being. This brings us to the somewhat surprising result that we will not know what reality or being is until we have made all the correct judgments that can be made, and we cannot be truly objective in our judgments unless we allow our unrestricted desire to know to unfold properly. To accomplish this means recognizing the four ways we bias our knowing and accepting that we exist in continuous tension between the limited horizon of what we know at present and the potential, unlimited horizon of what we could know. The sixth and last step was to set up an integral, heuristic structure through which metaphysical knowers could collaborate with scientific and common-sense knowers in moving toward a full explanation of the universe of being. Crucial in defining the six terms of this heuristic structure is the notion of being, since that notion establishes the intrinsic intelligibility of being or the basic premise that the structure of our knowing corresponds to the intrinsic structure of beings within being. This premise also grounds the ability of metaphysical knowers to reorient and transform the results of the sciences and common sense into a critically grounded and developing knowing of being. The next step is to establish how a metaphysical ordering of the different genera and species could be worked out in an explanatory way.

In discussing the notion of being in the last chapter, we shifted from knowing the tripartite structure of knowing to knowing the ultimate objective in all knowing, which means shifting from the acts of knowing to the structured contents known through these acts. Thus, we reversed the first stage of our study, which was to abstract from the contents of our knowing in order to focus on the acts of knowing. Now we are shifting from the cognitional acts to the structured contents that can be known through those acts, from the cognitional to the ontological structure, from experiencing, understanding, and judging to the experienced (potency), the understood (form), and the judged (act). Potency, form, and act constitute the structure through which proportionate or structured being can be known. This structure provides the medium through which beings become potentially, formally, and actually known. However, if, we want to know the actual forms of things, such as chemical or biological things, then we have to study chemistry or biology. What the metaphysician knows is that chemists and biologists do, in fact, know the actual forms of things because the metaphysician knows the explanatory structure of knowing as that structure is intrinsically related to the actual structure of beings. The metaphysician leaves the actual knowing of forms to the special scientists, and focuses instead on integrating the verified scientific explanations of these different sciences because she or he wants to know being or reality, or everything about everything. Metaphysics is not the whole of knowledge, but the whole in all of our verified knowledge.

This argument needs to be restated in terms of central and conjugate potency, form, and act.[3] What chemists know when they have attained the status of an explanatory science is a set of laws, implicitly defined and verified in particular cases. These laws can now be identified as the conjugate forms that relate chemical atoms to one another. Their verification, although probable and provisional, refers to conjugate acts, while the sensible situations and instances in which the laws have been tested refer to conjugate potencies. The metaphysician knows, first, that those chemical laws are intrinsic to the very structure of chemical atoms; second, that there are different types of conjugate forms – classical and statistical; and, third, that such conjugate forms can be combined into schemes of recurrence through which these atomic things interact with one another. These existing unities or chemical central forms, therefore, can be known as existing and operating through their recurrent schemes.

If we ask chemists whether the explanatory laws they have defined and tested reveal the real, actual structure of atoms, we are asking them a meta-physical question, and their answers will carry a set of assumptions about what makes knowing objective and about the relation of knowing to being or reality. Most, if not all, of these assumptions will be unknown and unex-amined by the chemists, yet they will be operative in the way they answer the question. It is not the business of chemists to know knowing, nor to know why knowing is what it is, nor what you know when you know objec-tively. That is the business of metaphysicians. And if metaphysicians have methodically set up their science as we have done, then they know that explanatorily, verified chemical laws are conjugate forms that intrinsically reveal the real structure of chemical atoms. Chemists are far from having a complete, explanatory science, but what they presently know correctly is moving them toward a fully comprehensive understanding of the actual concrete world of chemical reality. Chemical reality is only a small part of the complete universe of reality, but it is the part whose reality is being revealed by chemists.

The same is true for the other sciences, such as physics and biology, pro-vided that these sciences have moved into an explanatory stage of know-ing. Descriptive knowing does not reveal the intrinsic structure of the being of things and of the reality of their operating relations. Endless mis-leading questions can be raised by descriptive knowers who ask such ques-tions as, Is chalk really white, or does it merely appear white to human knowers? If we put the same descriptive question in terms of the explana-tory context of the electromagnetic structure of atoms, at least a probable and provisional answer is readily available. In setting up a metaphysical, explanatory theory of genera and species, it is important to know whether the science is still in a descriptive, descriptive-explanatory, or purely explanatory stage.

A second problem that needs to be examined is the difficulty of integrat-ing these explanatory sciences. The central idea for achieving this integra-tion is the notion of higher viewpoints, in which higher structures emerge from prior operating lower systems. These lower systems provide the potency in which the higher forms may emerge. Potency consists in a mul-tiplicity of lower acts that cannot be systematized on the lower level, and so these acts form possible opportunities out of which higher schemes of activities may come forth. For example, let us consider meteorology as an explanatory science of our atmosphere. Meteorologists know that the air surrounding us is composed of a mixture of different gases – nitrogen, oxy-gen, carbon dioxide, and so on. Meteorologists also know what percentages of those various gases are present in the wind currents as they circle the globe. But to explain the origin and maintenance of these various percentages of gases, meteorologists would have to resort to the biological sciences. To answer questions about the chemical balance of the various gases present in the air, meteorologists would have to know how the nitrogen cycle connects the biological activities of plants and animals with the chemical activities of the soil, air, and sea. This nitrogen cycle involves a vast web of interacting schemes, all mutually conditioning one another as they maintain the present balance of gases in the atmosphere. These atmospheric gases , like the soil, form a mixture of atomic and molecular compounds. This vast multiplicity of individual, existing atomic and molecular unities, operating in their respective chemical schemes, are the potency out of which higher biological forms are actually emerging. The potency for these higher biological forms emerge from the lower chemical conjugate acts, and what are actual events from the chemical viewpoint are potential forms from the higher biological perspective. Similarly, what are numbers or points from the lower viewpoint of arithmetic and geometry become potencies or variables to be co-ordered from the analytic geometer's perspective. Just as atoms pattern subatomic events into perduring atomic unities, cells absorb and transform atoms or molecules from the surrounding soil and atmosphere. Within the living cells, these chemicals provide the potency for the higher physiological schemes that nourish and support the metabolic activities of the organism. The conjugate acts of lower conjugate forms, therefore, provide the potential field for the emergence of higher schemes of conjugate forms.

This scenario of lower, individual existing unities operating in their respective schemes can be repeated until a series of generically higher things with their respective schemes emerge and evolve over time. Such a series of higher viewpoints can be united and integrated through the theory of emergent probability, which we discussed in chapter 4. But before we recontextualize emergent probability within our present metaphysical context, we need to clarify in a more differentiated way the role of potency in the dynamic unfolding of this universe.

4   Potency and Limit

In discussing the role of the metaphysical element potency, it is important to keep in mind the cognitional analogy which controls and specifies its meaning. We need to recall that the questioning of experience transforms that experience into a known-unknown. Experience as questioned reveals experience as the limit of our present knowing, but at the same time questioned experience becomes an opportunity since we can transform this known-unknown into a known through understanding and judging that experience. Thus, the conscious experiencing of the waxing and waning of the moon's appearance becomes a potentially intelligible experience when we wonder why the light of the moon changes the way that it does. Potency or experience means a limit from one perspective and an opportunity from another. It is a tension between opposites.[4]

As a tension of opposites, potency is a directed tension since it leads the knower toward the form or understanding that will resolve this tension. But this form or understanding will become, in turn, a potency for the higher act of judging, since form or understanding does not become fully actualized until it is judged as correctly understood or truly affirmed. Further, since the cycle of potency, form, and act is conditioned by an immediate, spontaneous desire or potency, any limited actualization of that potency will only whet the appetite of the knower to repeat the cycle and transform other aspects of experience or lower potencies into a conscious tension to another form or insight which will, in turn, be transformed by critical wondering into a potency or directed tension toward a judgment or conjugate act. Thus potency, form, and act form a cyclical process within every conscious knower, and this cyclical process corresponds to, and is structurally analogous to, the way every other being cycles and, as we shall see, the way the whole universe cycles in a 'dynamic, directed but indeterminate way.'

5   Vertical Finality

main point

Before considering the dynamic direction of the whole universe of beings, three points need to be discussed to clarify the structural analogy between the way that your own knowing being cycles and the way that any and every other being cycles. The first point is that there is a structural analogy between your own and other cycling beings, and that analogy should be understood vertically.[5] This means that your potency is to your form and your form is to your act as a plant's potency is to its form and its form is to its act. The second point is that the comparison between the two ontological structures is a comparison of the relations of the two structures, not the terms of those relations. This means that the pattern of relations of your potency to your form and of your form to your act is analogous to the patterns of relations of the plant's potency to its form and of its form to its act. The comparison is not between your potencies and the plant's potencies, but in the way your form is related to your potency. The potencies of people and plants are essentially different, but there is a structural comparison in the way the plant's form functions in its unconscious potencies and the way your understanding functions in your conscious potencies or experi-

vertical, not horizontal

ences. The potencies of plants and people differ because their forms differ, but if we abstract from these two potencies and forms and attend instead to the way these different potencies and forms are correlated, then we have established the basis for a metaphysical or structural analogy. It was for this reason we insisted in the earlier chapters that metaphysicians are not primarily interested in what the physicists or biologists know, but are interested instead in the tripartite structure through which they know. Just as you come to know that your own knowing is actually intrinsic to, and explanatory of, your being as a knowing being, so you also come to realize that biological knowing, if it is explanatory knowing, can reveal the actual intrinsic structure of biological beings. Moreover, because we defined potency, form, and act heuristically and explanatorily, we can anticipate knowing the way the intrinsic structure of any and all beings can be analogously related to one another, even though they differ individually, specifically, and generically.

The third point to be noted in considering potency, form, and act as dynamically and cyclically related is to understand how that cycling structure combines the four different methods of knowing which we have discussed in chapter 4. These four cognitional methods correspond to and ground four metaphysical methods which metaphysicians must integrate to form an integral heuristic structure. We have already differentiated form into central and conjugate forms; now we need to differentiate these conjugate forms into classical, statistical, genetic, and dialectical forms. The meaning of form has been specified by the act of understanding, and since there are different types of understanding, there are corresponding differences of forms.

Classical insights involve grasping invariant correlations among continuously changing variables, but such correlations are discovered by abstracting from the actual concrete conditions under which these correlates or conjugate forms actually operate. Statistical scientists attempt to understand how often these classical correlations occur in certain concrete conditions or, if they have already occurred and are recurring, then what the probability of their survival is. In verifying such frequencies or probabilities, statistical scientists abstract from the nonsystematic or random variations around these ideal frequencies. In brief, classical scientists deal with forms, while statistical scientists deal with the relations of these forms to acts. Genetic scientists deal with the way forms emerge from potencies, and dialectical scientists focus on the obstruction of emerging forms. I will discuss genetic and dialectical methods after I discuss the finality or indeterminate directed dynamism of the universe, but here I want to restate my earlier contrast between cycles and schemes of correlations or conjugate forms.

In chapter 4 I contrasted the traditional 'chain of being' world-order in which terrestrial cycles were attuned to the cosmic, celestial cycles. In the Aristotelian tradition, the cosmic cycles governed the terrestrial cycles; in the biblical tradition, the cosmic and terrestrial were subservient to the human cycles. In either case, the world was well ordered, and the splendor and complexity of this ordering revealed the presence of a divine designer, provider, and all-wise governor. The problem with such an account of world-order was that it operated within a descriptive and imaginative context that tended to conceive things as static essences, modified only accidentally and extrinsically in their relationships to one another. Such a world-order had two parts: the inner unchanging essences of things and the outer accidental, sensible properties of things that were contingent and changeable. Empirical scientists studied only the finite external appearances of things, while metaphysicians supposedly apprehended the intrinsic unchanging essences of things. Such a science of metaphysics was constructed on first principles that were considered to be universal, certain, and self-evident, and from such universal, necessary premises, metaphysicians would be able to deduce a series of certain conclusions concerning the order of the universe. The procedure we followed in setting up a world-order was radically different.

This study began, not with premises, but with an invitation to you, the reader, to examine your own cognitional activities. This was followed by a careful distinction between descriptive and explanatory frameworks, with which we distinguished ordinary practical knowing from scientific knowing. In the next step we combined the abstract, classical scientific methods with the explanatory-descriptive methods of statistical science in order to form the general notion of a recurrent scheme. On the basis of a conditioned series of recurrent schemes, we proposed an explanatory world-order, and only after this explanatory world-order had been articulated did we introduce the notion of things which exist and operate in and through their recurring schemes. Having established that things or individual concrete unities operate and cooperate through recurring patterns of activities, we turned to you, the knower, who exists and operates through your own concrete, conscious, cognitional schemes. In brief, we began descriptively and moved gradually to an explanatory context that elucidated and comprehended the ordering of the world, and then returned in chapter 5 to the original descriptive context of your own conscious self. But we returned to your knowing self in order to relate you in an explanatory way to every other knower in a common search for being. In other words, we mediated your descriptive self in and through your explanatory self. The reason for this approach was to bring the ordinary, familiar descriptive way of knowing under the control of explanatory or 'causal' knowing, so that we could set up an explanatory metaphysics that would account for, and comprehend in metaphysically analogous ways, how each and every being seeks to be and to behave. The basis for these analogies is the tripartite structure of your own knowing as analogous to, or proportionate to, the tripartite structure of any and all beings including yourself. Just as your own essence or central form exists and operates through your own schemes of conjugate or cognitional forms, any being's essence or central form exists and operates in and through its analogous schemes of conjugate forms.

In this view of metaphysics, it is scientists who anticipate knowing the essences of things, while it is metaphysicians who anticipate knowing the different analogies of different essences to their existences as they operate in their similar and dissimilar schemes of behaving. In short, the metaphysician can provide an integrated and heuristic view of the whole concrete universe of being, while the various sciences investigate generically and specifically similar beings within their respective fields of proportionate being. Because the metaphysician's integrating structure is defined in terms of the final objective of knowing, namely, being, and because that integrating structure is analogous to the structure of any and all being, the integrated view that the metaphysician reveals is a dynamic, open, and emerging universe of beings within being.

The source of this dynamism is potency, not only the potency of this or that level of being, but the total potency or possibilities of the entire universe of being. Any potency, as we have seen, is ordered to form as form is oriented to act. Another way of thinking about this metaphysical world-order is to think of it as the form that orders all the potencies (central and conjugate) of all the different levels of being to one another. The form or intelligibility which informs or explains the unity of these successive, higher levels of beings is 'emergent probability,' and that 'form,' which we have identified as emergent probability, is actually being realized 'in accord with successively changing schedules of probabilities.' In other words, the concrete universe of proportionate being is presently 'emerging,' and while the order of that emergence is intelligible as a whole, it is not a finished whole, and its actual unfolding is not certain but probable, and these probabilities shift from less to more as things and their schemes change. This does not mean that the universe is not effectively organized; probabilities are very effective ways of ordering results in the long run of events. It also means that, if the universal orientation of all potencies to forms is statistically variable with numerous possibilities, then a wide range of alternative forms may emerge. Some of these alternative orderings of things will have higher or lower probabilities of survival, and so those schemes of things with lower survival rates will gradually decrease and disappear, while others with higher survival rates will probably perdure.

Besides this extensive range of alternative orderings of world-order, there is also the potential that the multiple interacting of such forms will generate a vast manifold of aggregates of acts in which and out of which higher-ordered schemes and things may emerge. This further implies that the universe of beings is not only intelligibly ordered on any level of being and on successive levels, but this universal, emerging order is a directed ordering. What is the direction or the end of this universe of emerging things as they operate and cooperate in their respective schemes? This question about the directed and dynamic world-order is not primarily a question that focuses on the known schemes of practical living that have been recurring, nor is it about the religious purpose of this universe. We have defined being as that which becomes known through true judgments. The question of a direction in the present, concrete universe is a cognitional and metaphysical question. Moral and religious questions on the finality of the universe will be considered in later chapters.

We have already seen that potency is directed to form, form to act, and repetitive cycles of potency, form, and act lead to cumulative aggregates of acts that can form a potency for possible higher beings existing and operating in their schemes. Thus, besides the direction of single beings preserving their own unity and identity, there is the traditional horizontal tendency of groups of beings seeking to explore the range of possible variation within a species by dividing and branching out into a series of subspecies. In addition, there is also the vertical direction of a hierarchical series of higher genera of beings. The traditional 'chain of being' proposed a hierarchical world-order of higher and more perfect beings, but did not explain how lower aggregates of atoms and molecules could enter into, and participate in, the higher cellular schemes; nor did it explain how lower cellular schemes could participate in the higher psychic schemes of animals. In other words, the directed dynamism of the universe of being is moving both horizontally in the direction of new species and, at the same time, hierarchically in the direction of higher and more complex genera.

It is in this emergence of higher genera from lower genera, or in the way that horizontal finality serves to support and advance the emergent trend of successive higher genera, that the more significant direction in the universe is being achieved, since the lower orders are subordinate to and serve to advance the higher, more complex, and more differentiated schemes. Such vertical finality, however, while directed to a series of successive higher genera, is not a 'determined finality' because to be determined is to be limited to certain individuals, species, or genus. What is characteristic of vertical finality is an exploration of the full range of different ways of being and behaving. While some possible lines of exploration and courses of action will prove to be shortsighted and end in extinctions, others will prove fertile and flexible and lead to more resilient and resourceful results. Thus, while the finality of this universe is dynamic and directed, while it includes successes and failures, while it is flexible and resourceful, the end is undetermined because potency, form, and act are defined heuristically and unrestrictedly. The potency that grounds this dynamic unfolding of the universe is as open and unrestricted as the notion of being itself.

Just as the notion of being underlies, penetrates, and directs all questions toward an unrestricted objective, so the universe of being is unconsciously and consciously directed to the same objective. Again we see the importance of defining potency, form, and act in terms of an unrestricted desire to know the intrinsic, explanatory ordering of the whole universe of things as directed horizontally and vertically. Metaphysicians know the way the unrestricted desire to know underlies, penetrates, and motivates any and all knowers to know all being in a full, completely explanatory way, and it is the same directed dynamism that operates objectively and analogously in every being and at every level of being. This finality of the universe, therefore, is the objective counterpart to the notion of being. Just as consciously structured knowers seek to actualize their potential beings, so unconsciously structured beings seek to realize their respective potencies.

The 'form' that explains, orders, and directs this objective finality is 'emergent probability,' and it is that 'form' that needs to be further explored, since this metaphysical term embraces all the different types of intelligibilities, central and conjugate, as well as classical, statistical, genetic, and dialectic. Metaphysics has been defined as providing an integral heuristic structure for ordering the entire universe of being, but so far we have only discussed our metaphysical world-order in terms of a conditioned series of things existing and operating in recurring schemes in a dynamic, directed way. We have not asked whether that 'directed dynamism' of the universe is moving in a genetic or developing direction. There is a difference between a dynamic world-order and a dynamic developing world-order.

6   Genetic Method

Genetic method, as I noted in chapter 4, attempts to establish normative procedures for studying the problem of development. Such developments take place in singular beings, in populations of beings, and in the whole order of the universe. The basic difficulty in understanding such developments, whether singular, special, or general, is the same problem that has characterized our entire study, namely, the problem of moving from a descriptive understanding of development to an explanatory understanding, to shift from understanding 'what' development is to understanding 'why' it is what it is.

In a descriptive understanding, people tend to think of development as a pattern of changes that produce growth, such as observed in the growth of plants, animals, and people. Development is understood as a pattern of observable changes; there is no attempt to understand why those things change and grow as they do. An initial stage of a thing is observed, then a final stage; the final stage is compared to the former, and the judgment is made that a process of growth has occurred through some sequence of changes in the observable attributes of the things. To move from this extrinsic, descriptive notion of development to a more intrinsic, explanatory notion, we need to recall the way we summed up the three stages in the history of mathematics.

In the first stage, ancient mathematicians focused on numerical and geometrical objects and various ways of correlating them. In the second stage, Renaissance scientists transformed these mathematical objects into variables, which enabled them to shift attention to the unchanging correlations that co-ordered two sets of continuously varying terms into different types of series. In the third stage, scientists shifted their study from the unchanging correlations to the operations that generated and systematically correlated various series or sequences of changing variables. It was in this third stage that scientists discovered that any system of operations can raise questions that cannot be answered within the range of that system. Such questions tend to destabilize the balance of the system, thereby setting the conditions for the emergence of a higher, more complex system which will be able to answer the new questions by transcending the limits of the lower system. It was at this point in the history of mathematics that the problem of the infinite re-emerged, which opened up the possibility for establishing a conditioned sequence of systems of higher, more complex, and more expansive horizons.

These three stages in the history of mathematics illustrate how difficult it is to move from the descriptive to a strictly explanatory stage in knowing. In some sense, Euclid was a systematic thinker in working out the ordering of his twelve books of geometry, but he was not a strict systematic thinker because he was never able to break cleanly from extrinsic, descriptive correlations. The closest he came to this stage of thinking was in books five and eight where he set out a theory of proportion for ordering geometrical and numerical ratios. Later, Descartes broke away from such imaginable (descriptive) ratios when he discovered that geometrical problems could be solved by using the same set of operations (adding, subtracting, multiplying, dividing, and extracting roots) that were employed in correlating numerical objects or terms. However, while Descartes shifted attention from the continuous variables to the functions that correlated these changing variables, he did not succeed in specifying a system of operations as a group of reversible operations with a limited range of functions that could be transcended by the emergence of a higher system with a broader range of powers. This stage of thinking did not evolve until the nineteenth century. Where Euclid's axioms defined the terms he employed, nine-teenth-century mathematicians began to use different sets of axioms or laws to define the range of different systems of operations. It was this step that gave a clear, differentiated answer to the question of what numerical or geometrical ratios are. Numbers are what they are because of the opera-tions that generate them. The operations provide the 'why' of what num-bers are. This brief sketch of the three stages of mathematical history not only illustrates the long and difficult apprenticeship that scientists had to go through in moving from extrinsic, descriptive frameworks to intrinsic, explanatory frameworks, but also serves to illustrate the three metaphysi-cal methods of knowing we have been discussing: classical, statistical, and genetic.

The Renaissance discovery of functions as unchanging correlations that co-order changing variables in normative patterns exemplifies the classical method of explanatory knowing. Nineteenth-century scientists discovered that by sampling the actual, concrete variations, they could establish nor-mative, ideal frequencies which are unchanging for most cases, although every once in a while there will be nonsystematic variations from these ideal, normative frequencies. Such statistical norms reveal that, while the classic laws or correlations provide abstract norms, they can be combined with statistical frequencies to give the notion of recurrent cycles. The ini-tial emergence of such cycles has some probability, but once the cycle emerges, its probability of survival changes significantly. Such recurring schemes combine both classical and statistical methods of knowing. The history of mathematics is, however, especially remarkable in the way it exemplifies genetic method and the two different meanings of develop-ment that genetic knowers anticipate discovering. First, there is the hori-zontal development that takes place as the system expands by exploring its operating range; second, there is the vertical development that emerges when a new system moves beyond the boundaries of a lower system and opens up a further horizon of possibilities within which a new system is gradually differentiated and a new set of basic terms, relations, and opera-tions begins to be identified and defined. The second system builds on the first, but it also transcends the prior system with the discovery of possibili-ties or variations within the prior system that were left unexplored on the lower level. Thus, the analytic geometer sets up new terms, relations, and operations as he or she begins to explore numerical and geometrical possibilities that were unattended to in algebra and geometry. This vertical development can be repeated again and again as calculus emerges from analytic geometry and number theory from calculus; the result is a conditioned series of higher systems, each of which exhibits an operating range that is more extensive, versatile, differentiated, and complex than the previous lower system.

A systematic operator explores the possibilities of a system by developing the potential of that system. Potency, as we have noted, is a dynamic term since in its relation to form it sets up a tension toward a new form. Or, to state the reverse, form emerges from potency by resolving the tensions of its respective potency. However, the emergence of such forms reveals new possibilities within the prior potency, thereby setting the conditions for further emergence of forms. Thus, development can be defined as the emergence of a sequence of higher forms (higher intelligibilities) that resolve the tensions of lower potencies by moving upward to higher forms, while at the same time adjusting to the prior lower stages of achievement. This definition can be further refined and clarified if we apply it first to plant and animal life and then to the universe as a whole.

The example of development we have been using has focused on the conscious operations of a mathematical knower, but this case corresponds to, and parallels, the cases of unconscious developments as they occur and recur in plant life. The problem in establishing such a parallel is the difficulty of moving from descriptive to explanatory frameworks. There are three steps that must be taken in order to shift from the study of plants and animals as they are understood in relation to ourselves and the same plants and animals as they operate in relation to other things. The first step is the careful examination and description of their external and internal appearance, the anatomical stage. The next step is to identify the functions of the different anatomical parts of the plants and animals and how such parts may be related to one another. This takes us from the anatomical study of plants to their physiological study, namely, how the particular organs may be functionally related to one another. This sets up the third step as the study of cellular physiology leads to biochemical and biophysical studies. In these three steps – from anatomy through physiology to biomolecular studies – we move from describing plants to explaining why plants are what they are and why they do what they do.[6]

It is the shift from anatomy to physiology that forms the key step because not only do we move from the static study of the plant's structure to the dynamic performance of the organism operating in and through their different organs, but those functioning parts also co-order the organism's inner physiological activities to their outer environment from which plant organisms draw nourishment, reproduce, defend, and preserve their existence. Just as the analytic geometer understands numbers and points as dynamic variables which the higher operations transform into new numerical or geometrical correlations, so plants continuously transform lower, inorganic variables into the higher, organic correlations of cellular life. In this horizon, the outer surface of a plant becomes a functioning organ that controls the interrelations between inner and outer organic and inorganic processes. At this stage the extrinsic, common-sense, descriptive way of knowing the reality of plants begins to reveal itself as a very limited way of knowing the intrinsic reality of plants, and of knowing why plants actually exist in the various ways that they do.

This third step into biochemistry and biophysics of plant physiology suggests a parallel in the history of mathematics. Within and beyond the limited horizon of analytical geometry, calculus emerged to reveal new powers of the operations of adding, subtracting, multiplying, and dividing in forming different forms of series of sums, products, powers, quotients, and roots. These developments led to the emergence of the still higher forms of number theory and a further re-examination of the basic numerical variables with which mathematics began. So biomolecular and biophysical studies of plants bring the biophysical studies of plants back to a study of the basic constituents of the entire physical universe. Just as number theory uses the basic variables of mathematics in new forms, the study of bioelectrical processes within organisms can disclose how the lower potencies – chemical and electrical processes – are able to serve higher biological functions. This may seem as if biologists as biochemists and biophysicists are reducing plant life to atomic processes, but just the opposite orientation is at work. Biochemists are revealing how plants or organisms can reorganize chemical processes into higher emergent forms of life. Biochemistry and biophysics are not 'abstract' studies, but comprehensive studies that reveal how plants are actually integrating lower levels of chemical and subatomic activities into the higher functions of organic life. However, plants not only integrate lower molecular and subatomic processes, but also operate to take advantage of their environment to secure more and more surprising solutions to the problem of organic living within such environments. Organic beings not only live within an inorganic environment, but may actually surpass their environment in remarkably unexpected ways.

This notion of organic beings moving beyond their physical surroundings needs to be stressed since it tends to be overlooked or underestimated in the Darwinian tradition, which tended to treat adaptation only as an accommodation of organisms to their environment and not in terms of discovering variations that permit organisms to produce novelties. Richard Lewontin has pointed out that it is a misunderstanding of adaptation to think of it as implying a 'preexisting world that poses a problem to which an adaptation is the solution.'[7] Thus, Darwin himself was preoccupied with geological and climactic changes as they were occurring and recurring along the coastlines of South America and with the various ways that organisms responded to those physical and chemical challenges by evolving different ways of 'making a living.' For Darwin these various species of plant life had adapted their organic schemes of nutrition, reproduction, and preservation to fit into the surrounding lower chemical manifold. But this is only one aspect of adaptation. Besides the integration within the lower schemes, there is the emergence of the higher schemes. What Lewontin proposes is that organisms not only adapt to a changing environment, but in different ways constitute their own environment. In a sense, one may say that living organisms do not find their niches within an ecological system, but to some extent they make their own ecological roles insofar as they attempt to control their outer environment. For example, plants can change the gaseous atmosphere in which they live, and they can also change the chemical condition of the soil in which they grow as they shed their blossoms, leaves, saps, resins, twigs, fruits. In other words, there is upward, 'creative' movement to adaptation as well as the lower, integrating aspect.

This is even more evident if we move up to psychic adaptation on the animal level. In analyzing plant evolution, we moved from descriptive analysis to explanatory perspectives through the three-step process of anatomy, physiology, and biochemistry. At the animal level, we can extend this analysis to a four-step process of morphology, physiology, biochemistry and biophysics, and psychology. Plants are biochemical operators that systematically integrate lower levels to seek changing organic solutions to problems of living, while animals are psychosomatic operators that integrate higher psychic conjugates with lower organic, chemical, and physical conjugates. In animals, the higher system becomes a conscious operator, while the lower system remains unconscious. The unconscious pursuit of organic functions of feeding, mating, and preserving life among plants becomes consciously pursued by animals. If plants are able to some extent to control their outer environment and maintain their interior living, much more dramatically and effectively are animals able to do so as they achieve an essentially higher degree of freedom from their lower, limiting conditions. As the analytic geometer discovers new potential in the lower mathematical variables, so animals operate unconsciously to construct cells that make possible their conscious acts of living.

In commenting on the difficulties of his theory, Darwin confessed that explaining the evolution of the eye and its remarkable properties by natural selection must seem absurd to his audience.[8] No doubt Darwin was right. But such dramatic developments or adaptation can be viewed two ways: bottom-up or top-down. One can be astonished that animals have converted and transformed electromagnetic processes into neural cells for transmitting light stimuli through optic nerves to the brain, but one can be even more surprised that reptiles and birds pursue their practice of life through a conscious, systemic interaction with their environments.

To really appreciate why animals do what they do we have to take up the science of psychology and ethology.[9] Various species of animals differ morphologically and physiologically, but even more essentially and remarkably they differ psychically in the mode and manner of their conscious, aggressive, and affective behaviors. It is only recently that scientists have moved to study animals as psychic operators. The problem in appreciating animals as operators is the problem of understanding what a thing is. In chapter 4, we identified a thing as a unity-identity-whole that exists in and through its schemes of recurrence. A plant is a biochemical operator which functions in a set of mutually related, organic, chemical, and physical schemes of recurring activities. Animal operators, on the other hand, are concrete, consciously existing wholes which function simultaneously on four different levels. It is because animal operators have united their different parts into differently functioning wholes that paleontologists are able to infer the whole animal form by examining a single fossil part. These anatomical parts form an interlocking and interacting whole, and they are able to operate at higher levels by continuously integrating their higher level functions with lower levels.[10] Further, paleontologists are able to discover different interlocking wholes at different developing stages of an animal or in a sequence of different species.

The specific differences of animals, however, are in their conscious, psychic wholes, not in their anatomical or organic wholes. The distinguishing aspects of animals can be found in their various nerve endings and in their brain's capacity to receive and respond to various internal and external stimuli. The larger the brain capacity, and the more differentiated and effective the nerve endings, the more flexible is the range of responses that animals are capable of making to various external and internal stimuli. This is why we find in the higher animals, such as elephants and dolphins, the potential to acquire so many different skills and to learn how to develop different communicative schemes which permit them to form social schemes in order to cooperate in carrying out the various routines of practical living. Just how complex and how many levels of cooperations are involved in animal living can be further clarified if we consider the problem of development not as it pertains to single beings or to certain species, but as comprehending an entire ecological system. Such a complex, interacting system will provide a bridge to the question of the evolution and development of the whole universe of being.

In recent years, especially in the context of various ecological movements, most of us has encountered the notion of an ecological system as
embracing a vastly complicated web of interacting communities of animals
and plants operating in expanding and contracting territorial regions.
Darwin's problem was the evolution of species; more recently the problem
has become the evolution of a web of interacting species. Instead of a
developing being or specified group of evolving beings, there is the more
complex, dynamic whole of the grouping of many different species as they
set the conditions for one another's recurrent schemes.[11] Such mutually
conditioning schemes support, stabilize, and sustain a variety of different
species, functioning at different levels of being within the context of a
much broader world-ordering of all beings. In other words, an ecological
system is an example of the more general world-order that governs the
dynamic unfolding of the whole universe of beings.

Here I shall shift from considering development in plants, animals, and
the emerging universe of being to focusing on human development and
how human schemes of operating and cooperating may be integrated into
the emerging universe of being. In one sense, we have already considered
human development in many references in our look at the history of mathematics and science. Such examples may be misleading, however, since
they tend to focus on intellectual development while excluding lower psychic and organic development. Animal development involves both the
unconscious organic unfolding and the conscious psychic development,
and at the human level, going one step further, there is the three-fold
development of organic, psychic, and intellectual processes and their
respective functioning.[12]

Before proceeding further in looking at the three-fold development of
human beings, we need to examine the split in our ways of thinking about
conscious and unconscious development. On the one hand, there is the
tendency to consider conscious activities as unconscious and to reduce
them to lower-level conjugate forms; the other tendency is to consider conscious activities without any reference to the lower levels which set the conditions for the emergence and maintenance of these higher conscious
schemes. Behind these two tendencies is the foundational problem of integrating the higher human sciences with the lower natural sciences.

In discussing the vertical finality of the universe in the previous section, I
proposed that just as knowers are spontaneously and consciously oriented
to being, so all unconscious beings are oriented to being horizontally and
vertically. In other words, the human cognitional search for the meaning
of being is one instance of the whole universe's directed, dynamic finality
to being. The unconscious seeking of being on the different lower levels
becomes, on the human level, the conscious search to know being in a fully

explanatory way. The different disciplines of knowing seek to explain different regions within the universe of being, while metaphysics is the science that underlies, transforms, and unifies all these other disciplines in their search to fully explain the universe of being.

Besides the directed dynamism of finality, there is the directed development of the universe. Vertical finality refers to the continuously changing universe of beings as oriented upward to an indeterminate and open-ended goal. The notion of a developing universe is more complicated since development involves both the upward advance and the downward accommodations that have to be made to rearrange past achievements in terms of present advances. Vertical finality characterizes every level of being, whereas development begins at the biological level in the vast web of specialized kinds of organic beings. Lower physical and chemical unities emerge and operate in recurrent schemes in accord with probabilities. While there is a rich variety of dynamic changes to be observed and explained in these lower schemes, such as planetary schemes and weather patterns, the myriad molecular processes that make up weather cycles (as they pass from liquid to solid to gaseous states) do not develop from an early embryonic stage to a later adult stage. In brief, there is an essential difference between classical and statistical changes, on the one hand, and genetic changes, on the other hand, or between classical and statistical forms and their respective potencies and genetic forms and their potencies.

The difference is that genetic changes bring into existence new forms which successfully rearrange the potencies of the older forms. We have seen that organisms can do this unconsciously because they are biochemical and biophysical operators that are able to assimilate solar energy and employ it in synthesizing carbohydrates out of ingested carbon dioxide and water. Through various schemes of photosynthesis, organisms are able to establish their own inner vital processes which are, in varying degrees, more or less dependent on the external environment in which they exist, operate, and cooperate. These organic schemes of photosynthesis that cycle beyond and within the organism do not simply keep repeating themselves like the planetary cycles; rather, they develop from the early stage of immature organisms into the later stages of mature organic beings. This growth process means that the original cells keep subdividing and replacing themselves with more differentiated and more specialized cells, as the organism evolves different organs to perform different, functionally related activities. At any given stage of growth, the organism will be modifying its prior integration until it is replaced with a later, more differentiated and mature integration. For example, in the early stages of a growing plant, the central form of this organic being existing in and through its biochemical and biophysical schemes continuously operates on its present integration, developing that integration into a more complicated organic stage, which also includes the older, transformed integration. As an operator, the organism transforms its own integration into a more mature organism without losing its former identity, while at the same time significantly altering this former identity. We may explain a growing plant or tree as a continuously developing unity that is effected by a sequence of organic operators that rhythmically transforms any immature integration by operating on that integration, thereby setting up a tension within the biochemical process of its own cellular activities, which in turn make possible and probable the directed advance to a new, more mature stage of its subsisting unity. The growing plant keeps replacing its own developments with more differentiated and complex integrations until it reaches its mature state, when it stops growing and then attempts to sustain and preserve itself as a dynamic equilibrium system of higher and lower interacting schemes of recurring organic operations.

At the human level, the same law of integrator-operator functions, but it does so in three different contexts: organic, psychic, and intellectual, at one and the same time. There are not three operators, but one subsisting, central form that operates on three different levels. This means that there can be three different and related developments going on at the same time. For example, the growing child is undergoing significant organic development while also undergoing significant changes on the psychic levels as the assimilation of images, feelings, and memories set up psychic tensions that invite changes into new modes of affective living. The same child is learning how to think and speak in new ways. The problem that the child faces is how to coordinate these different developing levels into a single coherent unfolding. As an organic operator, the child has to be in tune with himself or herself as psychic and intellectual operator. Again, there is only one operator, one central form, uniting the three different levels that make up a human being.

Development in human beings may be initiated on any level, but on whatever level it originates, the other levels will also be affected, and so there must be a harmonious cooperation at all levels. For example, glandular changes in the unconscious sexual organs do not remain on the organic level, but rise through the nervous system to set up new flows of psychic feeling which, in turn, condition sensible and imaginative changes that may seem strange and disturbing to the person experiencing them. As we saw in chapter 4, the higher-level knower can prevent insights from emerging by controlling the images through which insights emerge, thus the higher-level cognitive operator can exercise control over the way psychic experiences are assimilated and accommodated into higher-level intellectual schemes. This also implies that lower psychic schemes are potentially variable and may be patterned in a range of alternative schemes, any one of which may meet the lower demand successfully. In other words, while there are lower, neural demands emerging on the psychic level, effecting various sensitive flows, these streams of sensations are open to a range of alternative modes of assimilations and integrations. Human development, then, is a very flexible affair involving three different levels which must be integrated, but at the same time there is a wide range of ways in which the higher intellectual operator may cooperate with lower psychic and organic processes. Just how variable the lower psychosomatic schemes are can be shown in the way that human knowers develop the different patterns of lower-level experiencing which we have already discussed, namely, practical, theoretical, and symbolical.

The basic difference between human and animal development is that animals have to integrate and operate on organic and psychic levels, while human development requires a three-level development. Animals operate in a psychosomatic world of inner and outer experiences in which they seek to satisfy the lower organic needs; human beings live in sensible and intellectual spheres in which the higher intellectual operators pattern the lower, inner and outer psychosomatic world in a variety of ways to meet a variety of purposes. While biological purposes of eating, mating, and preserving life tend to dominate animal operators, the human intentional operator may bring multiple interests and intentions in organizing and directing these lower psychosomatic experiences. Animals cannot significantly reorganize their psychosomatic experiences without acquiring new organs – eyes, ears, noses, muscles, nervous systems, etc. – through which they would then be able to receive different sensible stimuli and coordinate them into different responses. But even with specifically different psychosomatic experiences, animals cannot escape the purposiveness of biological living with its routines of foraging, mating, and self-defending. Despite the myriad species of psychosomatic beings ranging from lower to higher animals, none of these higher species seems to be able to move beyond the limits of biological purposiveness.

The transcending move from biological routines emerges in human development as the spontaneous exuberance and playfulness of children orient them to construct their numerous make-believe dramas of practical living in which biological needs are subordinated as new ranges of symbolic patterns of feelings, sensings, rememberings, and imagining emerge and eventually lead to the formation of the inner world of daydreams and fantasies. These symbolic make-believe dramas of practical living gradually yield to the central drama of human living as growing children begin to participate in the myriad common-sense schemes of their cultural community. This does not mean, an end to the symbolic drama; rather, it is the beginning of the human subject's ability to shift from one pattern of experience into another. How such symbolic and practical patterns mediate and transform their lower psychic and organic levels will be explored more fully in the next chapter, but here I wish to emphasize that such human developments in symbolic and practical patterns of experience liberate human communities from the animal-like schemes of feeding, reproducing, and defending, and allow them to invest these lower schemes with higher intentional meanings that both provide the community with a living and, at the same time, make that living meaningful and symbolically valuable to its members.

The emergence and development of these higher schemes of human living are to some extent still dominated by interested and practically purposeful desires. It was the emergence of the disinterested desire to know in Greek culture that liberated the intellectual operator to pattern lower psychosomatic variables in new schemes of lower psychic integrations that operated in correspondence with, yet were subordinate to, the higher schemes of theoretical knowing. A telling example of the different way that intellectual operators pattern their lower psychosomatic variables can be seen in the contrasting functions that psychic images play in patterning lower experiences according to different spheres of interest. As we have seen, patterns of experience unite internal and external sensory activities into consciously recurring flows that are organized and integrated according to the interest and purpose of the intellectual operator. In other words, internal and external sensing, remembering, and imagining are all interdependent activities in the continual flow of human consciousness, but the character and organization of that conscious stream depend on the interest and purpose of the higher operator who controls and governs the direction of these conscious flows with various degrees of expertise and mastery.

Auguste Rodin's famous sculpture, *The Thinker*, completely absorbed in personal reflection, is the outward embodiment of an interior knower absorbed in his own wondering as he evaluates his intentional world of meaning. In a similar way, professional scholars who have achieved a certain level of control and mastery over their lower psychic activities are able to summon appropriate and useful memories along with evocative images from their lower psychic stream, thereby setting the conditions for higher intellectual schemes.[13] Sculpting a statue like *The Thinker*, however, would require a quite different interplay of images, feelings, and memories than those needed by a scientist forming theoretical patterns. The history of mathematical science could be summed up as a liberation from imaginative thinking, or as a series of successful breakthroughs from imaginable worlds into strictly non-imaginable but highly intelligible worlds which are

176 Quest for Self-Knowledge

able to mediate in comprehensive and systematic ways vast amounts of sensible data. It was from such advances in liberating thinkers from images and replacing them with heuristic symbols that resulted in the art of implicit definitions and the discovery of a series of higher viewpoints. These nineteenth-century achievements in higher mathematics have been central in developing the present approach to metaphysics as an integral heuristic structure for explaining the universe of being.

More precisely, it was the ability to distinguish between the tripartite structure of knowing and the analogous structure of the known that permitted us to shift attention to the different desires and interests that organize and direct the cognitional activities of the knower. It was especially in the contrast between interested, practical knowing and the disinterested, theoretical knowing that we were able to clarify the character of the unrestricted desire to know and its corresponding unrestricted objective of being. This means that being orders all knowers to one another by an orienting desire that operates in each and every knower during each and every period of human history. Furthermore, the same notion of being underlies and penetrates each and every being as they seek, besides their own singular existence, a shared existence with every other specifically and generically related being through a horizontal and vertical finality. Finally, this directed, vertical finality is not only dynamic; it is a developing dynamism that begins on the biological level and rises through the psychic to intellectual levels. This implies that the vertical finality of the universe is a developing finality, or that this universe is incomplete and is still being formed. The destiny of the universe, therefore, is indeterminate, and it is indeterminate because the vertical finality of the universe, which becomes a conscious and developing finality in human consciousness, is grounded in the unrestricted desire to know with its unrestricted objective, being. It is this unrestricted objective, consciously orienting every human knower, that makes the goal of human history unrestricted, open-ended, and still to be determined.

What can be determined is how we will come to know that final objective, namely, through a completely correct set of judgments. It was on that basis that we have set up a metaphysical, heuristic structure through which we can anticipate a complete explanation of the universe of being. This structure has been solidly grounded in the concrete, factual judgment, I am a knower. This further implies that you, as a knower, will always be in a state of dynamic tension between what you already know correctly and what you could know in the light of your own unrestricted desire to know. This conscious dynamic state sets up within any individual knower a basic tension between the felt, lower, sensory-motor self, located in a particular sensible place and time, and the same self as an intellectual operator oriented to the full sweep of the universe of being through acts of understanding and judging. Any concrete, individual knower, then, is caught between a felt, sensory-motor self, centered within a surrounding experienced world, and a reasoning self who dwells in an ordered universe of being in which the decentered and detached reasoning self is but one tiny self in a vast universe of knowers in whom and through whom the whole universe of being comes to be known in some restricted fashion.

7   The Authentic, Objective Known

This basic contrast between the self-interested, sensing self and the disinterested, decentered self means that every single knower exists in a fundamental paradox. There is the self that you presently are and there is the possible self that you can become by replacing your present, actual self with a more integrated and highly developed self. But you already have developed an integrated self which is presently operating within a circle of recurring schemes that are combinations of habits or conjugate forms, and such habits are inertial systems for sustaining and preserving a range of alternative courses of action and interaction; whereas to develop is to change your habits and to change the self that formed these habits and who was, in turn, formed by the habits. To develop, then, implies that you are questioning your own acquired integration of lower and higher schemes as that integration presently operates within you. To develop, then, you as operator must question and destabilize yourself as integrator. There is no way you can prevent this cycle from repeating the same process again because you, the operator, are oriented through your own unrestricted desire to continually destabilize your integrated self as you keep ascending toward a higher, more developed, and better integrated self.[14] We have already pointed out that vertical finality as it dynamically orients the successive unfolding of different levels in the universe of being becomes conscious at the human level as each knower is caught up in this vast sweep of universal striving toward being. On the successive hierarchical levels, specifically different beings seek their own horizontal finality; at the same time, they also enter into, and become intrinsic participants in, the vertical finality of the universe which includes the whole of human history.

   In this scheme of vertical finality, metaphysical knowers may, through the explanatory schemes of physics, chemistry, and biology, retrace any prior integrated stage of the entire universe back to its original potencies, forms, and acts and, at the same time, unite these lower levels of the universe through the developing human sciences insofar as these sciences are moving toward a more explanatory stage. The basic tension between your transcending, operating self and your limited, integrated self is analogous to the vertical finality of the entire universe as that finality is being mediated and generalized through the integral, heuristic structure of your own or any other knower's potency, form, and act.

These reflections also provide us with a new context for considering the notion of objectivity. The foundation for this whole study has been to accurately define and affirm the concrete, factual judgment, I am a knower. At the same time, we have affirmed that each and every knower is oriented to the unrestricted objective, which is being. There is, therefore, the limited objectivity that exists between present known objects and your correct knowing of those objects, and there is the final unrestricted objective as well as your present openness to that final, remote object. To respond critically to the call of further knowing means you must know the four ways in which knowers distort and disorient their unrestricted desire to know. I will return to the dialectical critique of this desire to know, but in the present context I want to emphasize the metaphysical meaning of an authentic or genuine knower who operates between the restricted objectivity or authenticity of a limited knower and the potentially unlimited objectivity and authenticity of a fully realized knower.

To be an authentic, objective knower in the metaphysical context we have been discussing does not mean that you have and are making correct objective judgment in some limited context of knowing; rather, it means that you are in the paradoxical state between the limited authenticity or objectivity of a restricted context and the ever expanding and transcending context in which you keep questioning your present limited authenticity in terms of, and by the standard of, a remote, developing authenticity. This is what we mean by saying that objective knowing is the result of authentic subjectivity. As an authentic knower, I realize that there is a perpetual conflict between the knower I am and the knower I can be. Conflict, however, does not mean contradiction; it means a conscious tension between the concrete limited being I am and my conscious potential to develop beyond my present limits.

8   Metaphysics of History

We have proposed that methodical metaphysics can be seen as an integrating, anticipatory structure through which the whole universe of being can be completely known in an explanatory way. We have just discussed how that anticipated explanation includes you the knower playing a role within the gradual emergence and unfolding of the dynamic directed universe of beings as these beings seek their own perfection. That perfection includes participating in the perfection of other beings horizontally and on successive vertical levels in increasingly more controlled ways until the perfection of such controls reaches the level of human knowers, who not only share in the being of any and all beings but also learn how to control their own participation in the vertical finality of the universe as it heads toward its final objective, which is being.

However, human participation in vertical finality is a developing participation, and the development is in and through accumulating insights and critical reflection as orienting and responding to the disinterested desire to know being. Besides such accumulating insights that result in a developing participation in horizontal and vertical finality, there is the opposite accumulation of schemes that will block insight, distort the desire to know, and lead to recurring schemes that set the conditions for a succession of more restricted viewpoints with decreasing ranges of possibilities for alternative courses of actions. In chapter 3, we opened up a preliminary discussion of human historical progress through accumulating insights, as well as the dialectically opposed movement of decline based on the four different ways that human knowers may block insights and thereby set up recurrent cycles of distorting biases in personal, communal, and historical living. We also introduced the fundamental dialectic between our interested and disinterested desires to know, or the foundational difference between short-term and long-term cycles of meanings within cultural communities. More specifically, we discussed how interested cycles of practical living, since they are oriented by the pressures of more or less daily recurring needs as consciously experienced by a community, set up a basic tension and, most often, an open conflict with long-term concerns that respond to our disinterested desire to know. The example we presented was the play *Antigone* which dramatized the conflict between the social traditions of family and religion embodied in the character Antigone, as opposed to the public political traditions as embodied in the character Creon. The problem we raised was that the concrete, conscious tensions between the norms of these two traditions involved a more basic question of the historical context from which both traditions emerged. The problem we proposed was the various ways that long-term historical traditions precondition the short-term traditions operating within any cultural community. The challenge for any cultural community, therefore, is to understand and correctly judge the various ways in which past historical traditions precondition the alternative possible courses of operating and cooperating going forward, first, in any person; second, among the members of various groups; and, third, between different groups within the same community. In short, what is needed is a new, higher viewpoint that is transcultural or transhistorical and would therefore be able to provide methodical norms for critically interpreting and objectively judging the historical context within which a community is developing and/or declining. That was the problem we posed in chapter 3; the question now is whether the metaphysics we have been formulating can resolve this problem.

We have proposed a methodical metaphysics for integrating all the various specialized departments of knowing in order to move toward a complete explanation of the entire universe of being. This method of metaphysical integration is based on knowing ourselves and all other knowers as oriented by their disinterested desire to know being. We have just expanded this conscious orientation of knowers to being through the notion of vertical finality or the directed dynamism that underlies, penetrates, and goes beyond each and every being, uniting them through the horizontal finality of specialized beings and through the vertical finality of the successive hierarchical levels of being. This unconscious, directed dynamism operating on the lower levels becomes a consciously directed finality in human knowers. Furthermore, in plants, animals, and people, this vertical finality is not only directed to an indeterminate objective, but becomes a developing direction and, on the human level, may become a critically conscious finality as it constitutes and effects the basic tension between the knowers we are and the knowers we can become. Human knowers cannot escape this basic tension between their present knowing selves and their potential future selves since it is intrinsic and immanently operative in every human knower in whatever period of history and in whatever cultural community the person emerges and lives.

Every human knower emerges within a cultural community at some stage in human history and is thereby destined to play a role within that cultural world and, at the same time, to play a role in the unfolding of the total historical drama. Ultimately, the roles that people play are in tune with the vertical finality of the universe of being or, in different ways, they move against that finality. Just how human knowers play such a historical role in addition to their cultural roles needs to be clarified. In other words, we have now transferred the problem of a critical history raised in chapter 3 into a critical metaphysics of history within the context of the vertical finality of being. This finality of human history is a continuation and conscious development of vertical finality. Our earlier account of the order of emergent probability becomes, or may become, the consciously directed, emergent probability of human history insofar as knowers are able to understand and critically judge this emerging order of history. To accomplish this requires a collaborative alliance among historians, social scientists, and metaphysicians.

Metaphysicians know that human beings are intrinsically historical beings, but they also know that there is an important distinction between metaphysical knowing and historical knowing. The task for metaphysical knowers is to know what historical knowers are doing when they are doing historical knowing. Just as earlier chapters focused on what we are doing when we are knowing, in the light of those prior, more basic, and general considerations, we can now briefly sketch what we are doing when we are doing historical knowing. The point is not to do historical knowing, that is the business of the historian; rather, the point is to know what historical knowing is and, in the light of that knowing, to integrate historical knowing with social scientific knowing and natural scientific knowing and their corresponding knowns. The purpose of this integration is to specify the roles of cultural communities in the unfolding of the total historical drama.

In the light of the metaphysical context we have constructed, we may ask what metaphysicians do know about historical knowing. There are six major issues to be noted in answering that question.

(1) Metaphysicians know that all human beings are knowers and that they are ultimately ordered to know being as their final objective.

(2) All human beings are polymorphic knowers who operate at first in an undifferentiated horizon that only gradually becomes differentiated into three major patterns of knowing – practical, symbolic, and theoretical.

(3) Like plants and animals, all human knowers develop, but unlike plants which develop biologically and animals which develop biologically and psychically, human knowers also develop intellectually, and they do so by accumulating insights and critically testing the accuracy of those insights.

(4) All human knowers are caught between their own interested desire to know how to live practically and successfully and their own disinterested desire to know which, because it orients knowers toward an unrestricted objective, continuously destabilizes whatever stage of knowledge knowers may already have achieved, thereby opening up the possibility of moving to a higher stage. This implies that knowers may operate in a critically correct fashion within their limited, interested cultural context and still be inauthentic with respect to the transcultural context of their own unrestricted desire to know.

(5) All human knowers, in addition to spontaneously seeking insights within the various patterns in which knowers seek to know, may also disorient themselves. They do this by deliberately repressing or predisposing lower, conscious psychic events so that these events will emerge at higher levels of consciousness in patterns that will successfully block emerging insights and thereby restrict the range of possible alternatives available for consideration and realization.

(6) Human knowers not only are oriented to know beings in their various orderings to one another, but are also oriented to know themselves

and their participation within the vertical finality of human history as it unfolds within the universe of being.

In addition to these six principles, which we have already discussed in varying degrees, there is the problem of the expressions of human knowing, which is a central issue that historians must deal with in coming to understand and correctly judge past human knowings and doings.

8a Expressions of Meaning vs Truth of Meaning

It may seem strange to the reader that we have paid so little attention to the various forms of linguistic and other modes of human expression. Our concern has been primarily with the operations of knowing because these ground and explain the various meanings of human expression. It is not language that explains knowing, but knowing that explains language.[15] It is true that any knower, even a remarkably original knower, will have to use an inherited language to express his or her knowings and will therefore be conditioned by those former linguistic meanings. This implies that knowing and expressions of knowing interact and, to some extent, mutually condition one another.

A telling example that illustrates the difference between knowing and expression can be found in the way that Socrates went around Athens asking various citizens what they meant when they used words like 'justice,' 'bravery,' 'courage,' 'wisdom.' The Athenians were puzzled and embarrassed by the fact that they could use these words correctly but were not able to define what they meant.[16] The example illustrates several important points. In the first place, Socrates was attempting to develop a completely new pattern of human knowing – theoretical knowing – and he was using the inherited Greek meanings of these words to discover something that no one had ever known or attempted to express. Socrates, as Aristotle noted, was the first person who attempted to form universal definitions. He was using inherited linguistic meanings as instruments for triggering insights into new meanings. His quest in seeking universally defined meanings was to set up a new context of meanings for dealing with questions about justice, bravery, moderation, holiness, and similar moral and religious modes of behavior. For ordinary Athenian citizens to understand what Socrates meant by these terms, they had to shift from their practical, ordinary ways of wondering and assimilate an entirely new and quite different context of meanings. What do we mean by a 'context'?

In chapter 5 we noted that judgments arise from the question, Is it so?, and they do so within a context of earlier judgments. A context implies a set of related judgments that provide answers to a set of related questions. Since judgments emerge in response to questions, it is imperative in grasping an author's meaning to know the orienting desire that directed the questions that he or she was asking. For example, we find in Socrates' questioning the contrast between the practical, restricted desire to know, which characterized the common-sense knowing of Athenian citizens in their ordinary, familiar language, and the newly emerging attempt to develop a disinterested desire to know that leads to a line of questioning conditioned by that desire and the potentially unrestricted objective to which that desire was directed. A major problem for Socrates was that the words, through which the new contexts of knowing and meaning were to be expressed, were the ordinary, familiar words that were expressive of a quite different context of meanings. This problem illustrates that meanings, while carried in words, depend primarily not on the words themselves, but on the prior acts of knowing that explain and ground the acts of meaning. Meaning is the same as knowing, except that meaning adds to knowing the problem of expressing our knowing to an audience through different linguistic forms. Expressions of any knower's knowing may be adequate or inadequate, clear or obscure, but such expressions by themselves are not true or false. The truth or falsity of statements lies in the acts of judgments made by knowers, who then express those judgments in any language that these knowers may choose and in any appropriate combination of the words and phrases of that language.

There is an important distinction between what any knower knows and the mode and manner of the expression selected by the person to communicate that knowing, 'to mean that knowing.' Furthermore, because there is a distinction between knowing and the linguistic means chosen by the speaker or writer to express the known, there can be significant development in the modes and manners of expressions, just as there are major developments in knowing itself. This is especially true when exceptional advances in knowing have taken place, such as we have seen in the history of mathematics and physics. For example, the remarkable discoveries by François Vièta in mathematical algebra were expressed in a symbolic mode which he himself helped to invent and which eventually replaced the ancient Greek ways of expressing mathematical meanings. Descartes, who claimed to have picked up in mathematical knowing where Vièta left off, also made significant contributions to further develop this new symbolic language of mathematics. Similar developments occurred with the discovery of calculus. Newton and Leibniz both invented a new symbolic shorthand to express their discoveries but, because Leibniz's modes of expression turned out to be more appropriate and suggestive, Newton's attempts to explain the same discoveries in quite different symbols were eventually discarded.

This history in the development of modes of expression reveals that, just as knowers develop by differentiating their knowing into more specialized patterns and modes of knowing, there is a similar differentiation in the history of modes of expression and communication. For example, in the history of Western culture there has been a gradual development and differentiation of practical, theoretical, and symbolic spheres of knowing and a parallel differentiation of their respective modes of expression and communication. In the light of both of these developments – the metaphysical context we have been formulating and the distinction between the activities of knowing and those same activities as they are communicated to a specific audience through some form of linguistic or symbolic modes of meaning – we can now restate the meaning of truth that we set forth in the previous chapter.

A statement is known as true or false through a 'virtually unconditioned' judgment of our understanding of an experience. It is through such correct judgments that we come to an understanding of what certainly or probably is or is not true. Such judgments are both private and personal, as well as public and impersonal. While they are made by a knower in a particular place and time, they can still be asserted by any other knower in quite different times and circumstances. The reason is that the notion of being permeates, underlies, and transcends every knower, every audience, and every known object. Truth, then, may be defined as the correspondence of any knower's knowing to being. Being is what we grasp through correct knowing, or knowing is true by being correctly related to being.

Thus there are two norms of truth: the limited, absolute norm that is grasped in a precisely limited context of meaning and the remote norm that is immanent and operative in every context which can serve to correlate those limited contexts to one another by relating them to being. Because this desire to know can be distorted in four different ways, it stands in need of a dialectical criticism that will differentiate these different biases and especially the long-term general bias of common sense which operates in every cultural community, insofar as that community distorts its relation to past communities. This is usually done by developing commonly shared memories which screen out a community's dependence on past cultural achievements by degrading and distorting the meanings, values, and general cultural achievements that they have inherited from these prior communities. Such distorted schemes may tend to restrict that community's choices of alternative practical schemes. In brief, not only may a person distort his or her own unrestricted desire to know and become inauthentic, but communities can also set up cooperating schemes that tend to disorient the members of the community, providing them with distorted norms and practices that will successfully restrict their own personal ways of wondering.

However, this same unrestricted desire for unlimited knowing of an unlimited truth that can be distorted is also the source of unlimited development. A disoriented knower may pursue the self-correcting process that grounds the reflective process preceding judgments until that correcting process effects a fundamental reversal in that knower's own orientation to being. In other words, as a knower you may correct the inherited biases that are operating in your own conscious wondering and thereby reorient yourself to the final objective of human, historical knowing.

In the light of this discussion of truth and expression, we can now briefly sketch how a metaphysics of history could be developed, or how metaphysics conceived as an integrating heuristic structure can coordinate the efforts of historians, social scientists, and natural scientists as they attempt to achieve an explanatory patterning of any and all beings in their horizontally and vertically directed dynamism toward a higher undetermined and open-ended finality.

8b Resumption of Metaphysics of History

Let me begin with a general summary of how this objective can be accomplished. Metaphysicians have derived from their own unrestricted wondering the fundamental objective to which every person and every historical community is ordered – being. The general way to achieve that goal is through expanding the schemes of knowing that bring under comprehensive control the means to move successfully toward human historical finality, while at the same time reversing the cycles of decline that are operating in the cultural community. The basic problem in achieving this goal has been the failure to differentiate and distinguish the quite different objectives pursued in the various patterns of knowing. The failure to make such distinctions means that the short-term objectives of practical knowing tend to set up recurring conditions that disorient a community and its members; instead of encouraging and advancing historical progress, these conditions mislead community members into cycles of disorder and decline. To solve this problem, metaphysicians have to collaborate with historians and the human scientists in interpreting past human knowings and doings as they attempt to critically differentiate their inherited schemes of progress from the opposite disorienting schemes of decline.

Because metaphysicians operate with a basic anticipatory or heuristic structure of knowing through which corresponding structured objectives come to be known, they realize that they will be dependent on the various sciences for filling in that structure. These scientists have their own set of heuristic assumptions which need to be filled out by their own appropriate methods of assimilating data, hypothesizing explanations, and testing those hypotheses. Furthermore, there are significant differences between the natural and human sciences. A natural scientist like Galileo discovered an invariant correlation between variable distances, times, and velocities, and he tested that correlation in a number of different experimental cases. Historians, on the other hand, may be dealing with singular events and singular persons, such as Caesar's crossing of the Rubicon or the fall of the Roman Empire. Common-sense patterns of knowing deal with concrete particular cases in their singularity. Similarly, historians in dealing with concrete particular cases of history are attempting to know the common-sense world of a people who lived in particular places and times, as that world has been communicated to historians through the various records, documents, monuments, and whatever other data there are for revealing traces of certain past cultural communities.

Once such data have been accumulated, the historians then proceed to interpret it. Such data may carry a world of meaning, but by themselves the data do not speak. The dialogues of Plato, for example, are simply observable black marks on white pages. The problem for a reader is to bring the printed signs into the world of meanings. Interpreting is not just being able to read a text, but also being able to read it intelligently and knowingly. To do so a reader may require a long and remarkable development in learning. In other words, to interpret a historical text like Plato's *Republic* requires that the interpreter has to change his or her own knowing being in order to approach the level of Plato's knowing being as he has expressed his knowing in and through the various Greek texts. It means that the interpreter begins from the descriptive, linguistic, common-sense world of meaning in which that interpreter is presently living and develops his or her experiencing, understanding, and judging until his or her knowing approaches the experiencing, understanding, and judging that Plato himself developed. This also means that the primary source for interpreting any text lies within the interpreter's own knowing, as that knowing is capable of unlimited development. It also implies that the more the interpreter already understands, the more likely he or she will be able to understand the knowing that is being communicated by authors in and through the words they have selected to express their meaning.

The first task for interpreters is to make sure that they know what the author of the text is talking about.[17] Interpreters who know nothing about the subject matter of Plato's *Republic* are not able to interpret his meaning. They do not have to know all about the subject, but they do have to have some anticipatory ideas of what the whole thing is about. It may turn out that what an interpreter has in mind is not what Plato intended to express through the words he selected, and the interpreter will have to correct his or her original anticipations. Knowing what Plato had in mind does not

ensure that the interpreter will reach the correct interpretation, but without this preunderstanding, there is no possibility of knowing what is the
intended meaning carried by the words of Plato's text.

The second task in interpreting a text is to understand the words.[18] Here
the interpreter encounters the hermeneutical circle of ever widening contexts. The meaning of any word of a text will depend on the sentence,
which in turn depends on the paragraph and the essay as a whole. Furthermore, any text of an author can be interpreted in the light of his or her
other works. This widening circle simply reflects the way an interpreter's
mind moves back and forth from any given whole to the parts that make
up that whole; from understanding one part as related to other parts, the
interpreter returns to the unified whole as understood through those
interrelated parts. The procedure resembles the way we interpret a painting; we begin by taking in the picture as a whole, then we shift our attention to the parts, studying the various patterns of lines, colors, and tonal
gradients that interrelate and modify the parts, then we return to the unified whole as it emerges in and through these interconnected parts. This
spiral movement by which the interpreter cycles into the whole meaning of
that text eventually carries the interpreter beyond a text like the *Republic* to
the author himself.

A fuller and more comprehensive interpretation will include not only
Plato's other texts, but also the cultural world of Plato himself.[19] The concrete, myriad, ordinary meanings, which made up the Athenian cultural
world in which Plato grew up and lived, will provide a much fuller and
richer context for interpreting the Platonic texts. To enter this world
requires the same sort of common-sensical, self-correcting process of learning by which we gradually assimilate and master our own world of commonly lived meanings. However, in this case the self-correcting process of
learning may move toward a limit that requires a basic reorientation of the
interpreter's own self. To enter into the world of Plato in and through the
study of the author's texts may demand that a person undergo the very sort
of conversion that Plato attempted to describe in the parable of the cave;
or interpreting a text like Plato's *Republic* may also mean involving the
interpreter in a conversation much like the Athenian citizens experienced
in their encounter with Socrates.

In addition to this problem of understanding the text, there is the third
critical problem of judging the correctness or truth of the interpretations.
In judging, critical wondering operates with reference to a context, and
the context of understanding may keep expanding from the parts of a text
to the whole, from one text to another, from the text to the author of the
text, and from the author to the lived, meaning world of the author.[20] This
implies that, in judging the correctness of an interpretation, the context of

that judgment may likewise be limited to this sentence or this chapter or a whole essay. However, the fact that the meaning of a sentence depends on the meaning of the paragraph and the meaning of a paragraph on the meaning of the chapters of the book does not imply that different parts of the text cannot be correctly interpreted without understanding the whole text. The chapter of a book has its own limited meaning as distinct from the whole of the book. Seen in the light of the whole book, the chapter's partial meanings will have much fuller and more comprehensive meanings, but that fuller meaning does not have to contradict the more limited partial meanings, provided that those partial meanings have been carefully and accurately interpreted. It is true that the meaning of the whole text is more than its partial meanings, but the whole comes to light in and through the partial meanings provided that they have been understood and correctly criticized until they provide the sufficient evidence for the interpreter to make an absolute but strictly limited judgment.

Interpreters do make mistakes in overestimating the extent and accuracy of their judgments. But such a fact tells us two things: first, interpreters can make certain true judgments about their own mistakes; second, interpreters have to be very modest and parsimonious in stating exactly what it is that they have correctly understood and what they have not yet understood. In the example of Plato's *Republic*, a correct interpretation of the text can be accomplished by controlling the contexts within which interpreters make their correct judgments; interpreters must also make carefully restricted judgments with a critical awareness of the contexts within which they are understanding and judging. From the metaphysical viewpoint, there are four distinguishable contexts that should be considered. First, there is the text itself and the successive parts that interpreters move through as they attempt to understand the whole meaning through the successively related parts of the text. Second, there is the shift from a hermeneutical to a historical context, which occurs when interpreters attempt to understand the historical world of Plato and how that ordinary, common-sense world sheds light on the theoretical meanings of the text. Third, besides the task of historians who study the world of a particular place and time, there is also the task of social scientists who attempt to correlate successive historical worlds in order to explain what was going forward in them. Social scientists attempt to correlate through explanatory categories a series of historical common-sense contexts or historical worlds of meaning. Fourth, there is the metaphysical context that provides the basic integrating structure for uniting the prior three hermeneutical and historical contexts.

A methodical metaphysics, such as we have established by deriving our metaphysical terms and relations from a prior cognitional and epistemological appropriation, can integrate the sequence of hermeneutical and historical contexts because such a self-appropriated metaphysician knows that common-sense knowing and theoretical or scientific knowing are complementary patterns of knowing with quite different norms and objectives, which may be integrated by the more comprehensive desire and norms of knowing that have being as their objective. Such a self-appropriated metaphysician also knows that the social scientist attempting to construct a social history will be dependent on the historian who studies the lives of particular people in particular places and times. The social or political historian, on the other hand, will attempt to correlate a series of particular societies through more universal categories that the social scientist has developed in order to apprehend the recurring cycles of social behavior in successive societies. Like the social scientist, the metaphysician is also dependent on the scientific histories of the social historians. Just as the social scientist transforms particular histories into a series of successive social histories that attempt to interpret and explain the advance or decline of successive societies, so the metaphysician critically transforms the work of the social scientist by testing the correctness of the categories employed by the social scientists. Thus, the authentically appropriated metaphysical knower realizes that all human beings are historical beings who live in and through their historically received schemes of meaning which may or may not be partly true and partly false. This same authentic metaphysician knows why these meanings are true or false, and so can criticize, first, the categories employed by the social scientist; second, the results of their research; and, third, their interpretations and histories. The authentic metaphysician can then recontextualize the results of the historians and social scientists within the finality of human history, which is partly determined by past, authentic, historical knowing and partly determined in and through a patterning of the remaining totality of data of human history.

In brief, the authentic metaphysician knows the potency, form, and act of historical finality. The potency is the totality of materials that are pertinent to the interpretations of any and all texts, while the form is both hermeneutical and historical. It is hermeneutical insofar as the interpreter achieves a complete understanding of what the author meant, including the author's attitude and sensibilities that derive from the world of meanings in which he or she lived and which enter into the meanings of the text. The form is historical insofar as the prior interpretations are understood within a dialectical, developing, historical unity that unfolds through successive stages of human history. It is actual insofar as the hermeneutical, historical patterns of all authors have been truly and authentically judged.

This explanation briefly summarizes how authentic human knowers can cooperate in working out a metaphysical philosophy of history, but it has detached itself from a moral interpretation and evaluation of that history. In the next chapter, I will describe how this metaphysical philosophy of history may be expanded into a moral philosophy of human history.

9   Summary

The major developments in this chapter center on two themes: first, the correspondence of knowing and being and, second, the knower as an historical being who develops and declines.

We may phrase the first theme in cognitional terms in the following way. First, we established that you can know your own intrinsic reality as a knower in and through your own cognitional activities; second, we established that you can know the intrinsic reality of any other being in and through your own cognitional activities; third, we defined the traditional terms of potency, form, and act through your own cognitional structure of experiencing, understanding, and judging. However, it is important to insist that ordinary descriptive knowing does not reveal the intrinsic realities of things. Only when you have moved from extrinsic descriptive knowing to the different forms of explanatory knowing will you know the intrinsic structure of things in limited or provisional ways. When I speak of knowing as revealing the intrinsic structure of your own being and other beings, it is imperative to understand that this statement is meant in an explanatory context.

This same theme may be expressed in metaphysical terms. First, you know your own potency, form, and act through your own conscious potency, form, and act. Second, you know the conscious and unconscious potency, form, and act of other beings through your own conscious potency, form, and act. Third, you may also know the potency, form, and act of the entire universe of being – conscious and unconscious – through your own conscious potency, form, and act. This is because 'form' refers to understanding and you may be understanding this or that being or this group of beings, but you may also be understanding the universal ordering of all beings to one another through the theory of 'emergent probability.' The foundation for this argument centers on the notion of being, which provides the basic objective of all knowers in and through their acts of knowing and thereby grounds the objectivity and validity of the various limited schemes of correct knowing of potency, form, and act. The key to forming this notion of being is twofold: first, you need to appropriate and realize that you do not actually know the infinite but that you do have the conscious desire or potency to know it; second, you need to understand what a second-order or operational definition is, that is, the notion of being is defined not in itself, but in and through the operations by and through which being will become known. This procedure of defining what you do not know through the anticipatory structures of knowing depends on the ability to shift your attention from the known contents (variables) to the operations by which and through which those contents are made known. Only if this procedure is understood can you grasp the meaning of the metaphysical terms – potency, form, and act – and how they may operate as an integrating structure that relates the metaphysical structures of your being to the metaphysical structures of every other being.

There is an important aspect of this correspondence, or isomorphism, of your potency, form, and act with the potency, form, and act of every other being that must be understood and formulated in an explanatory context. This aspect again emphasizes the need to abstract from the descriptive contents of the known and to pay attention to the cognitional structure through which and because of which the contents become known. This same issue underscores the importance of chapter 2 and the achievements of Einstein in decentering the measuring frameworks of particular scientists, located in particular places and times, and co-ordering these particular frameworks to one another in terms of the way scientists may transform measurements from one framework to another. This means that the measuring frameworks of scientists can be correlated to one another through a set of transformation equations that can 'equalize' all the different frameworks. This procedure is analogous to the way the notion of being orders objectively the cognitive frameworks of any and all knowers, thereby completely universalizing the potency, form, and act of any knower. A key step in this overall argument is to decenter any and all descriptive knowers and their particular frameworks and to recenter them and their frameworks in the human quest for being. All human knowers are united insofar as they advance in their knowing of being and insofar as they communicate such advances to subsequent generations. This brings us to the second major theme of this chapter: the human being as a historical being who develops and declines in the historical quest toward the complete knowing of being.

To set forth a metaphysics of history as we did in the last section of this chapter, we first had to specify the notion of development and distinguish between descriptive and explanatory notions of development. Anyone may notice that flowers and trees gradually evolve from an early immature stage to a later fully mature stage. Such growth processes exemplify development, but such examples hardly explain why the notion of development did not emerge in full theoretical dress until the twentieth century. In analyzing development, we made a basic distinction between major and minor developments. Minor development takes place within a system as the student attempts to master the successive steps of a mathematical system of meanings, such as are worked out in analytic geometry. Major development occurs when the student attempts to move from one system to a higher, more complex system of meanings from analytic geometry to calculus, for example. Minor developments involve the horizontal expansion that occurs in working out the full range of problems that can be handled within a system, whereas vertical development emerges as the knower moves beyond the operational range of some lower system and develops a more comprehensive and flexible set of operations, thereby revealing within the lower systems the potentialities that were not explored on that lower level. Thus the higher system subsumes the lower system not by going against the earlier achievements, but by transcending their limits and opening up new possibilities for further advances. Any present civilization advances by modifying and building on past achievements. But such advances may be distinguished either as a horizontal broadening of the past horizons or as a vertical leap that opens up a new horizon. Development embraces not only the simultaneity of past situations with present settings, but also the way the present can bring the past into the present. Development means the formation of a new higher integration that becomes new by modifying and subsuming the old. Development is a process that cycles back and forth from the present to the past, continually renewing itself by remaking the old into new and higher unities.

In addition to an explanatory notion of development, there is a second major issue that needs to be addressed in order to articulate a methodical approach to a metaphysics of history namely, the problem of interpreting texts and other historical data. Here the most significant requirement is the interpreter's prior knowledge of the field. Let us take as an example the history of mathematics I proposed in chapter 2. A historian cannot write a history of Western mathematics unless he or she has been trained in the methods of historical research and knows the field of mathematics. Without a fairly advanced knowledge of mathematics, the historian will not be able to differentiate in the data the relevant and irrelevant issues and the various advances that have been achieved. In developing a methodical philosophy of mathematics, the metaphysician is dependent on the historian of mathematics, but must be able to criticize and select in the history of mathematics major philosophical issues. Thus, in commenting on Carl Boyer's *The History of the Calculus and Its Conceptual Development*, I picked out certain key epistemological problems that recurred throughout the historical development of calculus. I was especially interested in the way Boyer stressed how the imagination of mathematicians repeatedly prevented them from being able to define the key concepts and terms of calculus because they kept trying to imagine non-imaginable intelligibilities. This focus allowed me to select certain major advances and, at the same time, to indicate the need for inverse insights which would reorient the way mathematicians dealt with the problem of the infinite. The notion of the infinite is a crucial issue in philosophy for establishing a properly oriented theory of knowing, objectivity, and reality.

These observations further imply that, if we wish to write a methodical history of philosophy, we must know before we begin what the major problems are that a philosophy has to overcome. Thus, I have argued that metaphysical problems depend on prior epistemological and cognitional problems. The philosopher who has correctly identified the major problems in cognitional theory knows that the history of mathematics and the sciences provides an appropriate field, first, for clarifying these problems and, secondly, for resolving them. However, if a philosopher wishes to be able to criticize and integrate the various histories of the human sciences, such as economics, law, or sociology, it is imperative that he or she must have appropriated the similarities and differences between the patterns of common-sense and theoretical knowing and how the basic cognitional structure of experiencing, understanding, and judging grounds the metaphysical structure of potency, form, and act. Only with such an integrating structure will the philosopher be in a position to critically transform the history of human meanings as they have been, or are to be, articulated in the various human sciences.

If we are going to work out a metaphysics of history, we must first understand how knowers exist and operate in and through schemes of meaning which they have inherited from the past and through which they are advancing and/or declining historically. Or we must know how our own potency, form, and act as a knower can form an integrating structure for critically transforming and evaluating the potency, form, and act of human history as it develops and declines.

7

Ethics

It is in turning from metaphysics to ethics that we can further examine the significance and power of the method of self-appropriation in providing a new approach to the science of ethics. In the Scholastic tradition, metaphysics was considered to be 'first philosophy' since it provided the basic principles and the fundamental context for all the other sciences. However, we have insisted upon the historical importance of Renaissance science and the subsequent developments in recent centuries through the emergence of statistical and genetic sciences. Equally important was the rise of the human or cultural sciences during the nineteenth and twentieth centuries. Further, we saw in the last chapter that the notion of higher viewpoints introduced in the first chapter led to a theory of emergent probability in chapter 4, then to a metaphysics of vertical finality, and finally to a metaphysics of history. In this chapter, we will discuss an even more significant advance as we look at a major reversal in the relations between metaphysics and ethics. Ethics, rather than metaphysics, will come to provide the basic context for the other sciences.[1]

In the theory of higher viewpoints, we have seen how a lower context of meanings can provide the potential for a new, higher, and more comprehensive horizon without diminishing the importance of the operative range of the prior context. For example, we have seen how plants operate in systems of lower chemical schemes as they assimilate these chemical activities into higher biological functions. Now we are about to examine how a science of ethics can sublate and transform the study of metaphysics into a new and higher historical context.

The Western tradition which placed ethics within the context of metaphysics goes back to Aristotle and his distinction between practical and theoretical wisdom. Theoretical or metaphysical wisdom was contemplative rather than practical. It was not practical because metaphysical wisdom was a search for certain necessary causes which governed the eternal celestial cycles which, in turn, ordered the terrestrial cycles. If a science assumes a world-order governed by necessary causes, then that ordering cannot be changed, which also implies that such a science will not be directed to, and concerned with, 'praxis.'[2] Science, however, no longer seeks certain necessary laws, but seeks instead the best available explanations. And modern science assumes not a static, closed universe, but an open, dynamic, developing universe. The entire universe is evolving, and that evolution toward higher and more complex integrations becomes on the human, historical level a conscious, directed dynamism. In this context both the natural sciences and the human sciences have become dynamic, developing sciences; they also have become empirical and experimental. Scientists today do not contemplate eternal, necessary truths; they form hypotheses that are to be tested, altered, and improved. These tested and verified hypotheses must also meet the demands of further questioning by other scientific observers.

Similarly, the human sciences mediate the communal meanings of past, human, historical constructions so that human communities may learn from their successes and failures in order to manage more intelligently the future, lived meanings of people. Thus, human history itself has become the object of study, not to be contemplated, but to be completed by the collective responsibility of governments and nations which are invited 'to think globally and act locally.' History has become a grand experiment that calls for a quite different science of ethics than we find in the ten books of Aristotle's *Nicomachean Ethics*.

1   Methodical Ethics

Just as the metaphysics we assembled in the last chapter set forth a heuristic structure for integrating scientific and historical knowing and meaning, so our ethics will attempt to provide an integrating structure for scientific and historical knowing, deciding, and doing. And just as the integrating structure of metaphysics was based on the unlimited objective of our own cognitional activities, so the integrating structures of ethics will be based on the unlimited objective of our cognitional and volitional activities, as these activities are correlated to one another in a directed, dynamic, and heuristic structure.

To speak of our cognitional and volitional activities, however, suggests the more traditional vocabulary of a faculty psychology based on a metaphysics of the soul which, in distinguishing cognitional and volitional activities of the soul's potencies, tended not only to distinguish, but also to separate, knowing and willing. Behind this tendency to separate cognitional and volitional activities was the long-debated, medieval question of the superiority of intellect over will or of will over intellect. In the traditional Scholastic position, our intellect proposes (specifies) a course of action to our will. Our will is a spiritual appetite, which means it responds to and seeks spiritual objects. If the intellect proposes a reasonable course of action, which is a spiritual object, then the will ought to accept the intellect's reason as its own motivating good. Thus, our willing follows, or ought to follow, the lead of our knowing because the object we know should attract our spiritual appetite, namely, our will.

Today we speak less about will and more about choice and values. We speak of conscious subjects choosing this or that way of living, because this person values this particular lifestyle or career rather than another. Intellect and will, moreover, are potencies of souls, not of subjects, and souls are not conscious subjects. A soul is 'the first principle of a living body.' Such a definition assumes a metaphysics based on first principles, not a metaphysics grounded empirically on the concrete, conscious activities of the knowing subject, as we have been attempting to articulate them. To shift to an ethics of the concrete subject, then, is to shift to an ethics based on appropriating our own conscious activity of choosing, and not on the unconscious faculty of will. This does not imply that an ethics based on the metaphysics of the soul was necessarily incorrect, any more than a metaphysics based on first principles was necessarily mistaken. Rather, the problem with such a metaphysics was that it lacked empirical controls, methodical norms, and commonly accepted ways of proceeding and settling disputes. Similarly, an ethics of the soul lacked the methodical controls to solve such problems as the priority of the intellect in relation to the will, which had become a critical question in attempting to establish ethical foundations.

Following our method of self-knowing, we have seen that knowing is not a simple activity, but a structure of three distinct, interrelated activities. More important, these levels or spheres of activities are related to one another as lower to higher viewpoints. The activity of understanding sublates, transforms, and extends the range of the lower sensible and imaginable activities. Judging similarly introduces a still higher new level of operation that transforms understanding and initiates new sources of knowing that go beyond understanding. Finally, the activity of choosing or deciding operates on a fourth level which significantly transforms, subsumes, and goes beyond judging. Such a method readily solves the problem of the superiority of the intellect versus will since it discloses how deciding subsumes and transforms knowing. This means that choosing is a higher form of knowing than the structure of knowing as it operates through the first three levels of activities. It also means that ethics sub-sumes, transforms, and goes beyond metaphysics. Finally, the contemporary split between emotional and cognitive knowing will prove to be a misleading way of posing the problem.

To establish this new ethical foundation, I will follow the same basic questions we asked in developing a metaphysics. First, instead of asking, What am I doing when I am knowing?, I will ask, What am I doing when I am deliberating? Second, instead of asking, Why do I know?, I will ask, Why do I decide? Third, instead of asking, What do I know when I do knowing?, I will ask, What do I choose when I make choices?

2   First Ethical Question

Appropriating your own activity of deciding is similar to what you do when you are judging. Judging has three characteristics: (1) It is the reflective process that leads to the act of judging, and it begins when you wonder whether or not what you have understood about your experience has been correctly understood. You ask, Is it so? (2) Judging is a more personal activity than understanding or experiencing. You are more intimately involved in making judgments which makes you more sensitive about committing yourself to judging yes or no. (3) You judge in the context of prior judgments, and you spontaneously experience a need to make any new judgments consistent with your prior cognitional commitments.

Before you decide, you deliberate about and evaluate your plan of action. This process of deliberation, which ends in a decision, has certain similarities to the process of reflecting, which terminates in a judgment. They may be compared in the following three ways. First, instead of asking, Is it so?, you ask, Is it worthwhile? You take some time to consider the value of your plan of action in order to decide if it is worth doing. Second, in deciding, you will be committing yourself to the project, both as a knower and as a chooser, so your personal involvement is even more keenly felt. Third, any present decision will be made in the context of prior decisions, so part of your deliberation will be to accommodate your present deciding to past choices. There is a parallel, then, between the three defining characteristics of judging and those of deliberating.

Earlier I said that deciding subsumes, transforms, and transcends the prior three levels of knowing, giving birth to a whole new dimension of your being. While there are important similarities with the act of judging, which completes a particular act of knowing, the act of deciding has even more important differences that need to be articulated and appropriated.

In the reflective process leading to a judgment, you are seeking suffi-cient reasons to ground your assertion, and the standard for that 'sufficiency' is a reflective insight that transforms a conditional proposition into an unconditional one, because you judged that the conditions were or were not in fact given as you had understood them to be given. This 'virtually unconditioned' or 'limited absolute' motivated you to judge that the proposition as you had understood it was in fact so. In deliberating, there is no 'virtually unconditioned' or immanently generated term that brings the deliberative process to closure, thereby motivating your choice. In judging, we are dealing with what in fact is so, or probably is so. In deciding to buy a home or to get married, however, the deliberating can go on indefinitely because you are dealing not with a fact, but with a possible course of actions that will not be actualized unless you decide to do so. The home you are considering buying is a fact, but your buying it is not a fact and you know it; that is why questions of freedom, responsibility, commitment, and consequences are so significant in discussions of decision-making as opposed to judging. But, if deliberating subsumes judging, what are you judging when you are deliberating? You are judging the value or worthwhileness of doing what you are evaluating and trying to decide; you are wondering whether or not your proposed action is truly valuable. Deliberating raises the whole new question of values. If the first answer to the question, What am I doing when I am deciding?, is that I am evaluating or making judgments of value, then the next problem is to specify the difference between judging facts and judging values.[3]

To know something in a limited way is to experience, understand, and judge that thing. Judging is the activity in knowing which reflects on, and eventually asserts, the actuality of your experiences as you have come to understand them. Judging makes you cognitively present to the concrete reality of things, or to your own concrete reality. But the question may then emerge, Is that reality a truly 'valuable' reality? How do I judge the true value of things? In the traditional vocabulary the question would read, How do I know the goodness of things?, or more important, the goodness of a proposed course of action. Implied in this question is the further question of moral norms, What is the norm for making correct, moral, judgments? The traditional answer was 'right reason,' but this answer was dependent on a metaphysics of the soul and its faculties, not on the conscious, concrete, existing subject. In the latter context, the knowing subject has to be subsumed by the higher, choosing subject, which means that the problem is not only 'right reasoning,' but also true valuing.

Again, the basic clue can be found in the question, Ought I to do this?, or Ought I to continue to do this? To evaluate a project assumes you already know what the project is. Or, if you are evaluating a recurring scheme of personal behavior, then the question assumes that you already possess correct, factual knowledge, and that you are now asking an additional question about the value or values that are intrinsic to such a personal scheme. In other words, there is a reality to be known in correct judging, and there is the further and more complex reality to be known in correctly evaluating the intrinsic goodness and worthwhileness of certain personal courses of action and/or interaction. Judgments of value, then, presuppose judgments of fact. Assuming that you, as a chooser, have correctly understood the facts or have intelligently projected some course of action, then to evaluate this proposal, you must understand the feelings that are evoked in considering the project, since it is through understanding the feelings that you will judge the value of the project. To understand and identify feelings is a complex problem, but considerable progress has been made in this area during the present century, especially by certain phenomenologists.

A major distinction has been made between intentional and non-intentional feelings.[4] Non-intentional feelings are feelings that tend to direct you to specific goals and activities. For example, being hungry, being tired, being sick are conscious feeling states that emerge from changes in your unconscious neurophysiological system, and they lead you toward certain set goals, such as eating, or sleeping, or going to a doctor. But thinking about possible courses of action, such as changing jobs, buying a home, getting married, also evoke feelings, but these do not have such a limited and directed focus. Wondering about changing jobs can evoke a wide range of emotions which are not clearly defined. Such feelings need to be, and can be, understood, named, and differentiated. It is in wondering about whether you should or should not do something that you provoke in yourself these quite different types of feelings. Such feelings are intentional, but what their intention is needs to be attended to, apprehended, and evaluated. Some of these feelings emerge spontaneously, but what happens to feelings once they have emerged depends on you and your own prior emotional history. The key point is that, before you can judge the value of such feelings, you must understand them since such understood feelings mediate the values or disvalues of what you will decide.

Just as before making judgments of fact you must first understand and make intelligible what these facts are, before you judge the value of your feelings you must first understand what these feelings are. As felt, the feelings are experienced but they are not yet understood, although they are open to understanding and to judging. Only as understood and judged can feelings be asserted to be truly or probably worthwhile, or truly or probably not worthwhile. Thus, before you can answer the question, Ought I carry out this project? you must first understand and judge the project, and then understand and judge the value of the project. To know the actual value of the project goes beyond simply knowing what the project is.

Judgments of value transcend and reveal a further reality that is intrinsic to the actual or projected reality of a course of action. Such value judgments depend on the context of prior value judgments and on the prior development or distortion of your feelings. They also depend on the way you have scaled your values in the past. You have preferred certain values to other values because you considered them to be more valuable. And they are apprehended as more or less valuable because they were considered to be more or less limited. Just as arithmetic is a more restricted or limited way of dealing with numbers than algebra is, the values of your health can be considered more important than the pleasure of eating unhealthy foods or over-eating. The value of your own vitality, however, should not be preferred to the vitality and welfare of the whole community, which means that it is more valuable to set up a cooperative health system than it is to settle for the health of any single person.

Beyond vital values there are also social and cultural values which give meaning and importance to the whole social order. If we consider the social order to refer to the system of cooperative roles and tasks that are actually operating within a community, then culture may be defined as providing the why of that social order. The social order refers to what people do cooperatively, while their culture explains why they do it. Cultural values are more comprehensive and more important than the social order itself. Just as analytic geometry goes beyond the limits of simple algebra, cultural values surpass the values of the social order.

There is also the ontological value of the person who, not only values her social order and cultural values, but also esteems herself as a valuable being. She is a knowing subject oriented by a potentially infinite knowing and, as we shall see, a potentially infinite valuing subject oriented toward an infinitely valuable objective. The ontological value of a single knower and chooser ought to be preferred above and beyond cultural values. It is the knowing and valuing chooser who initiates, invents, and chooses the vital social and cultural values, and so the subject as originating chooser outranks these chosen values. Cultures may be judged valuable, therefore, insofar as they set the conditions under which authentic knowers and choosers may come to know and value themselves precisely as knowers and choosers. Finally, the supreme value is the unrestricted and completely transcendent value that is the orienting desire of all knowers and choosers and that therefore sets the conditions for all the different levels of valuing, or for the whole scale of values.

Every context of your prior value judgments within which you deliberate and evaluate includes a scale of values. For the most part, this scale of values is inherited from your culture. Before considering this cultural heritage, it is important to notice that judging the value of possible courses of action is not the same as deciding, but it does set the conditions for making such decisions. This is important to stress because it is critical to ask what deciding adds to evaluating. While you are evaluating possible courses of action, you have not yet made a concrete existential commitment through which you will not only judge that this would be a truly valuable course of action, but also choose to follow it. In deciding, you make a commitment, not just to know something, but to bring some course of action into being which, if you do not do it, will not exist. And, more surprising, it is not only the course of action that will begin to be, but you yourself will begin to exist in a way that you did not exist before making that decision.

Why do you choose to commit yourself to a particular course of action? Because you have decided not only that this is an intelligible and possibly reasonable way to be, but also that it is an intrinsically valuable and truly worthwhile way to be. You realize that you will begin to exist and to live in a more valuable way if you do this or, in doing this, you will make your own being a more meaningful and valuable being. Further, such a valuable way of being and living ought to be realized, and you are conscious of this 'ought-ness.' You are aware that you, as a chooser, ought to choose to live in this 'choice-worthy' way because you are spontaneously attracted to, and desire to be, a valuable being. In order to be the better being that you are not but could be, you feel that you ought to respond to the course of action that you have understood, judged, and evaluated and that transcends your present way of living and being.

Further, if you do choose to exist in this new way, you will become more truly responsible for the way you exist. You will become a concrete, existing being who chooses to live in a scheme of meaningful activities that you have understood, judged, evaluated, and chosen as a truly choice-worthy way to live. To live freely, therefore, is not to live in an arbitrary way, but to live in the critically judged, critically evaluated way that you ought to live. The paradox of freedom is that to live freely is to live in an obligatory way. But it is you who obliges yourself. Your own intelligence obliges you, as does your self-evaluating self; you command yourself to be and to behave in truly worthwhile ways. In other words, there arises a spontaneous desire to maintain a consistency between your knowing and doing. However, to oblige yourself does not mean that your actions will necessarily follow. It means that, if they do follow, it is because you did what you had decided was the right thing to do. Obligation is not necessity. To live freely is not to live in an indeterminate or arbitrary way, but to live in a self-knowing, self-evaluating, self-choosing way. A free self is a 'determined' self, but it is you who does the determining.

We are born not as actual knowers and choosers, but as potential knowers and choosers who need to develop biologically, psychically, intellectually, and emotionally before we can decide for ourselves what we are to make of ourselves. We are not considered reasonable until we are about seven years old, and we are not considered responsible choosers until we have reached a certain stage of maturity. In the meantime, what we do is not knowing and deciding, but believing that the knowing and deciding of others is truly worthwhile.

2a Belief

Aristotle adopted Plato's famous principle, 'the state is the soul writ large,' and 'the soul is the state writ small.' In our contemporary context, we would say that a culture sets the conditions for developing the character of its people, or a culture is the people writ large. Between culture and the person stands the family, and the early acculturation of children is through their families. It is this transmission of cultural schemes or habits of values from parents to children which brings to light the importance of belief or trust in the assimilation of a scale of value. As Freud and Erickson have noted, it is between the ages of four and seven that a child is taught the beginnings of a moral code and the manners of social behavior. The 'generalized other' of the culture is mediated through the 'super-ego' of the parents, and both become the inner voice of personal and social conscience for the child. Children do not develop their own standards of behavior; rather they obey the commands of their parents in doing this and not doing that. Children desire to do what is correct because they both fear and trust their parents. It is the authority of parents directing and controlling the behavior of children that provides the reasons or motives for children to choose their activities and ways of cooperating, which in turn provide them with their roles and respective tasks.

What needs to be stressed here is the role that belief plays.[5] Children do not develop their own norms of conduct, nor do they formulate their own ways of acting and interacting. They act and interact in ways set out by their parents, but such obedience can be quite reasonable even though it is not the sort of reasoning that emerges when you think through things for yourself, such as discovering the solution to a problem. To believe in the reasoning of other people is a much more common form of reasoning. The reason for believing in another is because you trust that person. How do you know if a person is trustworthy? Children know their parents are worthy of belief because they evaluate the trustworthiness of their parents through their own desires and fears. These desires and fears evolve and pass through stages, which have been detailed by scholars such as Piaget and Erickson.[6] The point is that such desires and fears provide the content for value judgments, which in turn form the motives for children to choose to believe. Children learn to trust their parents' code of prohibitions and permissions, and this code becomes the normative ground for their own behavior. Why do children trust their parents? They do so because their believing is grounded in their loving. Love is the ground that originates and orients their desires and fears. Since love seems to be an even more basic activity than choosing, we need to look at what love is.

2b Love

Just as knowing reveals the intrinsic reality of subjects and objects, loving reveals a new dimension of their realities that was not known prior to the state of being in love. Knowing reveals the intrinsic intelligibility of things, but loving goes a step further and reveals the intrinsic excellence or worth-whileness of persons and things. Knowing is the structured activity of a knower. But love is not only an activity; it is a way of being, a dynamic state that grounds, engenders, and orients all our other activities. Love also gives us a new context or horizon. When we speak of making judgments of value within a context, we mean that, for a person in love, it will be love that provides the horizon within which and through which he or she judges the value of various courses of action.[7] Such judgments of value provide reasonable motives for deciding to act or not to act in certain ways. Love becomes the motive that directs and guides the activities that lovers choose.

The state of being in love helps to clarify the contextual aspect of our judgments of value. It also clarifies how these values form the motives for choosing our courses of action. A brief look at the four different types of love will reveal that loving, like valuing, is also hierarchical.

The first is the love of intimacy, the love shared by husband and wife which blossoms into the domestic love of parents and children. This domestic love expands into social loving, the second type. The third type is the love of self that finds its ground in our own perfection as a domestic and civic lover. Finally, there is the love of a totally transcendent being who is the source and motive for all forms of loving. Implied in these four forms of love is a comparative judgment of the perfection implied in the different forms of loving. Just as true loving of family sets the conditions for the broader love of country and fellow human beings, love of self reveals us to ourselves, not only as social beings, but more significantly as historical beings whose origin and destiny belong to the beginning and end of all human history. To appropriate oneself as a potential lover of the total historical community is to set the conditions for seeking the infinite source of love in which history begins and ends, and to discover that a possible destiny of human history is to belong to a community whose love for others is grounded in the love of one's own being. Such a love may then lead to the supreme value, the love that begins and ends all loving. To establish an authentic scale of values, then, depends on appropriating the totally transcendent love that grounds the orientation of all other loves. This is religious love, the subject of the next chapter.

2c Symbolic Reasoning (Role of Imagination)

The key to persuading a person or audience to carry out a sequence of actions is to speak symbolically, using images that will reach down into a person's psychic underground and stir up subconscious vitalities which permeate higher levels of human experience, generating sufficient emotion to make an unwilling or indifferently disposed person become disposed to act. The result is that such symbols evoke feelings that are not only intentional, but also effectively intentional or motivational. How do such symbols or symbolic meanings operate?[8] What is the logic of symbols by which we persuade ourselves, or allow others to motivate us, to act in a certain way? Why is a single picture worth a thousand words? Because it is symbolic, not univocal. The picture gathers a host of different meanings embedded in a cluster of past experiences that are emotionally rich and that resonate their memories, meanings, and values deep within us. For example, the home you lived in, the school, stores, and neighborhood community where you grew up are all symbolic experiences reverberating with felt and remembered meanings which form part of that complex meaning world in which you live. Such symbolic meanings are spontaneous and primordial forms of valuing and meaning, and they operated in human history long before logic was invented. In fact, a convenient way to summarize how symbols operate is to contrast symbolic meanings with logical meanings.

Traditional logic seeks univocal, not multiple, meanings, and it does so in order to clarify assumptions and to argue consistently and carefully to conclusions that are reasonable because they have been proved by successive steps in a clear, consistent argument. There is, however, another form of an 'argument' in a story, song, painting, temple, dance, and statue. That argument is symbolic, and it reasons not inferentially, but the way the human heart reasons. Shakespeare, Beethoven, and Rembrandt are convincing, not because they prove their premises and conclusions, but because they overwhelm us with clusters of related memories and meanings that are not abstract, but evoke and condense endless lines of associative meanings and feelings.[9] Such patterns of associations may frequently be contradictory, such as we find in the symbols of the four basic elements: earth may symbolize the source of life, as well as the womb of death; water refreshes, gives birth, and nourishes life, but the same vast dark waters may swallow up life; air is the breath that sustains life, but it may also be the dreaded storm or cyclone that destroys; and while fire brings warmth and growth, it may also burn, consume, and destroy. Symbols do not follow the logic of propositions; they express, the contradictions, tensions, conflicts, and rages of the human heart. Symbols express not the logic of the mind, but the logic of motives that ground our actions and interactions, thereby revealing the logic of life itself as that life arises from, and is embedded in, the basic tensions of our deepest desires and darkest fears. While theoretical reason abstracts from images to deal in non-imaginable but highly intelligible meanings, symbolic reason employs images to evoke, direct, and pattern feelings; images speak simultaneously to our lower and higher knowing and evaluating self. Symbols provide people with emotional reasons that will nourish and supply them with the motivating meanings by which they carry on their life's work. And so we may distinguish between the institutional patterns which, woven together, constitute the communal practices of a people and their cultural patterns which permeate these social patterns to provide the motives that orient and direct their personal and social operating and cooperating in seeking personal and/or common goals.

Institutions are what people do; culture is why they do it. Because symbolic reasoning and deliberating are more spontaneous than, and prior to, the more familiar modes of reasoning, they form more universal and comprehensive patterns of knowing and meaning. To define a person as a rational animal is to define a person abstractly. In concrete terms, we are cultural or symbolic animals.[10] Just as the nineteenth century brought about a reversal in the priority of practical intellect over speculative intellect, in the twentieth century we have come to realize that symbolic emotional reasoning has a priority over cognitive or theoretical reasoning.

2d Culture

We experience the world spontaneously not as knowers or as choosers, but in terms of our desires and fears. Such desires and fears are transcultural, but how they are cultivated depends on the practices and symbols of the cultural world we are born and reared in. Culture is common to people at all times. While specific manners, customs, and beliefs are cultural variables, such schemes of meanings and values change genetically and dialectically throughout human history. What does not change is the fact that people must be born, grow up, eat, work, sleep, marry, dream, get sick, and die. These are the basic events of human existence, and they do not vary throughout history. What does develop and decline are the meanings and values that people give to these recurring human events. Such recurring meanings are expressed primarily in a people's stories and rituals. People and communities live in the past, present, and future schemes of meanings; they remember and anticipate, and such memories and expectancies are expressed in cultural stories that explain the meanings and values which they have come to associate with their historical origins, their covenants, their pilgrimages, and their final destiny.

While such stories may be partially known, they are lived and enacted in our daily routines, and thereby provide the basic context of motives that orient a people's private and public institutional living. We live in and through our languages, and these languages we live in are formed and reformed by the continual flows of our personal and communal knowings, choosings, lovings, and doings. Such cultural languages have a history, but that history as lived by its people is not known in the usual meaning of the word 'known'; rather, it is known because it is believed, and it is believed because it is considered to be credible, and it is judged credible because it is valued. Belief in history is motivated by the cultural symbols that incarnate and articulate this heritage. In other words, there is a fundamental distinction between the historical schemes of meanings and values of a people as they come to be written down and those same schemes as they are being lived by the people. In primitive societies, the only cultural history that people know is known through the recitals and ritualizings of their myths.[11] Written history as we know it began with the Greeks, but even people today know only a small part of their lived cultural history through reading, reflecting, and evaluating. Most history is lived, and lived in the ordinary and symbolic languages of stories, songs, rituals, and other mediating images and performances that evoke and cycle the emotional meanings and values that motivate our daily schemes of living.

If we now repeat our first question, What am I doing when I am deliberating and deciding?, the answer can be briefly stated in the context we have just articulated. When we deliberate and decide, we are doing so in the context of cultural norms and standards that we believe to be authentic and truly valuable. Such an answer reveals the significance of the ethical questions: Why do I decide? How do I know if I have decided objectively? How do I know if the cultural standards that ground my choices are truly objective standards? In other words, what we are looking for is a transcultural norm or standard that is independent of specific cultural norms but that is applicable to any and all cultures.

3   Second Ethical Question

The question we are considering corresponds to the question we asked about the objectivity of cognitional judgments, and the answer to that question was a theory of epistemology. The problem we are dealing with in this section arises because the normative grounding for making judgments of fact or judgments of value depends on giving free reign to our desire to know and love. As we have just seen, judgments of fact or value occur within a cultural context or horizon, which means that such judgments are limited by that horizon. But our desire to know and love is potentially unlimited. How can I be sure that I have set the limits of my judgment correctly?

We noted that reflecting leads toward a limit of mastery and familiarity when we grasp that the evidence accumulated is sufficient to assert, deny, or qualify the judgment we are considering. We have distinguished different patterns of knowing and, therefore, different patterns of judging. For example, if you intend to judge whether your understanding of the order of the universe is correct or incorrect, then you cannot make such a judgment until you have completely understood all there is to be understood about the universe which, while possible, has not yet been achieved. However, you can make a probable judgment and be certain about the fact that it is probable because you have accumulated sufficient evidence to assess that probability and, further, you have the 'mastery and familiarity' with the context within which you are reflecting to assert that this is probably true. In other words, whether you are making a practical judgment – the cat is on the mat – or a theoretical judgment – Newton's theory of gravity is probably valid in certain limited cases – you can always set your limits and judge correctly within those limits. What guarantees the validity of these limits is the proper development of the unrestricted desire to know as it unfolds in successive stages.

How do you know if this desire, which is potentially unlimited, is developing as it should? Because our desire for truth is unlimited and because our achievement of truth is limited, there is a continuous struggle in each human knower to move beyond the present state of self as knower and to replace the present self with a more highly developed knower who does not yet exist, but could begin to exist in virtue of each knower's potentially unrestricted desire to know. To be an authentic or genuine knower means you must not distort or disorient your desire to know, but consciously accept the fact that you must always seek to transcend your present, knowing self.

As we noted in the previous chapter, there are two norms of truth: first, the proximate norm, which was identified as a 'limited absolute'; second, the remote standard of truth, which depends on the proper development and unfolding of a person's unrestricted desire to know. In explaining the proximate norm of truth, we insisted on the significance of an invulnerable understanding – invulnerable because you waited until the question, Is it so?, had sufficient time to uncover sufficient evidence to ground your assertion within the limits you established. This means that setting the limits of any 'limited absolute' is the key for establishing the proximate norm, that is, letting questions arise and wondering long enough for them to arise. You know if your desire to know, as operating in a limited context, has properly developed by knowing the different ways that you can interfere with that desire and thereby block yourself from raising questions that you prefer not to consider. This is why we proposed three methods for dealing with the context or horizon within which you are judging. First is the method of logic that tests for clarity and consistency within any given context. Second is the genetic method that deals with the proper development of contexts by anticipating a continuous series of potential higher integrations; that is, by controlling a continually moving viewpoint or context. Third is the dialectical method that deals with the ways that you can block your proper development as a knower, as well as the ways by which you can not only correct a disoriented context, but also reverse it, converting yourself back to a genuinely developing knower directed toward an unlimited objective.

In summarizing the genetic and dialectical methods, we can state that, as a genetically skilled knower, you know how knowing develops through successive stages of intellectual growth. As a dialectical knower, you know the four different ways that you may distort your desire to know so that it does not develop properly. A genetic-dialectical knower is an authentic self-transcending knower who can critically judge the progress and decline of his or her own knowing, and can also do the same for other knowers as the human historical community moves toward its final objective of unrestricted knowing. But this explanation deals with cognitive epistemology, whereas the question we are now raising, How do I know if my cultural valuing is truly objective valuing?, deals with a moral, not a cognitive, epistemology. Can we make the same distinction between the proximate and remote norms of valuing as we have with those of knowing?

Our notion of cognitive objectivity depends on the notion of being, and so our notion of moral objectivity depends on extending our notion of being as true to a notion of being as both true and valuable. The transcendental notion of value, like the transcendental notion of truth, is unrestricted. As such, it anticipates all truly valuable decisions. When you have formed and chosen all the truly valuable choices that you are capable of making, you yourself will be, and you will have committed yourself to that which is transcendentally valuable. Such a transcendental notion of value is a second-order or heuristic definition just as is the transcendental notion of truth.

To know objectively depends both on knowing the notion of being as true, and on knowing correctly the tripartite structure of knowing through which the notion of being emerges. Similarly, choosing objectively depends both on knowing the transcendental notion of value and on knowing correctly your own fourfold structure of choosing: experiential, normative, critical, and evaluative. What unites these partial objectives is you, the chooser, who is oriented to an infinitely valuable objective. Just appropriating yourself as a genuine or authentic knower means becoming normatively and critically aware of your present limited actuality (as opposed to your infinite potential), as an objective chooser you must appropriate the same conscious tension between self as limited chooser and self as potentially unlimited. To become normatively and critically aware of your infinite potential as a chooser means you must appropriate and distinguish the two opposing norms that ground your deliberatings and evaluatings.

We identified the fundamental error in knowing as mistakenly assuming that sensible experiencing is the normative and critical component in the tripartite structure of knowing; in choosing, the foundational error is to mistakenly assume that sensibly affective experiences provide the normative grounding for making judgments of value. In other words, just as the correct knowing of objective knowing involves a reorientation of yourself from incorrect to correct judgments concerning the norms of knowing, a similar conversion is necessary if you are to establish within yourself a normative and critical foundation for a science of ethics. The fundamental mistake in choosing is to assume that sensible feelings and satisfactions are what make your choices valuable. To correct this mistake, it is necessary to appropriate and appreciate the difference between sensible and intentional feelings, which we discussed in the previous section. In one sense, this is a very traditional distinction since Aristotle and the ancients were aware that, while pleasurable or sensible satisfactions may be part of a good choice, they cannot provide the intrinsic, determining norm for making good choices. For example, you take nasty-tasting medicine because you are aware that being healthy is more valuable than the taste of the medicine, which may be intrinsically or truly valuable even if it does not taste good. Exercise may also feel unpleasant when you first attempt it, but the motive that orients you to take up exercise is not your present feelings, but the anticipated feeling of having a healthy body. You realize that the unpleasant feelings you first feel in exercising can be gradually transformed into feelings of satisfaction or even enjoyment. When that happens, exercising is not only valuable, but also pleasurable, and you made it pleasant by pursuing the intrinsically valuable goal of being healthy.

Even more valuable than the importance of being healthy is the value of establishing a good social order, which would provide recurring schemes of social, political, economic, educational, and religious values for a whole community of knowers and choosers. To choose to acquire the skills and expertise to participate in such a social order transcends your own individual vital values. A social order includes social, political, educational, economic, and religious values for each particular person, as well as for the community as a whole. Insofar as your social order operates in truly valuable ways, it forms and informs the actual intersubjective feelings people have for one another, thereby promoting civic loyalty and love among the members of the social order. Insofar as a social order comes about through biased judgments of values and false choices, the social whole tends to divide a community into hostile factions, thereby setting the conditions for recurring conflict, civic dissension, and social disorder.

Beyond the values of a social order are the cultural values that permit the members of the social order to question and criticize the social order itself. Every human being is a potential, metaphysical knower. But if you live in a society that has no science of metaphysics, you cannot wonder in any explicit, theoretical way about the nature of reality or of being. Similarly, if you live in a society that has no explicit moral theory, then you cannot wonder in any systematic way about the morality of the memories, meanings, and values that you and your community are currently living. For example, Socrates attempted to introduce the Athenians to new ways of questioning themselves and of criticizing the values of the social order. Only with Aristotle did these initial attempts at knowing self and society reach the systematic stage articulated in his *Ethics*. The problem with Aristotle's *Ethics* was that it was developed within the context of a metaphysics that placed contemplative wisdom above practical wisdom. We have reversed this ordering and given the practical wisdom of authentic choosers a higher and more comprehensively valuable position.

This reversal can be reconciled with Aristotle's own writings. Beyond cultural values that promote personal and social criticisms, there are the personal values that transcend such cultural values. In participating in a social order, you not only cooperate with others, but you make yourself into a virtuous or vicious person.[12] In choosing to cooperate with people in a truly valuable social order, you make yourself valuable, not just to other people, but more especially to yourself. If you cooperate in unworthy enterprises, you make yourself into an unworthy person. Thus, the value of a social order depends on whether it conditions and encourages its members to become valuable persons to one another and to themselves. This is why personal values are to be esteemed higher, and are to be preferred to cultural or social values. The intrinsic objective goal of a good social order is to make people lovable to one another and to themselves. People who lie, cheat, or steal are not being friendly to themselves. Lying is not only an unfriendly way to act toward others, but a personal betrayal since it makes you unworthy of your own admiration and esteem. Plato and Aristotle were both aware of this mutual relation between particular souls and their social order. Plato's famous maxim that the state is the soul writ large also implies that the soul is the state writ small. The social order does not necessarily determine the character of its members, but it certainly does set the conditions and disposes them to behave in socially approved and disapproved ways.

Beyond the question of your identity as a knower and chooser operating and cooperating in a social, civic, and cultural community, there is the question of your history and the history of your community. How do you know if being an American, a Canadian, or a Mexican cultural chooser will make you a good friend to yourself? To answer this question in a normative, critical, and evaluative way, you need a transcultural norm to serve as a standard for critically evaluating the cultural meanings and values that presently motivate the members of your social order to value and choose the 'goods' that they do. The first step in developing a transcultural norm is finding a transcendental notion of value that applies to any and all human choosers and to the choices that they may possibly make, as contrasted with the actual choices they have or are making. The foundation for this transcultural norm can be found in the conscious tension between your own personal and cultural identity and the potential identity that you may develop if you were more discerning and responsive to your orientation to an unlimited value. While personal values transcend cultural values, the ground of your evaluation of yourself as a self-chooser depends on your own openness and your ability to respond to a transcendental objective that orients you to the potentially infinite self that you are not, but could be.

In chapter 5, we established the 'virtually unconditioned' or 'limited absolute' as the proximate norm for judging truth. In chapter 6, we established that the 'remote norm' for judging truth was to be found in the proper development of your own unrestricted desire to know. Now we are making the same distinction between the proximate and remote standard for making truly valuable choices. Earlier we defined cognitional authenticity in terms of the conscious tension between what you know and your potentially unrestricted desire to know; as an authentic chooser, you are to be defined in terms of a conscious correlation between your present limited choices and your infinite potential to choose. Only insofar as you are committed to a continual transcendence of your present knowing and choosing self will you be an authentic or truly objective knower and

chooser. There is a foundational difference between the cultural conscience, which you have inherited and assimilated from your own lived cultural meanings and values, and your truly authentic moral conscience. You
may be faithful to your present cultural conscience, and still be unfaithful
to your authentic moral conscience, as we have just defined it. Becoming
an authentic metaphysical knower involves a conversion of yourself as a
knower from the basic mistake made in knowing knowing and in knowing
objective knowing; to appropriate yourself as an authentic moral chooser,
you must know both what you are doing when you are choosing and why
you choose the way you do, which means knowing why you scale your values the way you do.

To be an authentic moral chooser is to choose in the context of a true
scale of values. And to set up such a scale of values – vital, social, cultural,
personal, and transcendent – it is necessary to have an absolute on which
to lay the foundation. This absolute foundation is your own self as chooser
oriented to a totally transcendent objective. Just as the norm for being an
objective or authentic knower is your own subject as a self-transcending
knower, the norm for an authentic chooser is your own subject as a self-
transcending chooser. How do you know if you are a self-transcending
chooser? By appropriating the conscious tension between yourself as a cultural chooser and yourself as transculturally oriented to an objective that
transcends your cultural community. To do this, you must know the cultural history of your community, and from that context you must be able to
discern and evaluate within your culture those recurring schemes that are
generating progress and those that are orienting your cultural community
toward decline. For example, when you ask, Should I do this?, you tend to
evaluate the merits or demerits of such projected courses of action within
the context of the culture in which you live. As an adult you do not experience the world with an 'empty-head,' that is, without a cultural context.
You experience people and places culturally, which means that you judge
facts and their values, you deliberate and decide, within the cultural context in which you live. The world you live in, therefore, is not the immediate physical world, but that same physical world as a culturally mediated
world of meanings and values. In other words, you do not ask, Is this
project worth undertaking?, as if you were Adam or Eve. Rather, it is
because Adam and Eve and other men and women made the decisions and
did things the way they did that you wonder the way you do and decide the
way you do. These ancestors were responsible for setting the conditions
under which you experience other people and the world, as well as the way
you remember the world that came before and anticipate the world that is
to come. You are a cultural being, which means you are a historical being.

Human history does not start afresh with each generation. We inherit our history and hand it on to posterity with our own added improvements and deformities. How, are we to evaluate our actual, lived cultural history? How are we to know if our culture is setting the conditions for its members to become authentic or inauthentic knowers and choosers? To answer that question we must transform the methodical metaphysics of history into a moral metaphysics of history or a moral philosophy of history.

4   Moral Philosophy of History

In the previous chapter, the emphasis was on the history of human know-ing as that knowing was communicated to audiences through various modes and manners of human expression. The problem was to correctly interpret the meaning of different historical records and authors through various scholarly procedures that transformed partial, limited contexts of interpretations into more comprehensive, historical perspectives which metaphysicians can then criticize and transform in the context of a histori-cal world-order that subsumes the natural world-order. Granted that we are in possession of such an explanation of world-order, knowers may then ask: Is this universal world-order truly valuable? Is the present concrete order-ing of the universe, including human history, a truly good order? To answer this question, it is necessary to specify more precisely what a good order is. But before we can do this, we must further differentiate how prac-tical common-sense knowing operates and communicates itself in and through various, concrete human performances. We have already specified common-sense knowing as a pattern of knowing that specializes in under-standing what to say and do in different, concrete, particular situations as they emerge in the day-to-day business of ordinary living. Here we wish to emphasize knowing not so much what to say, but what to do. We are all familiar with the fact that people express their meaning in and through speaking and writing, but we are much less familiar with the fact that peo-ple also express meanings in and through schemes of bodily gestures and behaviors. The failure to appreciate and properly evaluate the role of embodied meanings conceals an even more important difference between our knowing and doing.

In the preceding section I drew attention to the difference between what people do and why they do it. Culture – the set of symbolic schemes that motivate people to believe and behave the way they do – is not only a set of known schemes, but also a set of motivational or effective schemes of meanings. Our cycles of knowing are distinguishable from our cycles of doing, or the habits of our minds are different than the habits of our hearts. It is one thing to plan and project a reasonable course of actions, but quite another to execute it. Just as people do not become piano players or golfers by reading books, they do not become generous, caring, and courageous individuals by studying those who have acquired such virtues. Athletic skills and moral virtues are 'known' in the fuller sense of knowing in and through the repeated performance and gradual acquisition of such habits. What courage means can be apprehended in and through the actions of courageous people who express its meaning by actually doing courageous acts. Just as actors incarnate meanings in the postures and gestures of the roles they play in staged dramas, people also embody meanings in the particular cultural roles they play within their social order. Such cultural meanings cannot be seen, but they can be interpreted in and through the particular ways that people operate and cooperate with one another as members of a cultural community.

Besides interpreting the embodied meaning of particular people playing particular roles in a cultural community, there is the much more complex and difficult meaning to be interpreted and evaluated in the way the society as a whole unites and organizes itself in and through such repeating patterns of roles, tasks, and goals. In the example in chapter 3 of the person going to the butcher or baker to buy a particular product, the actual performance of a particular baker selling and of a particular customer buying is just one single event in a system of similar exchanges being repeated by millions of other particular people in their own concrete places and times. Such singular exchanges are part of a vast ordering that cannot be apprehended, explained, and evaluated except by social scientists who have developed a systematic understanding of how singular economic exchanges participate in the more extensive recurring economic schemes. There is a significant difference between a person deciding to buy this particular type of bread or cut of meat and a person understanding and evaluating the economic order through which millions of different types of objects are produced by millions of workers for potential consumers.

This contrast between particular desired objects, such as bread and meat, and the economic ordering that generates the flow of such particular goods brings to light a fundamental distinction between two meanings of the term 'good' between the particular goods that people seek and the publicly ordered good that governs all the different economic activities, uniting them into cooperative schemes that will effectively sustain the flows of particular goods. Just what is this public order or 'good of order'? To understand the good of order, we must shift from a common-sense patterning of knowing into a theoretical perspective.[13] In the practical, common-sense pattern, the butcher and baker as well as their customers are able to understand and evaluate the flow of economic goods only insofar as these particular goods are related to their own buying and selling, to their own personal advantage or disadvantage. Economists, on the other hand, want to understand how to correlate the buying and selling of any and all sellers and buyers as they are related to one another throughout the community. This contrast between common-sense and theoretical knowing is analogous to the different but potentially complementary perspectives between the way the ordinary people perceive the movement of the sun, earth, and moon and the way Newton was able to correlate these same movements through his universal gravitational theory. Both perspectives may be objectively correct, but they are significantly different contexts of meanings. To integrate them, we must know how theoretical, explanatory correlations ground, generalize, and mediate the particular descriptive correlatives that relate the movements of different planets to the sensory-motor experiences of human knowers. Similarly, there is a remarkable difference in knowing particular goods as they are related to our own evaluative choosing and those same goods as they are systematically produced by an economic ordering that integrates all the various roles and tasks of producers, buyers, and sellers into a functioning whole that will satisfy or dissatisfy the economic needs of the whole community.

To carry this analysis somewhat further, let me differentiate the economic ordering of goods into short and long-term schemes and analyze how such cycles interact with one another. In the example of buying a loaf of bread, the baker sells you bread that was distributed to him by the wholesalers, who in turn bought it from some central bakery. The bakery produced the bread, first, by purchasing the building and equipment needed to make the bread and, then, by buying the ingredients required to bake bread. Ingredients like flour can be traced back to the wheat growers and those who store and mill the wheat. In other words, there is a series of interrelated steps that have to be taken in order for the wheat that was sown and harvested to end up on the family table as bread to be consumed. At each step there are various tasks requiring certain skills that must be performed to complete the process of transforming so much wheat into so much bread.[14] At each stage in this productive process there are various means employed – factories, equipment, machines, light, heat, power, transportation – that form an integral part of the economic process but do not enter into the product itself, since they are only the 'means' for making products. These 'means,' such as machines for grinding wheat into flour and trucks for transporting it, are not objects that are desirable in themselves; rather, they are desirable because they accelerate the successive steps that are required in the total productive cycle. There are, therefore, two cycles that operate in an economic order. The first is the more familiar productive cycle that generates a regular recurring flow of the different products that are bought and sold in the marketplace, and there is the much less familiar cycle of the means that are produced not for ordinary consumption, but to be sold to the people who produce consumer goods. This cycle serves to sustain and/or accelerate the regular flow of goods and services that are to be sold and consumed. Since this second cycle is less familiar, a few examples from the course of history will help us realize why this cycle is actually the more important one to identify.

Simple examples can be seen in such activities as the production of spears, knives, fishing nets, and similar tools. People take time to fashion spears, forge knives, and make fishing nets not because such things are desirable in themselves, but because hunters and fishermen are intelligent and know that their need for food is a recurring need and spears and nets will serve that recurring need in a practical and effective manner. While particular fish and meat are consumed, the spears and nets perdure to sustain a regular flow of desirable objects. Similarly, the domestication of animals and the invention of plows, harnesses, and new modes of farming significantly accelerated the planting-harvesting cycle of food production. Such improved farming methods provided medieval society with surpluses of wheat which not only could be stored and bartered, but could also provide the conditions for the development of small towns and new trading routes, which in turn created new roles and tasks for workers to perform. These economic trends eventually transformed the medieval modes of making a living; they made possible new productive and distributive economic cycles that in turn generated a wide variety of new modes and manners of living. The most striking changes came in the Renaissance, as Europe shifted from an economic order based primarily on agrarian modes of making a living to more commercial modes based on a widespread use of money. This shift has been characterized as the transformation of a pre-market economy into a market economy, in which there emerged a major differentiation between labor and capital, which in turn set the stage for the even more remarkable changes in production and distribution that is familiarly known as the industrial revolution.

The word 'revolution' may be misleading since it tends to suggest that the industrial revolution established new economic schemes of production and distribution which opposed or broke away from prior cycles of production and distribution. However, these new industrial cycles depended on, and emerged from, the prior economic schemes, just as Newton's calculus emerged from, and was dependent on, Descartes's coordinate geometry. The industrial revolution was a development from prior cyclical orders of production and distribution, not a reversal.[15] And like all development, it brought the past into the present in a way that established a continuity with the past economic cycles, but it also transformed them in significant ways as it changed the economic roles people performed, the tasks that had to be accomplished in performing these roles, the new products that resulted from them, and the goals that they intended to achieve in and through their cooperative performance. There were also some important changes in attitudes and motives that emerged in this new economic order which will be discussed later.

To underscore my general theme here: economic development occurs not primarily in the productive and distributive process itself, but in the economic scheme of activities that accelerates and transforms the range of the productive capacity of the society. Just as the making of fish nets speeds up the capacity to catch fish, the making of more efficient fish nets speeds it up even more. If a machine can make fish nets ten times faster and with ten times fewer laborers, not only is there greater production of fish nets and more fish catching, but there are workers who are now free to do different tasks. Such a development can be taken a step further if a machine is designed that can make fish net machines. The point is that economic schemes develop in two different ways: by organizing the people who produce goods in more effective ways (division of labor, mass produc-tion, etc.) and by changing the very means of production itself. The latter development will result in long-term changes that are not predictable; the former developments can be foreseen and planned because, for the most part, they require not new discoveries, but new ways of organizing old dis-coveries.[16]

My reason for making this very basic distinction is to point to a general development in human history that was going forward at the time of the industrial revolution during the eighteenth and nineteenth centuries of Western history. In the early chapters I suggested that the scientific revolu-tion of the seventeenth century may be the single most important histori-cal event of the last two thousand years. During that period the development of mathematics and physics moved from a descriptive to an explanatory stage, which resulted in a differentiation between the descrip-tive, practical world of everyday living and the remarkably different theo-retical world of highly intelligible but non-imaginable meanings. These discoveries of the seventeenth century were further developed and spread in the eighteenth century throughout the intellectual world of England and Europe, thereby conditioning the major cultural expansion of the Enlightenment. At the same time, the economic ordering of production and distribution was transformed by the industrial revolution, first in England and then expanding into Europe and America during the eigh-teenth and nineteenth centuries. The history of how scientific discoveries had an impact on economic productivity during this period is a task for a specialized historian, but I would like to discuss briefly one example that will serve to show how the human sciences can be integrated with the natu-ral sciences.

The example is the rise of the technology of heat power as it evolved primarily in England during the eighteenth century.[17] What is so significant about the development of heat power is its relation to the emergence of the science of thermodynamics, on the one hand and, on the other, the extraordinary impact it had on the emerging industrial revolution, producing long-term effects on the production and distribution of a vast number of products which elevated the standard of living of many people. What is especially interesting about this example is that it corrects our tendency to consider the long-term theoretical interest of scientists in explaining the cosmic order as independent of the short-term practical interests of the inventors who construct the machines that transform our ways of working and living. There is an important distinction between practical and theoretical patterns of knowing, but there is also a complementarity, and it is magnificently illustrated in the interplay between the series of attempts to build a more efficient heat engine and the emergence of an autonomous science of heat. The history of this interplay between science and technology and the various reciprocal contributions that practicing engineers and theoretical scientists made to each other's fields is a long, complex, and fascinating study. My purpose here is to draw attention to several general methodological issues that are illustrated in that history.

In outlining major events in the history of physics, I mentioned the shift from Newtonian conception of force to the Einsteinian conception of energy, or the shift from $F = ma$ to $E = mc^2$. I also pointed out that the pivotal discoveries in thermodynamics between the times of Newton and Einstein changed the scientist's understanding of the cosmic ordering of the universe. The Newtonian world-order tended to be closed and static, while the new thermodynamic ordering was more open and dynamic. The same contrast between static and dynamic systems can be found in two different ways of thinking about machines. There are machines like levers, pulleys, clocks, and wheel barrows that are used to move bodies from one position to another without effecting any significant change in the bodies being moved. But there are other types of machines that work by transforming one form of energy into quite different forms, with these second forms of energy providing the power to do work. This is how a heat engine works as it transforms the stored chemical energy of coal into the energy of heat and light. The heat and light then transform water into steam at high pressures, which in turn drive a piston, thereby converting thermal energy into the mechanical energy that drives the piston up and down. This-up-and down motion creates a vacuum in a pipe which is then capable of sucking water up from the mines where coal is being excavated. Or the piston can be connected to a rod that spins a wheel which can perform a variety of different tasks in textile factories, lumber mills, tool-making factories, coal mining, and other industries that emerged during the industrial revolution. Thus, the gradual perfection of a cycling heat engine – primarily by James Watt and other engineers – accelerated the production schemes of a wide variety of industries, thus multiplying the power to produce economic goods in a vast range of different fields. The same heat machine also significantly accelerated the entire distribution schemes of these economic goods as the engines were fitted into steamships, which significantly accelerated the national and international delivery and exchange of goods from one international market to another. Such widespread transformations changed the roles, tasks, goals, and daily routines of millions of human workers. If, instead of the piston in the heat engine rotating a rod that then performs some mechanical work, the rod turns an electric generator, then we have electric power that can be sent through wires to do mechanical work in running machines in homes, factories, businesses, etc. The same power can also be transformed into light and heat.

From this brief description of how a major transformation can take place in the economic ordering of production and distribution within a social order, I want to make three observations. First, the example illustrates how long-term developments in scientific thinking can cooperate with short-term changes in practical cycles of working people to bring about major shifts in the flow of human history. The more important changes are not in the productive working cycles of different communities, but in the 'means' by which societies produce goods. Heat engines are bought not by ordinary consumers, but by the industries that use them to transform and accelerate the production of goods and services. Major economic advances arise primarily from the people who supply the producers with their means of production. Ordinary people buy plows and wrenches to do work; they do not buy machines that make plows and wrenches, nor do they buy machines that make machines that make tools, etc. There is a basic distinction between long-term consequences and short-term ones, between inventing a new mouse trap and discovering an internal combustion engine. My second observation is that the gradual perfection of the heat engine was coordinated with the discovery of a new scientific world-order. Because the natural scientists were gradually advancing in their ability to explain how the universe works, the engineers were able to set up human economic cycles that worked in a way that was analogous to the way the natural order operated. The example exemplifies how the natural science of physics can be integrated with the human, explanatory science of economics, which deals primarily with universal economic schemes as they operate in a series of successive historical situations. Historical scholars deal with the concrete, particular details of those successive situations. It is the business of moral metaphysics to explain how all three contexts can be integrated in the more comprehensive and basic context of historical finality.

My third observation is that our example illustrates how decisions made two and three hundred years ago can set up recurrent cycles whose consequences are present and operative in our own lives. Certain economic roles, whose tasks require certain skills so that certain goals can be achieved, are operating in our lives because of choices made by people and communities many years ago. The past continues to live in the present, predetermining in many different ways the conditions under which we make our personal choices. These preconditions are for the most part unknown to the people making these choices. As Hegel put it, history takes place behind our backs. This does not mean that the consequences of those prior historical choices necessarily determine our choices, but it does mean that in varying degrees these past historical choices precondition and predispose us to choose and live in certain ways. Our present short-term choices are being made in the context of many different long-term historical undercurrents, which flow into and permeate our living in all sorts of unsuspected and unknown ways.

There is also the complementarity between social scientists and historical scholars in moving from descriptive history toward explanatory history. The short-term common-sense contexts in which people live are preconditioned by long-term historical currents which continue to influence these short-term lived contexts. For historians to explain any given historical context, they must interpret and evaluate that context within the larger historical horizon which includes the long-term trends that social scientists study. This means that historians are dependent on social scientists as they attempt to move beyond historical descriptions of what happened to an explanatory history of why it happened. Social scientists, on the other hand, are dependent on historians to discover what actually happened; while long-term trends predispose a community to behave in certain ways, they do not determine what particular people do. There is, therefore, a complementarity between the scholarly activities of historians and social scientists, just as there is an analogous collaborative effort between scientists and philosophers who are attempting to answer the basic question of the ultimate value of human history. To move ahead in answering this question, let me now return to the distinction between good and value.

People have spontaneous desires for sweaters, but they do not desire textile industries. Yet it is the textile industry that produces the sweater they intend to buy. Here are two distinct meanings of good: there is the good object , a sweater, as it is spontaneously desired, and there is the same particular object as a product of the textile industry. The textile industry is a good, but it is a good that must be understood as a vast multitude of people playing roles, cooperating, performing different but related tasks, and seeking certain goals. The difference between these two goods is the difference between concrete, particular goods that people desire and the systematically ordered good that is also concretely operating through a complex system of cooperating members of an economic order.

The notion of value results from a combination of these two distinct notions of the good, as they are brought together in a personal choice. Value is the good, not as an object spontaneously desired, but as intelligently understood, judged, and chosen. The ordinary consumer purchasing a sweater does not know that sweater as part of an ordered good any more than the ordinary person observing the mist rising from a pond knows the rising mist as part of a thermodynamic world-order. How do ordinary consumers desire, evaluate, deliberate, and choose particular products as valuable objects to be purchased and possessed? The answer depends on our distinction between immanently generated knowledge and knowledge based on belief. Most people, whether they are highly trained professors or textile workers, base their decisions on belief, not on immanently generated knowledge. Such choices can be quite reasonable, but they can also be mistaken.

This same distinction between choices based on belief and those that proceed from an intelligently apprehended understanding of the good of order also underscores the difference between a short-term and a long-term context of meanings and values. We make choices within the context of our personal and communally lived meanings and values, but those meanings and values are conditioned by the long-term historical trends that provide the condition under which and through which we deliberate and decide. The challenge for the human community is to bring those long-term historical currents out of the background of the meanings and values that precondition our deliberating and deciding and into the foreground of our knowing and choosing. To explain how we may proceed to achieve such a goal in a methodical manner, we need to transform the theme of ourselves as cultural knowers and choosers in the light of the distinction between the good as experienced, the good as intelligibly ordered, and the good as evaluated and chosen.

I have defined culture as the motivating ground on which the members of social order make their decisions. If the institutional schemes of roles, tasks, and goals define how communities operate and cooperate, their cultural schemes explain why they choose, and have chosen, to organize their communal living in the concrete ways in which they cooperate. Now if we apply the distinction between the producers of an economy and the means by which the producers generate an economic order to the realm of culture, we can articulate a basic methodological procedure for critically controlling the development and decline of cultural contexts of meanings and motives as they emerge and operate in the unfolding of the human historical drama in successive cultural stages.

The distinction between economic producers and the means by which they generate an economic order is an application of the basic distinction that has been at work throughout this study – the distinction between the operations by which we know and choose and the contents that are known and chosen through those operations. Applying this distinction to the topic of culture, we can differentiate the cultural meanings and motives that make up a people's way of living from the operations through which those cultural meanings and motives were developed, along with the many different ways those meanings and motives were and are expressed. Such expressions are through ordinary speech and stories, but they are also in the actual 'doings' of people, in their various and multiple forms of behavior, rituals, ceremonies, songs, dances, as well as in all their private and public buildings, their streets and cities, highways and seaports. Human culture comprises the totality of all those meanings and modes of expressions.

Human culture is distinct from human nature. People are born with natures, but culture is what they make in and through their natures. Nature is the constant, and culture is the genetic and dialectical variable. All people are by nature knowers, choosers, and lovers, which implies that human history is the series of cultures that have been produced, developed, and distributed through what people have known, chosen, and loved, as well as what they have refused to know, choose, and love. On the basis of this distinction, scholars of history and human scientists can study human history as the history of cultural achievements, while philosophers can study operations by and through which the history of culture was and is being advanced or allowed to decay. The philosophic way to differentiate cultures is to know our own knowing and choosing and both how those activities function to reveal different realities to us and, at the very same time, how they also function to constitute our being and motivate our choosing and loving. These cognitive, constitutional, and motivational functions of knowing and choosing operate in every culture and in every period of history. We can mark off major periods in the history of culture by the way different historical communities control these functions of knowing and choosing, or by the different methods that cultures have developed to govern their personal and collective making of history.[18]

In the first period of human history, cultural communities were certainly able to know, choose, and love, but they had not developed any special reflective controls over these operations. The second stage emerged with the Greek philosophers, who knew their own knowing and choosing in a somewhat systematic way and conceived these meanings in metaphysical terms, employing logic to control the way they reasoned with these meta-physical terms, and with logic they were able to focus on the contents of knowing, not on the operations through which the knowing is generated. As a result, philosophical scholars tended to concentrate on the proposi-tions of their system and not on the operations of their own knowing and choosing. In the third stage, beginning with Descartes and Kant, attention shifted from the metaphysical questions to the prior epistemological ques-tions. In the previous chapters, we have discussed how moving from cogni-tional questions through epistemological to metaphysical problems permitted us to control both the development of metaphysical and moral positions based on these prior epistemological and cognitional positions. Such a procedure defines what we mean by 'method.'

Method is a normative procedure for reaching a goal. If the goal is to determine the clarity and coherence of our propositions, then the method to use is logic. But if the goal is to discover whether we are an authentic knower, then we need a method for knowing our knowing, knowing its basic objective, and knowing how to advance toward that objective and, at the same time, how to reverse dialectically the various biases that block advance and bring about decline. The same method can be extended to appropriate ourselves as authentic choosers. Such a method does not inval-idate the legitimacy of logic as a method; rather, it uncovers its foundation and also why it has such a limited role in dealing with basic questions. This same method not only reveals and makes possible the integrated collabora-tion of natural and social sciences with historians; it also discloses that the central problem in achieving authenticity as a knower and a chooser lies in distinguishing between the short- and long-term cultural cycles of meaning and motives as they are operating both in the concrete and lived meanings of a culture and in the reflective and deliberative procedures of theoreti-cians in understanding and evaluating their own and others' lived mean-ings. The basic problem in such reflecting and deliberating is to appropriate the scale of values that has been inherited from the past and is still operating, not only in the personal, practical roles and goals people perform but also, and more significantly, in the public ordering of the institutional schemes that organize the many different ways that the mem-bers of a cultural community cooperate or fail to cooperate in seeking their common destiny.

5   Third Ethical Question

The first ethical question was, What am I doing when I am choosing? The second question was, Why do I choose it? Our answer to this question focused on the motives that ground our choices and the various cultural and historical contexts within which we make our decisions. The third question is, What do I choose when I make a choice? In the light of the cultural and historical contexts just articulated, we can answer this question with a brief, but surprising, answer. Whenever we make a choice we commit ourselves to play a personal role in the cultural and historical world-order in which we are living. In the examples of buying a sweater or loaf of bread, the buying and selling are part of a vast economic ordering which involves millions of people playing various roles, performing their respective tasks, and seeking their own personal goals. The purpose of the interplay of all these roles goes beyond the personal goals of the individuals involved to include the larger public order that embraces and patterns all the various roles into a cooperative effort organized for the benefit and well-being of all the people. Whether or not a particular economic order is operating to the advantage or disadvantage of a particular community, the point is that the purpose of this order surpasses the particular personal goals of the individuals who contribute to, and participate in, the overall order. In purchasing a sweater, the purchaser is cooperating in a social order that is the result of decisions made centuries before. This also implies that every present decision-maker is participating in various ways in setting up the conditions for future human choices. Every social order participates in the larger historical world-order since it receives, from prior historical communities, public and cultural institutional orders which it further develops or distorts, and thereby transmits to future societies its contributions to historical finality. In addition, every social order takes a position with respect to the overall cosmic order of horizontal and vertical finality.

In discussing the heat engines as part of the technological advances that transformed nineteenth-century social and economic orderings, we suggested ways in which the Western social and economic orders entered into a new relation with the cosmic order. Cultural communities have always been dependent in various ways on the natural order and its seasonal cycles. But in the gradual unfolding of the human historical drama, that relationship has been significantly altered and perhaps no more dramatically than during the emergence of the industrial age when communities learned how to control the flow of heat and electrical power. Throughout history, human communities have been constructing economic orders that transform the potencies of nature into different forms of practical living, thereby transforming and subsuming the natural order into becoming part of their own higher human orders. The more advanced these communities are in the understanding of the natural order, the more control they are able to exert in making natural processes serve the human community. The goal of the human community, however, is not primarily to set up social orders. Rather, it is to construct cultural orders that will permit and encourage the community's members to discover their own authentic identities as disinterested knowers who desire to know being. As well, the goal of the human community is to discover the members' identities as authentic choosers who are aware of their cultural identity as an historically inherited identity, which is or is not in tune with their own unrestricted desire to choose the most valuable social order that they can cooperatively establish through a more comprehensive and concrete understanding of the development and decline that is going forward in their cultural community.

What we choose when we make choices may be concrete particular goods, but these choices also make us participants in our own social and cultural order as that order is at present operating in ways that may or may not be in tune with the authentic order of the entire universe of being. Our final moral reflection concerns the question of human freedom.

6   Human Freedom

There is a further dimension to this problem of becoming an authentic chooser, namely, the problem of our freedom in executing what we know and value to be better ways of being and behaving personally and collectively. Our moral conscience is a conscious correlation not just between our knowing and choosing, but also between what we choose to do and what we actually do. The much more serious and intractable moral problem is that we do not do what we know we ought to do. Smoking provides a good example. Millions of Americans smoke. We do not have to educate them about the verified statistical correlation between smoking and cancer; for the most part, they believe the experts. Smokers know why they should not smoke, and we do not have to convince them to try to stop smoking – most have already tried and failed. They are free to stop, but they are unable to actualize their freedom. Smokers are essentially free to exist as non-smokers, but they are unable to bring their being as non-smokers into existence. And so smokers have to exist in an inauthentic way since their actual recurring schemes of smoking cannot be reconciled with what they know and would choose as a more valuable way to behave. Such people exist in a self-contradictory way. They may escape the contradiction by seeking various forms of rationalizing, but they cannot completely silence their questions. Unless they meet their own conscious demand, a certain unease accompanies such rationalizing. Thus, the spontaneous demand emerging from our own evaluating and deliberating is that we actually do what we think is truly worthwhile doing.

Freedom is not indeterminism. Quite the opposite: freedom involves determinism, but it is we who do the determining, or it is we who ought to determine the worthwhileness of ourselves as self-choosing beings. Ironically, to be free is to oblige ourselves to become a truly valuable self by doing truly valuable deeds. Only then, as Aristotle said, will we be a true friend to ourselves and become a source of other people's admiration and affection.

The same dialectical tension between choosing and doing which emerges in our personal lives also characterizes our communal living. Political leaders already know more intelligible and worthwhile ways to arrange our social order, but they also know that such plans and policies are impractical. By 'impractical' they mean that such courses of actions are actually practical, but they have to be agreed upon and chosen by the governing body, and there are not sufficient votes to pass such policies. There are vested interest groups within the body politic that will block these truly worthwhile policies, because they do not serve their own interests. Such interest groups are free to back such policies, but they refuse to actualize the making of a more valuable social order. Just as self-knowers try to make reasonable their unreasonable courses of action, so dominant social classes rationalize their unwillingness to construct a more intelligible and valuable social order because it might be disadvantageous to their own way of living. The evidence of such behavior in history is massive; groups of people who initiated and sustained conditions for a successful and truly valuable social order will frequently change from a creative minority into a dominant minority that refuses to adapt to changing social conditions.[19]

Human freedom is a radical problem, and just how radical it is can be disclosed if we again ask, Why do people fail to do what they know they ought to do? The biases we form are simply our own elaborate and very effective cover-ups and the cultural rationalizations that we have inherited and will hand on to the next generation. What makes this problem so radical is that it cannot be solved by a better education or a more comprehensive intellectual enlightenment. Nor can it be solved by assimilating the moral and metaphysical theory that I have been setting forth here. The intrinsic tension exists between what we know and what we choose to do in light of that knowing because our willingness to act in a certain way is an acquired, not a spontaneous, willingness. For example, you may spontaneously desire to play the piano, but you cannot play the piano spontaneously, nor can you learn to play the piano simply by reading books on how to play the piano. You must practice until you have acquired the habit of playing. Once you have formed the habit, then you do not need to be persuaded to play, nor do you have to persuade yourself, since you have acquired, beyond the natural spontaneous desire to play, the newly formed spontaneities that flow from such acquired habits. People are not born naturally courageous or cowardly. Such personal characteristics are acquired. Similarly, people are born, not with a culture, but with a nature. Culture comes from the acquired habits of meanings and motivations that we develop by growing up and living within culture. Finally, we are not born free. We are born choosers, but we are not born with habits of choosing. We must develop the habits that will make our choices more or less effectively free. There is, therefore, a fundamental difference between our potency to be free – the essential freedom that comes from our natures – and the effective freedom we have to win by doing what we know we ought to do. Potential freedom becomes actual freedom only when we make it actual. In doing so, we bring our potential being into actual existence.[20]

To solve the problem of personal and collective bias, we need the love that would provide us with spontaneous willingness. One of the most obvious effects of love is the new spontaneities it gives us to do things for the person we love. Our problem is not choosing to do good things for one person, but choosing wisely and willingly within the whole ordering of history. To solve the problem of evil or bias, we need a new ordering of our cultural and historical way of being. In short, the problem arises as a moral problem, but there is no moral solution. Only through some higher form of human living can the problem of moral weakness be resolved. The next chapter will raise the possibility of a religious solution to this problem of moral impotence.

7   Summary

This chapter not only extends the method of self-appropriation into the field of ethics, but also reveals the sources of certain key disputes in twentieth-century philosophy. Such issues are numerous and difficult and beyond the scope of this chapter which attempts to articulate how the disputed issues may be dealt with in a methodological way. Most of these philosophical problems stem from the way the traditional Scholastic philosophy evolved in the late medieval and early Renaissance periods.

I have suggested that the traditional distinction between metaphysics and ethics needs to be reordered. While presupposing and conditioned by metaphysics, ethics is in itself a broader and more comprehensive study than metaphysics. Implicit in this traditional distinction between metaphysics and ethics is the distinction between intellect and will, which are considered to be the defining faculties of the human soul. In the method I have been following, the concrete, conscious relations between these two faculties can be empirically, normatively, and critically grounded as you differentiate the ways in which as a knower you advance to become a chooser. Just as metaphysics grows out of knowing your own knowing, so ethics can unfold by knowing your own choosing and the ways choosing operates to subsume and carry knowing to a higher plane of perfection.

In addition to reordering the relations between intellect and will, as well as reversing the relation of metaphysics and ethics, this methodical approach brings to philosophical attention the fact that moral choices are made within a cultural context or horizon which has been and is assimilated by all cultural choosers from their earliest conscious living. This cultural context is mediated primarily through the language of symbolic forms. This focus on cultural ethics, done in a methodological manner, has some significant consequences which I shall summarize in four parts.

First, the method of self-appropriation makes it clear that, while choosing is a higher form of knowing, it still depends on the lower activities of knowing that occur on the first three levels. The 'ought' of your moral choosing is a consciously experienced correlation between your knowing and your choosing.

Second, the method brings to light the essential role of motivational meanings and values and the distinction between judgments of fact and judgments of value, which leads to the difficult problems of understanding and judging your feelings, and the way these emotional meanings are communicated through various symbolic forms. This in turn opens up the problem of 'symbolic reasoning,' or the logic of images and feelings, which becomes the central problem in appropriating, not what you choose but why you choose the way you do. The simple answer is culture. Not only does culture provide you with a context of meanings, but cultural meanings also provide the motivating values conditioning and guiding your decision-making.

Third, the methodical appropriation of your choosing self discloses the central role that believing plays in assimilating a cultural horizon. The word 'belief,' or 'faith,' is usually associated with religious truths and practices that a person accepts on the basis of religious authority. But most of what scientists know they know by trusting in the knowledge and truths acquired by other scientists, who are assumed to have been in a position to discover such knowledge and to have communicated their findings in a truthful way. The foundational reason for trusting in someone else's truths is that truths are public as well as private.

This chapter extends the role of belief into moral living. Everyday you read and hear about hundreds of events, accidents, births, deaths, marriages, scientific discoveries at home and abroad. In varying degrees, these events become part of your storehouse of knowledge, yet not one of these events has emerged from your own personal experiencing, understanding, or judging. To know your own knowing and choosing, in the way these seven chapters have set forth, results in immanently generated knowledge, but such immanently generated knowledge is only a tiny fraction of what you know.

The fact that the cultural horizon within which we deliberate, evaluate, and choose is composed of meanings and values that we know only by belief may surprise many Americans. Among Tocqueville's remarkable insights about America is the line: 'Descartes is the least read but most practiced philosopher.' In America, people believe that they do not believe what other people tell them; they assume that they form their ideas and choose their values through their own personally generated meanings and values. The American cultural horizon leads Americans to assume that they do not know and choose within a vast context of inherited motives that have been symbolically mediated and assimilated by them. Just how that cultural horizon conditions and motivates this or that person or this or that group of people is another problem. My point is that moral decisions are made within a cultural horizon, and that cultural horizons are communicated and assimilated as a set of beliefs. This does not necessarily mean that these beliefs are false or misleading – quite the opposite.

In chapter 5, I established precisely how you can make a true judgment and know what, in fact, is or is not. Beliefs can be based on someone else's true judgment precisely because a person is capable of making true judgments and sharing them with others. Believing is not blind trust in the word of another person; it is the reasonable assessment of whether the other person has carried out the required steps to reach a true judgment. We are cultural choosers who deliberate and evaluate within a cultural horizon that we have assimilated and accepted through belief and trust. The defining character of any cultural horizon will be the scale of values that has been received, assimilated, and practiced by the members of that cultural community. This implies that the cultural scale of values which sets the conditions for you to make choices has, for the most part, been inherited from past cultural communities.

This brings us to the fourth issue, namely, to be a cultural chooser is to be a historical chooser. Because every chooser has the potential to move toward an unrestricted objective, any cultural community may be critically evaluated as authentic or inauthentic insofar as that cultural community sets the conditions for its members to differentiate between the proximate goals the culture seeks at present and the remote, unrestricted objective that choosers naturally desire. In other words, the scale of values that is operating in the actual performances of any historical community is either open or closed to the remote goal of human history. Just as the previous chapter established the conditions for being an authentic, objective knower, this chapter specifies the conditions for being an authentic, objective chooser. However, to critically evaluate the basic cultural orientation of any community is a problem in historical research, interpretation, and evaluation.

In chapter 6, I established an integrating heuristic structure for understanding and judging the history of human knowers; in this chapter, I sketched the method for subsuming and extending this integrating structure to a history of human choosers. Such a moral history depends on appropriating, first, what you are doing when you are choosing; second, why you choose to behave the way you do; third, what you actually become by doing it; and, fourth, why you so frequently fail to behave the way you know you ought to behave (moral impotence).

8

Religion

The previous chapters described the successive steps by which you can transcend yourself as you move from being a sensor to being an understander, from an understander to a judger, from a judger to a believer, chooser, and lover. These movements are not only successive modes of being, but also enlarging and encompassing modes of being where each prior mode of being is assimilated into the higher stage. This higher integration must accommodate itself to the lower by respecting and accepting the advances of the preceding lower stage. In these sublating transformations, we witnessed a significant advance over traditional Scholastic philosophy.

Traditionally, epistemology and cognitional theory were derived from metaphysics, while metaphysical meanings were controlled by the method of logic. Metaphysical meanings also provided the terms and relations for formulating specialized theories, such as physics, biology, and psychology. Ethics was also conceived in the context of metaphysics. In the first six chapters, however, we developed a cognitional theory and then constructed an epistemological and metaphysical theory based on the cognitional theory. The cognitional theory was controlled not by logic, but by an appeal to your own conscious experiences, inviting you to know your own knowing and to know the ways in which your immediate conscious experiences can be mediated through your own understanding and judging. This mediation or appropriation reveals the way that you, as a knower, can keep surpassing yourself in each successive cycle of knowing. For this reason, the method of self-appropriation or self-knowing can be referred to as a transcendental method.[1]

The key step in learning this method is to discover that, in every correct judgment, you are not asserting what you think is so; you are actually affirming a fact that is true or probably true independently of your saying so. Such independent judgments commit you to a realm of factual realities that other knowers may in turn verify for themselves. Even the most personal or private facts, if they are facts, are public and communally verifiable. This leads to the surprising, and, at first, paradoxical, fact that to be a truly objective knower of what is so, you must be faithful to your own immediate, spontaneous desire to know and its objective. Your desire to know provides you with the immanent norms and directives for knowing what reality is, including the reality that constitutes you. The norm for being an objective knower is achieved not by being a faithful observer of the sensible realities surrounding you, but by mediating such immediate, sensible realities through your own acts of understanding and judging.

On the other hand, if you accept the immediate public domain of sensible objects as what makes knowing real objective knowing, then understanding and judging are activities that simply rubber-stamp the reality already present and known on the sensible level. But if the objectivity of knowing depends on being open to the intentional and objective field revealed in and through questioning, then the immediate, sensible field provides only one part of a three-part field of objectivity: sensible or empirical objectivity; intelligible or normative objectivity; critical or absolute objectivity. In appropriating these three aspects of objectivity, you discover the tension between them and the ways in which you can mistake and overemphasize empirical objectivity as the norm and critical base for being an objective knower. In distinguishing these three aspects of objectivity, you realize that there are three opposed views of what reality is, and from that can follow three different views on what objectivity is. The transcendental method of self-appropriation reveals that to be an objective knower involves a continuous struggle between your present, actual knowing of self and your potentially known self, which can only be actualized by transcending your present, realized self. Truly authentic knowers are continually struggling knowers, always on the alert for further questions that will advance their accumulated knowing or reverse their mistaken assumptions and judgments. Further, authentic metaphysical knowers will be converted knowers who have reoriented themselves from their habitual, mistaken assumptions concerning what knowing is; what objective knowing is; and what is known when we know objectively. The same transcendental method that grounds an authentic metaphysics can be extended into a metaphysical ethics.

In the context of transcendental method, ethics goes beyond and subsumes metaphysics. To speak of the human person as a knower or rational animal, as was customary in the Scholastic tradition, is to speak abstractly about the human person. In more concrete terms, you are a chooser who exists in and through your choices, and you transcend your knowing selves when you choose. However, to appropriate yourself as an authentic or objective chooser is more complex and difficult than appropriating yourself as a authentic knower. The problem is that, in evaluating the worthwhileness of a course of action, you must make judgments of value in the context of a cultural scale of values, which you know not by your own immanently generated knowledge, but primarily by your cultural beliefs. Further, your cultural heritage is carried in a system of symbols which provides the motivating meanings that effectively ground and orient you in day-to-day decision-making. Being an authentic chooser is being able to evaluate how your decisions are advancing the progress of human history or undoing its decline. But in evaluating yourself and your cultural community, you find yourself faced with the radical problem of being unwilling to choose and execute the policies and courses of action that you know are in fact truly worthwhile. The problem is that you cannot provide yourself with sufficient motive or willingness unless you develop that willingness, but to do so takes time, and while you are taking the time, you must live with your unwillingness.

The problem is both personal and social. To solve it requires is a further transcendence that will make you willing to develop and execute more reasonable and valuable ways of cooperating with others. The most effective motive in making you a willing chooser is 'falling in love,' since love opens up a new and transformed context of living. In short, love transcends and changes your past attitudes, creates new spontaneities, reveals values never felt before, and provides motives for doing things that previously seemed neither possible nor worthwhile. The three different types of love – domestic, civic, and religious – are differentiated in terms of the subjects that are loved. In domestic love, a woman falls in love with a man, or vice versa; in civic love, we grow in the love of our political communities. But, who is the subject of religious love? The subject of religious love is unknown. How can you be in love with someone you do not know?

The traditional name for the unknown object of religious devotion is god.[2] The significant issue here is not how many gods there are, who they are, and what they do. These issues refer to answers that are given at different historical stages of human meaning. What is important to note, first, is the question about god and, second, that it is natural to ask such a question.[3]

1   Questions about God

Questioning transcends cultural stages and characterizes people at every stage in cultural history. Questioning is the initial movement of mind that takes you out of yourself and draws you into a quest for knowing what you do not yet know. The object of this quest is reality or being, and in correctly knowing any reality, you go beyond the possibly real to the actually real. You do so through a commitment to a reality that does not have to be, but does in fact exist because the conditions for its existence have been given, formed, and realized. If such contingent or conditioned realities do exist, the further, transcending question arises: Why do such contingent realities in fact exist, and exist in the different ways that they do? Is it worthwhile for these beings to be?

Your questioning carries you beyond the actual reality of things to the fuller reality of their worthwhileness. It is in apprehending and in appreciating their values that you discover that things do or do not exist in truly worthwhile ways. Such truly valuable realities that you come to know and value only serve to reveal that the final objective of your knowing and valuing is a further unknown, and will not be known until you have brought your questioning to rest and fulfilled all your desirings. God, then, can be defined heuristically and implicitly as the completely valuable objective of all your questioning and desirings that you do not yet know and have not yet loved. Further, the only way to be an authentic knower and an authentic chooser is to appropriate the foundational tension between the knowing and choosing being that you now are and the more intelligent and worthwhile person that you can make yourself come to be in virtue of your capacities.

Against this position, you may say with Pascal that this god of the philosophers, this god of metaphysicians and moralists, is not the god of Abraham, Isaac, and Jacob. Pascal's objection is partly correct since it points to a new sphere of human experience by suggesting that metaphysical experiences are not moral experiences, and moral experiences are not the same as religious experiences. What is already appropriated and established is that, as a moral chooser, you transcend your knowing self. Now what needs to be examined is how, as a religious lover, you can further transcend your choosing self. It is important to underscore that experiencing is not knowing. You may experience yourself understanding, judging, choosing, and loving without knowing what you are doing when you are knowing, choosing, and loving. Frequently, the term 'experience' is used to mean knowledge, as when we say that a person is inexperienced and will need considerable training before he or she is able to do some job satisfactorily. In such a context, experience means practical knowledge. As I have used the term in this study, experience means to be aware without attending, understanding, and judging that experience. Experience is an immediate, undifferentiated awareness. To know that immediate experience, it must be mediated through understanding and judging. Anyone who understands does so consciously; that person experiences his or her activity of understanding. But, as we have seen, understanding understanding is at least as difficult as trying to understand what Einstein understood.

We experience inwardly and outwardly and on many different levels of activities, and the difference between these inner and outer experiences, as well as the four levels of experience, are for most people a polymorphic, undifferentiated conscious field. This study began by inviting you to begin to differentiate inner and outer experiences by shifting attention from the contents to the operations that actualize these contents in very different ways. In moving on to the third and fourth levels of conscious activities, the purpose was to find the differences and relations among these functionally related activities, and to lead you into appropriating the many levels of your own being and the ways they can combine into different recurring patterns or schemes of meaning and choosing.

These conscious levels of knowing and choosing do not emerge in any set sequence, and usually all four levels are present and interacting simultaneously. To differentiate your own levels of experience is like listening to a motet or madrigal with four voices singing in different registers. To differentiate four simultaneously heard voices is difficult enough, but after attending to and differentiating their melodic, rhythmic, and tonal differences, you must go further and attend to their blending and integrating patterns which are producing the changing textures and harmonies that you are hearing. Similarly, your own field of conscious experience involves four levels of ongoing activities that can gradually be appropriated as remarkably different from, yet functionally related to, one another. The basis for the unity of these different levels is the transcending and transforming relations that each successive level engenders as it subsumes the lower levels.

I have continually emphasized the breakthrough of Renaissance science since it was this development that revealed in such a dramatic fashion the power of the intellect to surpass the sensible world and that began, with Descartes's philosophy, the shift from the theoretical world of science to the intentional world of the transcending knower. With Kierkegaard, Marx, Schopenhauer, and Nietzsche, attention shifted to the transcending chooser. Finally, with Scheler and other phenomenologists, the person as transcending lover also became a focus of philosophical attention. To appropriate these successive selves – knower, chooser, and lover – is to know how the interior world of philosophy keeps expanding both by incorporating the prior fields and by introducing new methods to pursue new intentional objectives.

The philosophical problem in this journey has become the problem of being an authentic knower, chooser, and lover, the problem of reconciling the spontaneous, immediate objectives of knowing, choosing, and loving with the mediated meanings and values of the different worlds that are made through these activities. Finally, a further and more complete transcendence emerges when authentic choosers fall in love with other persons and with their communities. But beyond loving any single person, beyond communal loving and even historical knowing and loving, there is the experience of a much stranger and more mysterious state of feelings when people find themselves in the presence of a totally other being. This experience of a totally transcendent reality can be called 'religious consciousness' or 'experience.' To appropriate your religious self is to ask, What am I doing when I am having a religious experience?

2   Religious Experience

In the Western tradition, reflection and evaluation of religious experience has usually taken place in the context of a community's beliefs about the tradition and origin of its religious stories, rituals, and doctrines. The tendency was to defend the reasonableness of such beliefs in the familiar precept of Augustine's 'faith seeking understanding.' But understanding tended to be identified with reasoning, and reasoning tended to be associated with syllogistic thinking, which in turn was oriented to establishing proofs for conclusions that could be demonstrated and defended against anyone who did not share those beliefs or who attempted to deny them. There was a tendency to think that religious beliefs could be translated into demonstrable conclusions which any reasoning person could and should judge to be true. The central truth was the existence of a god who revealed these truths or beliefs to a past historical community, who then handed them on through oral and/or written traditions, which may or may not have been under the authoritative control of a formally organized religious community or church. Since these truths were communicated by god to a specific person or community, the truths were divine and permanent and did not vary from one cultural period to another. Such truths were assumed to be transcultural and transhistorical; they were also static and immobile. Missing in this way of reasoning about faith was an appeal to the subject's own experience of reasoning, choosing, and loving. With the method we have been following, it is possible to go behind various people's religious beliefs and discover the common religious ground from which these different beliefs emerged.

Knowing engages a person on three different levels simultaneously and successively. The same is true of choosing, except that this activity engages four different operating levels of the chooser's being, all interacting and contributing to the activity of choosing. When we speak of experiencing a person, thing, or the world about us, we respond to such objects on all our conscious levels simultaneously. We have a spontaneous experience of ourselves and the world about us that is immediately conscious through wondering. However, it is not the inquisitive wonder that leads to insights on the second level, nor the reflective wonder which conditions judgments, nor the deliberative wonder that orients us to choices. Rather, it is the undifferentiated, elemental wonder which can be differentiated into these different, specialized levels of wondering. Our different levels of wondering become specialized as the concerns of the intending subject become differentiated. Thus, to appropriate yourself as a religious subject having religious experience, it is necessary to appreciate the radical openness of this elemental wondering in an immediate field that is not yet differentiated into the different worlds of experience we have discussed.

There are three notable difficulties in identifying and appropriating such religious experience. First, the notion of experience, like the notion of awareness, can be taken as referring to mediated knowledge, and not to the immediate awareness that precedes knowing. Experience, like consciousness, refers to an immediate, preconceptual, prejudgmental, preevaluative experiencing. Second, the term 'religious' is a term loaded with affective meanings that are personal, social, and historical, and that vary according to a person's cultural traditions. For centuries, people have been fighting wars about religion, and so it is usually discussed in an emotionally charged context. Third, 'religious experience' refers to an immediate, prelinguistic experience, and since clarity comes from illumination and formulation, the term 'religious experience' is undifferentiated and can only be approached indirectly or tacitly. This can be done by attempting to identify the engendering experiences behind various religious traditions which have developed as evaluative responses to, and expressions of, these engendering religious experiences.

Since the late nineteenth century and during this century, the field of religious studies has blossomed, and there are now significant publications that can be used to clarify the notion of religious experience. The most important and frequently cited study was done in the early part of this century, Rudolf Otto's *The Idea of The Holy*.[4] Instead of focusing on the nature and existence of god, or on religious morality, Otto attempts to describe the 'engendering religious experiences' that provided the sources for specific religious writings and practices. He characterizes these engendering experiences as an awareness of something 'mysterious' which is both 'tremendous and fascinating,' 'terrifying yet attractive.' It is like no other experience, and so he referred to it as an experience of the 'wholly other.' The religious term 'holy' refers to experiences that are utterly strange, that can make people shudder with fear as if they found themselves in the presence of an overwhelming and powerful reality or force that was felt to be superior to any natural thing in the entire universe. To emphasize that these experiences are not primarily abstract, rational experiences, but rather that they permeate the whole person, affecting even the neurophysiological system (causing goose bumps, shudders, etc.), Otto referred to these experiences as 'irrational.' But he also uses the term 'numinous' to suggest the overpowering surplus of feelings which transcended the rational and ethical aspects of ordinary human behavior. Similar characteristics are implied in the phrase, 'totally other.'

Besides Otto's work in the history of religions, which attempts to fix the core or essence of religious experience in the 'tremendous and fascinating mystery' that is 'totally other,' there have also been a number of interesting studies on the psychology of religious experience beginning with William James's classic, *The Varieties of Religious Experience.* A more recent study that may help to clarify and advance our appreciation and appropriation of religious experience is Abraham Maslow's *Religious Values and Peak-Experiences.*[5] This book was first published in 1964, but a new edition with a new preface was issued in 1970. The more recent preface is especially interesting since Maslow both summarizes his book and also offers a criticism of it in terms of reflections he made during the six years following the earlier publication. Unlike Otto's book, which is based mainly on Western biblical writings, Maslow's study is based primarily on data assembled from his own work as a clinical psychologist. Furthermore, while Maslow, like Otto, is trying to identify the 'essential core' of religious experiences, he is also concerned with overcoming the dichotomy between science and human values, especially religious values. In a word, Maslow is trying to establish a 'methodical' approach to the study of human values and especially religious values. He speaks of the need for scientists to develop for their society experimental norms for making choices from among many possible values. What humanists, artists, and religionists need, Maslow states, is 'the firm criteria of selection, which they now lack, to choose between the many value possibilities which clamor for belief, so many that the chaos may fairly be called valueless.' In the next two paragraphs, I shall sketch the major themes of Maslow, which will be followed by his own criticism of these themes.

Maslow proposed that the intrinsic core or essence of the 'high religions' emerges from a 'private, lonely, personal illumination, revelation, or ecstasy of some acutely sensitive prophet or seer.' It is because of such 'founding experiences' that the high religions refer to themselves as 'revealed religions.' In order to communicate this 'mystical experience' to the masses, the church officials tended to express such 'transcendent experiences' in various systems or codes of ordinances that regulate the religious beliefs and behavior of the church members. The result is that the original 'mystical experiences' tend to be neutralized and transformed into external symbols and ceremonies.

Maslow developed a tentative vocabulary of the mystic or prophet, as opposed to the religious 'legalist' or 'bureaucrat,' in order to contrast the sort of person who has mystical experiences with people who feel insecure, threatened, or overwhelmed at the thought of having such ecstatic experiences. Organized religion controlled by the religious legalist may suppress or discourage truly religious experiences among its members. Further, these mystical experiences have been and are now being studied by psychologists under the heading of 'peak-experiences.' The premise of such studies is that these 'illuminations' or 'mystical experiences' are not supernatural, nor are they rare experiences. Rather, these experiences are natural and are shared by many people, and others can be encouraged and taught to experience them. Finally, these non-supernatural 'peak-experiences' can be identified with religious happenings, and Maslow provides a brief description of twenty-five characteristics of these peak-experiences that traditionally have been associated with religious experiences.

In the preface to the more recent edition of his study of peak experiences, Maslow admits that in the earlier edition he was excessively critical of religious organizations and his arguments relied too heavily on individual experience. In the 1970 preface he writes that 'basic human needs can be fulfilled *only* by and through other human beings, i.e., society.' The need for belonging is itself a 'basic need.' Furthermore, in 1970 he views religious experience as a much broader category than he judged it to be in 1964. Besides 'peak-experiences,' there are also the 'plateau-experiences' and 'nadir-experiences,' which are also identifiable as religious experiences. Plateau-experiences are more 'serene and calm' than are the more sudden, miraculous, and awesome feelings characteristic of peak-experiences. More important, plateau-experiences have a cognitive and volitional quality to them and, therefore, are more under the control of the experiencing person, and may even be produced at will.

My intention here is to underscore that we are dealing with scientific research that has just begun taking the question of religious experience as a valid and serious research question, and that the need for methodical norms and procedures in the field is clearly recognized. My purpose is to begin to clarify those norms and procedures. To do this, I will turn to historical expressions of religious experience, first, among primitive religions, then, among biblical religions. Finally, I will focus on specifying the notion of stages in the history of religions.

3   Primitive Religion

There has been remarkable growth in the study of religious history, and especially in the field of primitive religions, in the past hundred years. Perhaps no other scholar has been able to summarize and communicate so effectively this extensive research into primitive and archaic religion than Mircea Eliade. A comparative historian of religion, Eliade espouses a phenomenological approach to the study of religion. His special gift has been to identify the transcultural structures in the religious myths and rituals of different religions of the same period and in the successive historical stages of religions. Equally important, he has reversed the basic meaning of myth from a fanciful, illusory explanation of the world and society to an archaic ontology that purports to present an absolute, true account of the intrinsic reality of all things, from the perspective of their origins or beginnings.[6] Such myths provide a people with an explanation of how and why things began to be. Because these myths account for the origin of the being of things, Eliade refers to them as 'ontological' stories whose meanings are expressed and communicated symbolically. In phenomenological language, Eliade's research may be described as a 'hermeneutics of retrieval': he attempts to recover the actual meaning and value of certain religions, insofar as those meanings and values were being lived by the people who recited and dramatically enacted them. Probably more than any other scholar of this century, Eliade is responsible for making people aware that knowing a community means understanding their myths, not in any abstract way, but as those myths were or actually are being lived by the people who have come to believe them by living and performing them. For Eliade, a myth can lose its 'lived meaning'; when it does it becomes just a story or tale that is no longer considered an 'ontology,' a 'real' story.

As a 'phenomenological' historian of religion, Eliade realizes that people 'live in language,' and the languages expressive of primitive religion are myth and ritual. Eliade is especially helpful in bringing out how dramatic gestures and rituals of archaic religions are expressive of meanings that are of 'surpassing value' to the people who perform them in cultic songs, dances, and dramas. Archaic religious ceremonies may be said to ritualize or dramatically enact the myths, while the myths explain the ritual. Primitive religious ceremonies are mythico-ritual, symbolic forms of worship. To understand how these mythico-ritual forms of meanings function for the people reciting and performing them, we must remember that the further back we go in human history the less differentiated are the social, political, economic, and religious modes of communal cooperating. In archaic societies, the cooperative roles that people played in their communal living were very restricted. For primitive communities, there was only one sphere of being; as a result their everyday world was infused with religious mystery since it was for the most part an undifferentiated world of meanings, motives, and values. In his book, *The Sacred and the Profane*,[7] Eliade points out that the purpose of myths and rituals was to preserve society in its sacred mode of being since the 'sacred' was the source of its power and reality. To conserve their very being, primitive people desired to be with, and to remain close to, these sources of the different forms of being. What modern societies may consider as secular activities, such as fishing and farming, would have been sacred activities for primitive societies. They were 'sacred' activities because the people engaged in performing them believed that they were repeating and reenacting the very same activities, not of their human ancestors, but of their supernatural ancestors who had performed these same activities at the 'Great Time' when the universe had passed from 'chaos to cosmos.' In other words, any social, political, or economic activity of primitive communities had an origin that was analogous to the origin of the cosmos out of chaos.

In primitive societies there are different myths and rituals, but they are all interrelated. They are all in some way analogous to the cosmogonic myth and ritual, which is a retelling, reenacting, and reliving of the creation of the world. The nature of this creation story or cosmogonic myth varies according to different cultures and times, but these culturally or historically 'variable meanings' are grounded in a transcultural structure of a cyclical passage from disorder or chaos to an ordered cosmos, or from death to rebirth. The cosmic solar, lunar, and seasonal cycles exemplify this basic passage. Everyday the sun dies at night, only to be reborn in the morning; every lunar month the life (light) of the moon 'wanes' toward death, only to be brought back to life three days later; every winter the earth with its vegetative life dies, only to be reborn in the spring, which blossoms into summer, only to fade and decay in fall, and finally die in the winter. These various repeating cycles of nature provide the basic cyclical experiences that are interpreted and symbolized in various cultural mythico-ritual scenarios.

It is important to stress that, although for primitive cultural communities these religious ceremonies were considered to have metaphysical meanings, the people did not think they were creating the cosmic cycles. Rather, they thought they had a sacred obligation to participate in these creating events brought about by supernatural beings who did actually recreate, and periodically restore and reform, the cosmic, animal and vegetative cycles, as well as the community's social and political cycles. In other words, while performing these ceremonies, the people were collectively involved with the divine powers and forces that formed the being of all beings. Such a metaphysical myth, however, was not a cognitive or moral metaphysics, but a sacred metaphysics, an undifferentiated ontology. In living in and performing these sacred ceremonies, the community was sharing in a supernatural death and rebirth; for just as the universe was periodically regenerated, so also were the social structures that constituted the community's collective and personal ways of existing. The significance of such participation can be seen in its dialectical opposite, since a failure to participate and reenact the appropriate rituals would result in a loss of being or 'fall' from being.

In our post-Enlightenment period, it is difficult for us to appreciate these primitive attitudes. The extraordinary achievement of Renaissance science was to put aside questions about the origin of the being of things, and attempt to understand these things in terms of their own intrinsic structures. Strange as it may seem, for Eliade the scientist in one important sense discovered 'nature,' because for primitive people who do not have a differentiated consciousness, there is no 'natural or demystified world.' The 'natural world' of science is a desacralized world. Scientists are not trying to discover the sacred origin, meaning, and value of this universe. Put in an even more paradoxical way, for Eliade human beings are religious, which means they are in some sense supernatural. In the previous chapter we spoke of the person as a natural knower and natural chooser; here we are focusing on the same person as 'naturally religious.' The problem is the word 'supernatural.' For many modern and postmodern people, 'supernatural' frequently means something weird or spooky, which also implies that the supernatural is opposed to the natural. Especially prone to holding this view are academicians, who have a differentiated awareness of the world about us and who live at a time when the 'hermeneutics of doubt and suspicion' of the Enlightenment period has been significantly developed and advanced by Freud, Marx and Nietzsche. What historians of religion like Eliade are attempting to do is a 'hermeneutic of retrieval' of primitive religious experiences, and of the symbolic expressions of those experiences in myth and ritual. They have provided a basis for understanding the supernatural and the natural, not in opposition, but as fundamentally and primordially related in the human being.

Because of the dramatic developments in 'scientific reasoning,' Enlightenment thinkers like Kant tried to work out a religion within the limits of reason. It would be a secular religion with appropriate ethical laws that would fall within the limits of reason. Kant explicitly excluded 'numinous experiences' from such a 'reasonable' religion and morality. Unfortunately, when Rudolf Otto, under the influence of the Kantian tradition, reintroduced 'numinous experiences' as the core or essence of religious experience, he also described such experiences as 'irrational' in order to emphasize that they permeated the entire being of a person and caused such neurophysiological reactions as goose pimples and shudders. While such effects may be common in the presence of strange and spooky happenings, and may also be present in authentic religious experiences, they are not essential to religious experience.

The critical reflections on clinical data by Abraham Maslow suggest that, in addition to the so-called peak-experiences, there are also plateau- and nadir-experiences which he also classified as religious experiences. In clarifying the notion of supernatural experiences as religious experiences, the work of Eliade is much more helpful because his studies embrace such a wealth of historical data, including so many different cultures and such different historical periods. The recurring theme in these mythico-ritual scenarios is a symbolic passage from chaos (or disorder) to cosmos (or order) which occurs in analogous forms in different cultural myths and rituals. Thus Eliade describes supernatural experiences as a symbolic passage from one way of being to other. Just as in creation the cosmos passes from nonbeing to being, so at birth the embryo passes from the womb of the mother (earth) to life. In sickness, a symbolic burial is enacted in order to regenerate and restore life; and in marriage ceremonies, where the conjugal ritual reenacts analogously the creation of the cosmos, the groom is symbolically identified with the sky god and the bride with the mother earth.

In the preceding chapter's discussion of symbolic meanings, I pointed out how symbols can embrace contradictory meanings. Water may be associated with death and with life. Water has the power to dissolve forms and return them to their formless state and, at the same time, it contains the power to generate life. Thus, in all initiatory rites like baptism, the person is immersed in water and dissolves in death, only to come forth a new and higher being, that is, from a natural way of being and behaving to a supernatural way of living. Similarly, sins may be ritually dissolved in water so that soul may be restored as the 'old man' is dissolved or absolved and 'new man' is reborn. Eliade's writings are replete with such examples which he refers to as ritualistic 'homologies' or analogies. The central issue for Eliade is that, for archaic and primitive people, there are two modes of existing: the profane and the sacred. What myths and rituals mean for these people is a passage or transformation from a lower way of being to a new higher mode of being, from the natural to supernatural mode, from the secular to sacred.

The precise meaning and values of this passage or transformation will depend on the cultural context in which it occurs. What I am emphasizing is the transcultural structure that can be discerned within these cultural variations. Religious experience, as expressed in archaic myths and rituals, can be identified with a passage from one way of being or not-being to a higher mode of being. Each religion will have any number of different myths and rituals, but these 'cultural variations' can be understood as specific forms of this transcultural passage. 'In other words,' Eliade says, 'the ideal of humanity that the primitive wishes to attain, he sets on a super human plane.' This means, first, that 'the primitive' does not become a complete man until he has passed beyond, and in some sense abolished, 'natural' humanity, for initiation is reducible to a paradoxical, supernatural experience of death and resurrection, or of second birth; and, second, that these initiation rites, entailing ordeals and symbolic death and resurrection, were instituted by gods, cultural heroes, or mythical ancestors. These rites have a super-human origin, and by performing them, the novice initiates a super-human, divine action. It is important to note this, for it shows once again that the religious man wants to be other than he finds himself on the natural level and undertakes to make himself in accordance with the ideal image revealed by the myths. Primitive man undertakes to attain a religious ideal of humanity, and his effort already contains the germs of all the ethics later elaborated in evolved societies.[8] There is a normative, transhistorical, and transcultural 'ethics' that is manifested both in primitive myth and rituals and in the modern theoretical ethical systems.

Archaic religion can be defined as a set of mythic rituals that specify various personal and social passages which are ontological transformations in that they involve a conversion from one mode of being to a higher way of existing. These ritualistic transformations of the various aspects of communal living are analogized to the celestial and terrestrial cyclical passages, thus providing the people with different ways of staying in tune with the divine ordering of the whole universe. This is why Eliade speaks of primitive myths as an archaic, ontological world-order. Ontology or metaphysics, as we saw in chapter 6, is a heuristic structure for ordering and integrating the beings of all things to one another in being. There are two major differences in Eliade's 'archaic ontology.' First, it is a religious ontology and, second, it is a symbolically ordered ontology that is being lived by the people. The problem with this lived religion or archaic ontology is that it remains undifferentiated. The meanings of such symbolic expressions need to be brought under reflective and evaluative control so that basic differences between the being of human beings and the super-human beings of the cosmic order can be differentiated.

In Eliade's terms, the problem is in the movement from the mythic time of 'eternal return' to the historical time that is irreversible. Eliade sees the religious experiences of Moses and Abraham as qualitatively different types of experiences than those of primitive and archaic religious experiences. For example, for the Israelites to remember and recite events associated with Moses was not to step out of profane times and enter into a mythic time, but rather to return to a historical event that happened at a particular time and place to a particular person.[9] Where the primitive community tried to escape history by living in a non-historical eternal present, the Israelite community began to live in the context of historical events that had not happened in some prior repeatable time, but were part of an irreversible sequence. The meaning and value of these historical events had meaning and value as the revelation of the will of Yahweh, who had personally disclosed himself to Abraham and Moses, and who had chosen to enter into human history to govern and direct the unfolding of successive historical events. As a result of this revelation of Yahweh to Abraham and to Moses, the Israelite community began to live in a historically sacred time, in a 'saving time.'

4   The Bible as Sacred History

The bible is not the history of a people's actions, but the history of a people's response to the divine initiatives of Yahweh's actions in the concrete historical course of their communal living. The usual way of explaining this shift, from the primitive myth of 'the eternal return' to the sacred or biblical history, is to refer to it as a shift from cyclical time, which periodically permitted the community to participate in the permanence of eternity, to linear time, in which people lived in a sequence of successive, historical events. Such a contrast of circular and linear images is seriously misleading since living in a historical form of existence also means 'living in a language,' which in turn involves living in the past, present, and future times, at one and the same time, as well as in successive times.

All human beings are 'historical beings.' All people, once they have learned a language, live in the meanings and values of that language, and that language has a history. To be a 'linguistic being,' then, is to be a 'historical being.' Human beings do not live simply in a sequence of 'nows'; rather, they live in some limited range of different times according to the memories and expectancies of the cultural community which they live in and have inherited as part of their living tradition.

Today historians of culture have begun to reconstruct some of the more proximate sources and aspects of that living tradition. And even more interesting, historians of religion like Eliade are expanding our awareness back into their more remote sources. It is this continually expanding horizon of past, present, and future meanings that provides us with the model for interpreting and evaluating the way the Old Testament came to be constructed. Eliade has identified Abraham and Moses and their religious experiences of Yahweh as key turning points in the history of religion because these religious experiences were interpreted, not in terms of the repeating cosmic cycles, but in terms of the lived religious history. The question we now need to pose is, How did the Israelite people develop the symbolic expressions that transformed their prior myths and rituals from static, cosmic cyclical forms to changing historical forms?

Old Testament scholars of this century have gradually discovered that this transformation of the religious symbolic meanings and values of the Israelite community took many centuries of continuous reinterpretation and reconstruction. Here I want to look at the basic outlines of how a people shifted from living in tune with cosmic cycles to living in tune with the personal presence of a revealing god who had entered into the hearts of his people, while still remaining 'transcendentally other' and 'tremendously mysterious.' The complexity of unraveling this radical religious transformation from natural cycles to historical schemes can be grasped if we realize that lived stories and rituals of a community reach back into the tradition of a people, from very recent sources to extremely remote sources, as well as to myriad in-between sources. These densely stratified sources are not woven together in a neat, chronological sequence. What turns out to be the major motivating center for arranging these strata of past meanings is not only the present experiences of a people but, more importantly, how they regard their future destiny. Paradoxically, future meanings tend to control the interpretation and evaluation of present experiencing and past rememberings.

Thanks to Kierkegaard, as well as to Heidegger's adaptation of Kierkegaard's insight, we can begin to clarify the paradoxical suggestion that the way we face the future tends to control the way we remember and experience ourselves in the past and present.[10] As soon as we are born we are old enough to die, Heidegger reminds us, and so silently and disturbingly the fear of death continuously enters into our interpretation and evaluation of our past, present, and future meanings and values. To live historically is to live in a present and past that is, to a large extent, determined by the way we anticipate the future. In the archaic culture, the 'future' was in the ritualistic possibilities of repeatedly returning to the past, and thereby transforming the chaos of present disorders back into the pristine orderings of divine creation. To put the future in the future and not in a return to the past would seem to 'straighten out' the temporal sequence and provide us with a historical narrative. But there is the more subtle, ontological problem that we live in past, present, and future meanings simultaneously, and yet experience them successively. While our future orientations may ground our basic attitudes, we are constantly cycling back and forth between past, present, and future meanings as we 'do' our daily living. To live in symbols and language is to live in many different temporal meanings both simultaneously and successively.[11] Moreover, the range of that simultaneity will vary considerably.

The writers or redactors of the Old Testament texts were continually altering and expanding the range of their past, present, and future lived and written meanings. The basic problem in such advances was that not only did they have to discover these new meanings and values, but they also had to invent or adapt the new symbols and languages for effectively communicating those meanings and values to their communities. In the context of these problems, I can briefly indicate how certain scholars have explained this shift from 'nature to history' in the construction of the Old Testament. For these scholars, the central event in the Old Testament was the covenant promise that Moses made with Yahweh to live in accord with his divine order. The Mosaic covenant was a solemn agreement to live in the tension of a limited participation which was also permanently open to a more perfect partnership with Yahweh. Moses presented this 'calling' to his community in the form a fundamental decision for right living under Yahweh. Live according to the revealed plan of Yahweh, Moses said to his people, and you will prosper and grow, but betray your promise and you will die. This 'covenant commitment' also involved a 'future promised land.' When the Israelites finally took possession of the 'promised land,' the 'future' of their covenant was transformed, and became symbolized as the establishment of a royal empire. The empire, however, turned into a corrupt political order, which meant that the people had betrayed their covenant promise to Yahweh. In this context, the second decisive event of the Old Testament occurred as the prophetic revolt emerged, and there followed a major reconstruction and retrospective reordering of the symbolic meanings and values that the Israelite people had been living.

Two principal aspects of the prophetic revolt need to be emphasized: first, a new differentiation of the person of Yahweh who had first revealed himself to Moses and Abraham; second, a reformulation of the nature of the covenant order which had grounded the Israelite entrance into their new historical form of existence. It was during the prophetic period that the problem of monotheism came to the foreground and, with it, the problem of the character of Yahweh. In the early history of Israelites, Yahweh was a personal god, the god of Abraham or Moses; he was also a tribal god who belonged to a specific community. Gradually, as the Israelites, through their imperial political order, entered the stage of world history, Yahweh became a more universal god. With the prophets, Yahweh became not only the lord of history who governed and directed the destiny of all the nations, but also a totally 'transcendent other,' or in the phrase of Rudolf Otto, 'a tremendous and enticing mystery.' In other words, while the core of religious experience may be identified as a 'transcending experience,' there are many different meanings and values in the history of religious expression that may employ the same expression but mean something quite different. In religious history, there is a sequence of significant advances in the interpretation and evaluation of the religious experiences of persons and communities, as their symbolic expressions become more and more differentiated, refined, and reevaluated. In some cases, new symbols are invented to express developments that cannot be communicated in the traditional modes of expressions. This is what happened in the imperial and prophetic period of Israelite history. But quite similar developments occurred in the other 'high religions.'

These developments and reevaluations are exemplified in the writings of Eric Voegelin, who has identified three stages in the prophetic religious experiences and in the expression of those experiences.[12] In the first stage, the prophetic attack was directed against the reigning king and was articulated in the context of a reform of the political regime and a return to the right ordering of the covenant. In the second stage, the disorders became so staggering that a reordering of the present regime became impossible, and the prophets shifted the vision to a future king who would reorder the society so that it could live in tune with the commands of Yahweh. In the third stage, the prophetic call becomes intensely personal, as the covenant drama shifts to the soul of the prophet himself, who is called to a reordering of his own person in response to a divine calling. This 'new covenant' calls for the prophet to become a part of a redemptive reordering, not just of his own people, but of all the nations. This new covenant will no longer be 'written in stone' but be written 'in the hearts' of every person.

This is only a mere sketch of a long and complex reinterpretation, redescription, and reconstruction of the religious meanings and values achieved during the lengthy prophetic period. But it is sufficient to serve my purpose, which is to indicate what it means to live in a sacred history as opposed to the primitive religion of 'eternal return.' The central problem is to grasp how we live past, present, and future courses of action simultaneously while we live and perform these simultaneously understood courses of actions successively. Such 'courses of action' as conceived and projected symbolically, become the 'story' of our personal and communal history. If we change the future goal of our intentions in some significant way, we will gradually reconstruct our present and past meanings and values to correspond to this new intended destiny. Thus, the Israelites first became a 'pilgrim people' leaving Egypt behind as they set out for the 'promised land' in a religious partnership with Yahweh. Once they arrived in the promised land, their goal shifted to building a royal empire. It was in this second phase under King David that the Israelites began to expand their past back beyond Egypt into a history of the whole human race. In the third phase, the prophets began their major critical reinterpretation and revalorization of their past religious history as they distinguished the kingdom of Yahweh from the kingdom of David. The new destiny of the kingdom of Yahweh was to be realized not through force and power, but through a conversion of the hearts of all people.[13] Again, the purpose of this sketch of different stages in Old Testament history is to show that historical living, as a moving horizon of narrative meanings and values, keeps cycling forward and backward expanding and contracting as the Israelites progress or decline in their interpretations and evaluations of the original contractual promise or covenant between themselves and the god of Moses and Abraham.

What changes in this 'saving history' is the community's interpretation and evaluation of who Yahweh is and who they themselves are. Both cooperating partners develop new identities as the narrative of their interaction with one another advances or recedes. Yahweh begins as one of many divinities or nature gods and evolves into the totally transcendent god who also dwells in the hearts of the converted person. Similarly, the community begins as a tribal community of liberated slaves committed to the god of Moses, only to undergo numerous changes ending with the possibility of receiving God's own spirit in their heart, thereby becoming the 'sons of god.' However, while these identities change in dramatic ways, there is a transhistorical identity, if we distinguish between the actual identity of a person and the potential identity, or between the proximate and remote identity, or between the natural and historical identity. Nature is what we receive at birth, the sum total of various possibilities or potentialities; our history is what we make of those possibilities during our lifetime. Thus, at any time in our lives we are between what we are now and what we may become. Thus Eliade has argued that we are 'naturally religious,' meaning that we have a potential for religious experiences. The history of religion is the history of what persons and communities have made of their religious nature in responding, and giving expression, to their religious experiences.

I have briefly indicated two stages in that history of religion, a primitive and a more advanced stage. Eliade proposes that the 'core of religious experience' for primitive people is to be found in the mythico-ritual practice of an 'eternal return,' as people ritualistically transform themselves and nature from a state of chaos or disorder into a well-ordered, well-attuned, cosmic community. For Israelites, this primitive passage from darkness to light becomes the passage from slavery to freedom, but this mythico-ritualistic transformation takes place at a particular time and place as they become the chosen people of Yahweh. This covenant or religious promise made with Yahweh gives them a new communal identity which eventually becomes a personal covenant written in the hearts of all those who choose to accept this 'word of god' spoken in the inmost recesses of their being.

This more advanced stage in religious history is not peculiar to the Jewish or Israelite community. Friedrick Heiler, a historian of religion, has identified seven characteristic features that can be found in all the world religions: Judaism, Hinduism, Buddhism, Taoism, Islam, Zoroastrian-Mazdaism, and Christianity.[14] Very briefly, these characteristics include the notions that there is a totally 'transcendent other' who is the reality of all realities, that this reality exists in a way that transcends our understanding, and that this same 'holy other' is unlike anything in the whole of nature and is 'nearer than our pulse,' as the Koran phrases it. This 'supreme other' is both totally transcendent and wholly immanent. The way to seek this transcendent mystery is through sacrifice and renunciation, the way of purgation and moral discipline. The same way is to be followed in dealing with our neighbors. We are to love our neighbors as ourselves, even to the point of forgiving our enemies. By following this way, we will pass through a state of illumination and enlightenment to a final state of purified love and supreme happiness. Thus, we come to know through love the 'transcendent other,' achieving perfect union with the being who is infinite love and wisdom. This is what characterizes the religions of the world. There are also negative aspects of religion. We are all familiar with wars of religion, where people destroy one another in the name of Yahweh or Allah or Christ, the so-called holy wars. Furthermore, the history of religion is replete with bloody sacrifices of woman and children, cannibalism, sexual orgies, and even exultant self-destruction. How do we account for these supposedly religious events?

5   Dialectic of Religious Expression

Love comes to us as a gift. It is not like calculus which may take years to learn. Love can be sudden, overwhelming, and profoundly passionate. But it is not so overwhelming that it robs us of our liberty, unless we choose to allow it to do so. Similarly, while religious experiences may be majestic and awesome or mysteriously silent, they usually leave us wondering about the real meaning and value of such experiences. There seems to be good reason to think that Moses or Abraham could have refused their 'calling,' refused to give their promise, and refused to enter into a sacred covenant with Yahweh. Moreover, besides the 'true' prophets at the time of Elijah, there were many 'false' prophets. How did the people know which prophets to believe and which ones to distrust? The brief answer is that while, the core of religious experience is a transformation of the person from a natural way of being to a 'supernatural' way of being, it is 'beyond' or 'above' the natural not in the sense of being contrary to nature, but in the sense of raising the natural to a higher level of perfection. Just as choosing trans-

forms, completes, and extends knowing, so religious loving can perfect
and enhance human loving. But just as we can know the right thing to do
yet choose the wrong thing, so we can correctly evaluate a religious experience yet refuse to respond. A frequent characteristic of the 'prophetic call'
in the Old Testament is the strong resistance to the call of such a religious
vocation. Just as our choosing can be distorted by our biases, religious loving can also be debased and become destructive either of ourselves or of
other people whom, because of our biases, we despise and desire to
destroy.[15]

In examining love, we noted that love expresses itself primarily in
actions, not in ideas, because love transforms us and becomes a new powerful, motivating center for our behavior. Loving also provides us with a special illumination of understanding of the person or persons who are the
object of our love; but if such love and 'loving illumination' are to grow
and develop, they need the ordering that comes from wise choices and
practical understanding. While the biological schemes of the plant move
beyond the chemical schemes of stones, the deprivation of the proper
chemical schemes of soil and water can gradually destroy the conditions
for biological living. Similarly, religious schemes of recital and worship, if
they are to grow as the new motivating centers for higher personal and
communal living, need the proper growth of moral and cognitional developments to underpin and support them. If these fail to advance, religious
living may seem to be interpreted as an authentic expression of the Mosaic
covenant, but upon prophetic, critical evaluation, it may turn out to be a
basic betrayal of the community's originating promise and commitment.
The rituals are still performed, the words are recited, but the sacred gestures and solemn sayings are vain and empty, or worse, an elaborate cover-
up for one group to exploit another and make a mockery of the authentic
meanings and values that were once the motivating centers of well-
ordered, religious communal living. Just as human knowers and choosers
are open to the four biases which set up the long and short cycles of
decline that block cognitional and moral development, so religious knowers and choosers are not immune to the same cycles of stagnation, breakdown, and decay.

The problem of being authentically religious is the problem of living
with a limited, actualized, religious self who has an unlimited potency to
love the totally other being who sets up the silent tension that calls for a
non-stop critique of our religious, moral, and cognitional self. A key characteristic of all the world's religion is the discipline of asceticism and purgation. If religious conversion calls us to a transcendence of self, that call is
also a denial of our former, inauthentic self, the self that needs to be
purged and disciplined. Religious development is through purgation to

illumination, and through illumination to a growing communion and union with a transcendent other.

In discussing primitive religious experience, I identified the core experience as a passage from disorder to order. In discussing here the dialectic of an inauthentic and authentic religious living, I have characterized religious development as an analogous passage or conversion from the disorder of religious inauthenticity to a growing authenticity that embraces our total self – cognitional, moral, and religious.

6   Faith and Beliefs

In the context of the discussion of religious experiences and their expressions, it is now possible to introduce a fundamental distinction between faith and beliefs. In considering Pascal's famous saying, 'the heart has reasons which reason does not know,' it was noted that loving is a way of knowing that is more perfect and superior to ordinary forms of reasoning, but not contrary to them. Similarly, religious love is frequently spoken of as an 'illumination' or 'revelation.' What is revealed is the value or worthwhileness of being-in-love in a totally transcendent way, and of behaving in certain ways and/or believing certain truths. This religious illumination which proceeds from being in love may be named 'faith,' as opposed to specific religious beliefs and behaviors that are judged to be valuable because of this prior inner illumination.[16] Faith is the motive for believing in, and belonging to, a certain religious tradition. But it may also be the motive for rejecting a religious tradition because it is not worthwhile when evaluated by the standard of a person's religious illuminations.

Faith is a revelation, 'the eye of religious love' by which a person discerns the value of belonging to a tradition because that tradition fulfills and enhances his or her religious loving and living. Faith reveals the object of my religious love, directing me to discern how to develop a more perfect communion and union with the 'transcendent unknown other' who has entered into my conscious being and dwells within me in some mysterious way. Thus, the Israelites chose to believe in the 'outer word' spoken or written by the prophets as the 'word of god' because of the 'inner word' of their own discerning faith. They discerned that, in accepting this 'outer word of god,' they would be perfecting their own communion with Yahweh, the object of their religious love. Similarly, the Mohammedan community chose to accept the 'outer word' of the prophet Mohammed because they discerned that, in following the word of the prophet, they would be perfecting their love and worship of Allah.

It was in the context of this distinction between faith and beliefs that we looked at the research of Friedrick Heiler who identified certain common

characteristics of the world religions. Prior to the traditional beliefs and rituals of different cultural communities, there is the transcendent source
and origin that may be discerned in the religious commitments of various
religious communities. Furthermore, it is this transcendent value and mysterious ultimate goodness that conditions, orients, and makes valuable all
other forms of value.

Thus, the transcendental notion of value we discussed in the last chapter
arises here again, but in a new form. Here it is not just a notion of value,
but 'an ultimate and mysterious other' to whom people choose to commit
themselves, living in communion with this 'divine other' through a set of
beliefs and practices which constitute their religious tradition, and which
they share with a past religious community. This is the 'god of Abraham'
which Pascal opposes to the 'god of philosophers.' The god of Abraham is
not known as the ground and source of questions of truth and value;
rather, he is the personal god encountered by Abraham, the god Abraham
knew by receiving within his own being the gift of love that gave him a new
being, and to which he responded with his own personal commitment.
The god of the philosophers is not the living god that Abraham and Moses
encountered, for without the initial calling and gift of a new being
bestowed on Abraham and Moses, they would not have been able to
respond in the deliberate way that they chose. Moreover, it was in the light
of Yahweh's inner word given to the prophets that inspired them to speak
their 'outer words' which they identified as 'god's word.' Illuminated by
this inner word of god's presence to them, the prophets developed their
criticism of the social and political values which were being practiced by
the 'people of god.' The prophets preached a hierarchy of values based on
the transcending value of their encounter with the living presence of Yahweh. This transcending value was intended to transform and revalorize the
cultural and personal values the people were living.

Such religious experiences are immediate experiences, and once the
prophet chooses to speak or write about these immediate religious experiences, they must be mediated through some mode and manner of expression. When such religious experiences enter the world mediated by
meaning, the prophet's audience may be puzzled by his words and begin
to wonder what Jeremiah and Isaiah mean by those words. Does the
prophet expect us to evaluate these meanings and to discern the value of
what he is saying? To do so, the audience must share the prophet's commitments, since the word he speaks is not a 'human word' but the 'word of
Yahweh.' Such a word can only be understood by a person whose heart and
mind have also been illumined by the Yahweh who speaks through the
prophet.

While the word of the prophet is a 'revealed word' that can be discerned only by persons who have received the same religious love and faith, it does not go against a person's own 'natural' reason. Instead, 'revealed reason' perfects natural reason, drawing and directing it to desire, to understand, and to judge who this 'transcendent other' who bestows on us the gifts of love and faith, and who makes it possible for us to believe that such religious practices as prayer and worship will actually put us in communion with a totally transcendent realm of divine reality. If a person believes that god is the creator and conserver of the universe, then that universe becomes a gift of god, which may make the task of understanding and correctly judging the nature of this universe an infinitely valuable project.

If religious values are totally transcendent values, then other values become more valuable insofar as they can be integrated and harmonized with these higher religious values. To do this, religious believers must work out basic ways of cooperating with one another, ways that are more reasonable and valuable, or more in harmony with the higher religious realities and values they have come to discern as truly worthwhile. However, to develop valuable public ordering of their cooperative living, religious believers must first know whether they are authentically religious believers, which in turn depends to a large extent on the historical stage in which they are living.

7   Stages of Religious History

In the preceding section we identified a distinction between a faith that proceeds from religious love and the beliefs that are being lived and performed by an historical, cultural community which is grounded in and based on that religious love. Because of that distinction, we were able to get behind the religious beliefs and practices of a community to the 'engendering experiences' on which these beliefs were based. We were also able to discover certain common characteristics of world religions. By identifying religious experience with being in love with a 'transcendent other,' we can underscore how religious love can be understood as a gift that may be received by any person and, if accepted, may transform that person into a 'new being.' Further, it is the interior faith or illumination, flowing from that gift, that provides the motive for evaluating and choosing to believe the 'outer word' of the religious tradition to which the person commits herself or himself. That illumination or revelation does not take the place of our 'natural' reasoning and choosing, but can enhance and perfect our reasoning and choosing, as we feel the desire, and begin to value the need, to know who this 'divine other' is and how we might incorporate our religious love of that 'transcendent other' into our day-to-day modes and manners of cooperating with one another.

The ability to integrate and harmonize religious loving with patriotic and domestic loving and living depends to a large extent on the historical, cultural stage in which we are born. For example, for the Israelite people it was only after two hundred years of the prophetic revolt that some Israelites were able to begin to distinguish the Kingdom of Yahweh from the political kingdom in which they were living. It was equally improbable for people living in a primitive religious culture to clearly distinguish present and future religious events from past historical events. Primitive people were actually living historically, but they had no written history of that lived history. Instead, they had only their recited myths and dramatic rituals to interpret and evaluate the realities of their lives. Furthermore, these myths and rituals tended to discourage any primitive believer from considering the possibility of major developments occurring in their religious beliefs and practices.

While Western Christianity was aware of itself as a new development, as well as a historical continuation of an older historical religion, it was unlikely that a Christian believer would wonder about a continuity between the biblical traditions that they were living and the earlier primitive religions. Nor was there, before the late nineteenth and early twentieth century, any significant opportunity for discovering a common grounding of the different world religions using the distinction we have made between faith and beliefs. The ability of a twentieth-century Christian believer to raise new questions about the integration of Christianity both with other world religions and with the whole history of religion has changed remarkably from the cultural situation of Christianity during the preceding nineteen centuries.

Before examining the major reasons for the changes that have emerged in the nineteenth and twentieth centuries, I will clarify the notion of historical stages by comparing and contrasting it with the term 'state.' A person goes to a doctor to discover what the 'present state' of her health is. The president or chief executive officer will give an account of the 'present state' of the nation or of a corporation. By comparing a sequence of different states of a corporation, an economist may determine whether the present state of the corporation represents an advance or decline in terms of prior states. This means that the present state of a person's health may be interpreted in terms of the stage of her life. Thus, the doctor may tell a patient that for a person of her age the state of her health is normal. A person's state of health is a cross-section of a dynamic changing process. A stage is a state viewed within a developmental process.

Human history is a similar dynamic process which orders or disorders the successive advances and/or declines in the meanings and values that mediate and motivate the lives of the different historical communities that are living those meanings and values. The stages of human historical process will depend on the methods that people have developed to deliberately control their lived meanings and values. Through such 'controls of meaning' communities may become more reasonable and responsible in the various arrangements of their cooperative and personal living. In the first stage of a religious history, we are dealing with cultural communities who are not 'literate' and do not have a 'religious book.' Thus, they will simply recite and ritualize their religious meanings and values.[17] A second stage emerges when the culture becomes literate, and not only possesses a religious book like the Koran or Bible, but may also develop their own literary and artistic culture. The first stage is not eliminated in this second stage; rather, it is extended because a 'book culture,' besides reading and writing, also recites and listens to its religious meanings. Unfortunately, at this second, literate stage most of the population still remain in the first stage. As the third stage emerges an even smaller élite group begins to develop and practice a new spirit of critical reflection on the literary and religious writings. This results in the formation and formulation of a new kind of theoretical writing and conversation about both the religious and literary works and the day-to-day practices of the people. In this stage, there is gradually built up a new theoretical language and, by means of this new theoretical language, a theoretical system of religious meanings may be constructed. This new 'theological system' is developed by scholars interpreting the religious writings and practices of their cultural community. We come to the present stage as the religious scholars recognize the difference between their own lived history and their theoretical, reconstructed, and recorded history. This may involve not only their own religious history, but also the broader field that encompasses other religious histories.

I noted that these four different stages of religious history were distinguished on the basis of reflective and evaluative controls of meanings and values. What are these different controls? In chapter 5 I discussed the self-correcting process of learning which is present in every human being from the beginning of human history. The problem with this control is that its reflective range tends to be limited to the community's daily cycle of common-sense activities and modes of cooperating. In the second, oral and literate cultural stage, the range of critical reflection is significantly extended, as the written text permits a sustained examination and evaluation of religious writings and practices. Accompanying these newly developed critical powers, there emerged during the 'axial period' a new sense of personal responsibility, as the various modes of literary expressions and different social classes of people began to form and provide new possibilities for critical reflection.[18] The major advance occurred not only when scholars discussed and argued about what other people were saying and/ or what they had written, but when they began to reason systematically and, at the same time, to develop the first explicit method for controlling these systematic meanings and values, namely, the method of logic. We have discussed the nature of systematic thinking in the second chapter, as well as the advantages and disadvantages of logic as a method. What I wish to stress here is that there was, in this third historical stage, no explicit method of dealing with symbolic modes of expression and of the ways that symbols express religious experiences and provide motivation for behavior. And, most important, there was no theoretical science of history.

The great step forward in this third stage was the differentiation between the descriptive, cultural world of common sense and the theoretical world of explanation. This successful advance, however, created the problem of relating these two worlds of meanings. Unfortunately, the world of theory tended to be interpreted as a universal, necessary, non-historical world, which governed both the lived, practical world of the people as well as the world of nature. The concrete, particular changes in the lived meanings and values of the community were interpreted and evaluated as only 'accidental' changes, making them seem unimportant, non-essential changes. That such small day-to-day changes of meanings and values could accumulate and effect major historical transitions, resulting in a new historical stage, did not seem very probable and thus was disregarded. As a result, classical culture in this third stage tended to think of itself as a permanent and normative achievement without any significant need to develop a critical, evaluative science of history by which it might reflect upon the changes that were occurring in historical meanings and values that they were living.[19] The emergence of just such a critical, evaluative science of history, and especially of a history of religious experience, marks the transition to the present fourth stage of cultural history.

In this fourth stage, philosophy is no longer a theory as it was for Plato and Aristotle and medieval thinkers. Philosophy becomes a method that attempts to integrate the other specialized methods by appropriating the basic operating structure of knowing, choosing, and loving that grounds them. The practice of these specialized methods gradually brings about the construction of different realms or worlds of meanings and values. Such different, but relatable, worlds of meaning have gradually emerged during the successive stages of our cultural history. The first two worlds to be distinguished were the sacred and profane worlds which, as Eliade suggests, were present even in the first, oral stage. This somewhat vague distinction between the sacred and profane becomes clearer in the literate stage. Yet, even in the third stage where the world of theory is clearly differentiated from the familiar common-sense world, the sacred world of transcendence is still not thematically differentiated, and does not become so until philosophy shifts to the world of interiority and identifies the centrality of transcendent, religious experiences as a fundamental category in interpreting and evaluating human history. This, in very broad outline, describes the four stages of religious history.

8   Summary

In the preceding chapter I discussed the reversal of the primacy of speculative intellect over practical intellect and the consequent subsumption and transformation of metaphysics by ethics. In this chapter a similar transformation and subsumption has been suggested between our moral and religious living. My intention has been, first, to distinguish between religious and moral experiences and, second, to provide a methodical basis for critically appropriating the religious beliefs and practices of the reader, whatever those religious beliefs might be. Just as in chapter 5 I set forth the method for appropriating self as a transcultural knower, just as in chapter 7 I set forth a method for appropriating self as a transcultural chooser, so this chapter extends this same method to self as a transcendent, cultural, religious lover and believer.

The method for achieving this goal is basically the same you followed in appropriating your cognitive and moral experiences. The key to such appropriation is to move from expressions of knowing and choosing back to the engendering experiencing from which cognitive and moral expressions emerged. This same shift is required when it comes to appropriating self as religious subject. This is not an easy step to take since it involves the difficult process of acquiring the habit of distinguishing between what you know and choose and the four levels of operations through which you know and choose. Once such a step has been achieved and clarified, you can proceed methodically to make the same distinction between religious expression and the engendering experiences from which religious expressions have evolved through a historical sequence of evaluative interpretations. It is not necessary to proceed, as I have in the earlier chapters, by appropriating major events in the history of mathematics and sciences, but without such a methodical approach, it is difficult to clarify and criticize what has been going on in religious studies during the past several centuries with scholars like Rudolf Otto, Abraham Maslow, Mircea Eliade, and Eric Voegelin. All of these scholars in different ways are attempting to describe the sources from which various religious traditions have emerged, developed, and/or deteriorated.

Immediate experiences are neither subjective nor objective. Such distinctions as subjective and objective are mediated expressions emerging through some form of knowing as articulated and objectified through various linguistic and symbolic modes of meaning. Sensible experiences are immediate, but so are wondering experiences. The immediate awareness of wondering is awareness of a potentially unrestricted objective, while sensible, immediate awareness offers the subject only restricted objectives. This distinction between mediated and immediate experiences is critical in specifying religious experiences since such experiences are both sensible and wonderable, engaging us on all the different levels of our being. Religious experiences, then, are prelinguistic, preconceptual experiences, and they involve the whole being of the person. Responses to such experiences depend on a variety of factors, but central to these factors is the historical culture in which the person attempts to interpret and evaluate such experiences.

I noted Rudolf Otto's pioneering attempt to find the essential core of religious experience in an awareness of a 'totally other' – the experience not of a natural other, but of a mysterious and absolutely transcendent other. Eliade's history of archaic religions places Otto's work in a far broader context as he attempts to describe the 'sacred' in much more nuanced and historical detail. Focusing on the rich variety of religious myths and rituals, Eliade finds the central core of these myths in a renewal and cyclical restoration of the earth and all of its living members. Through these rituals, the people believed they were able to return to the 'Great Time' when everything had come into existence. Without these sacred rituals the earth could not again become powerful and energetic, and so the people believed they had a sacred obligation to their deities to carry out these rites of renewal and worship. Left to themselves, worldly things wear down, get old, become barren, and lose their life-giving energy. At the core of such religious stories and practices is the notion that living things can be recreated, reordered, and made new by being made sacred, and thereby participating again in divine life. Religion, in its earliest manifestations, expresses a passage from one way of being, namely, being old, worn out, disordered, and chaotic to being reborn and passing into a higher, more perfect, and timeless way of being.

In sketching the major developments in the history of religion, I noted that the meaning of this religious passage from the way of natural being to the surpassing, sacred ways of being underwent significant changes in meaning during the course of different religious traditions. However, all of the higher world religions share certain basic characteristics which may be summed up in terms of our description of the experiences of being in love with one or more persons. Love may be experienced as a rebirth that illuminates and orients the person or persons in love. Common to the higher religions is a god that is love and that desires to redeem and save all people. The religious response to god's gift of love is an experience of a new willingness to trust in and believe god, whether in terms of personal response or in relation to a set of particular religious beliefs and practices. Love affects the whole person, mind and heart (intellect and will), immanently and transcendentally. Just as love discloses and reveals the goodness and dignity of another person's whole being, so you in turn love that person in and through your whole being. But when the beloved is love itself and infinitely valuable, then that love may be absolute, unlimited, and the ground for all other limited forms of love. Therefore, such love may form the basic motive and direction for other lesser loves. It transvalues all other values and provides a people with motives for carrying out the personal and communal goals that are deemed to be truly worthwhile.

It is imperative to underscore that, while religious loving may ground and motivate political, domestic, and personal loving, just as moral reasoning depends on an expanding, practical, and theoretical reasoning, so religious reasoning, while it may subsume and motivate moral and cognitive reasoning, also needs to develop and perfect both patterns of reasoning if it is to achieve its higher goals. For example, for members of a political community to express their love of one another in truly valuable ways means that they must be able to reason practically and wisely. You may love your neighbor, and such love may reveal in a special way the intrinsic dignity of that person. But in trying to help a neighbor in trouble, you may misunderstand and misconstrue his situation and actually make matters worse. The same goes for religious and political leaders. They may truly love their people and be sincerely desirous to lead them to better ways of living, but they may also be morally obtuse and intellectually stupid. As a result, their moral and religious idealism may lead to disastrous policies and dreadful consequences.

While religious love has the potential to motivate a person or a community to meet the problem of moral impotence, it still requires sustained moral and intellectual development if it is to succeed. Religious history is filled with bizarre and even destructive ritualistic practices, as well as extravagant and utterly fanciful religious stories. Just as moral idealism without intellectual development can blunder badly, religious development cannot advance without the support and steady evolution of moral and intellectual development. In other words, the basic human challenge is to become religiously, morally, and intellectually authentic. For any concrete knower, chooser, and lover, to be authentic is to have appropriated the basic tension between unrestricted capacity and restricted achievements. More concretely, this means that individuals or a community have to have appropriated the distinction between their lived, cultural selves and their potential selves, which may always be further developed. Such development in turn depends on a dialectical interpretation of the inherited, historical currents of meanings and values that form the context or horizon of that community, and such a dialectical interpretation assumes a metaphysical, moral, and religious integrating structure.

Epilogue

Method as Conversion

The usual meaning of 'method' is some sort of orderly procedure that is established to carry out certain tasks in a systematic, efficient way. It can also mean following a set of rules to solve a problem, as is found in mathematical textbooks which teach students to solve problems by learning rules without explaining why the rules work. In either case, the method is extrinsic to the procedure itself. 'Method,' as I have used the term, refers not only to the operations required to carry out a project and the orientation that normatively directs these operations, but also to you the operator who performs the operations, which is why I have referred to the method as 'self-appropriation.' The method is intended to guide you toward an ever-expanding awareness of your own knowing, choosing, and loving and of how you operate in and through these operations to achieve certain goals.

There is also a basic difference between the method of self-appropriation and the method of logic which Aristotle developed to control the way we reason from one proposition to another in a coherent and orderly way through various syllogistic patterns. The foundation for such systematic reasoning was grounded in the initial premises that provide the first principles from which sequences of premises and conclusions could be concretely deduced. There is nothing inherently wrong with such an account of systematic reasoning, but it does not bring to light that the propositions, whether initial or derived, depend primarily on the way a thinker understands and judges these propositions. The propositions, whether cognitive, moral, or religious, arise from the operations that generate those propositions, and so, two moral or religious thinkers may articulate the same propositions but understand, judge, and value them in quite different, even opposed ways. Logic, then, is a very limited way of controlling meaning.

The much broader method is to control, not the clarity and coherence of the contents that are meant, but the operations that originate and generate the meanings and the orientation that directs those operations. The key to constructing such a method is to identify the basic objective of meaning or to answer the question, What is the meaning of meaning? and, What are the norms that guide knowers, choosers, and lovers in attaining that objective?

I began this study by identifying the objective of wondering as an unknown that becomes known through successive, cognitional operations. These operations, as functionally correlated, could provide dynamic, normative procedures for revealing the unknown objective. I contrasted the restricted, cognitive operations and their proximate objectives with the unrestricted, remote, and unknown objective that would become known only when everything that could be known correctly actually became known. This contrast between proximate and remote objectives permits us to contrast further the difference between a basic method oriented to a remote objective – being – and specialized methods seeking limited objectives within being. I identified four different specialized methods – classical, statistical, genetic, and dialectical – with four different normative procedures for reaching their respective, specialized objectives. This contrast between specialized, normative procedures for achieving restricted objectives and a foundational method for achieving an unrestricted objective provides a new way to think about and define metaphysics. In this context, metaphysicians who have appropriated their own structured operations of knowing, as well as their remote and proximate objectives, realize that metaphysics as a science of being will be dependent on other knowers who seek specialized, limited objectives. But this dependence will be critical and transformative in the sense that metaphysicians can critically understand and dialectically judge the categories through which these knowers proceed and the objectives to which they are oriented through their specialized categories. For example, the task of metaphysicians is not to verify and further develop Galileo's and Newton's laws of gravitational motion. That is the task of physicists. It is the task of the metaphysicians to correct certain foundational mistakes made by scientists who fail to remain within their own autonomous field and attempt to articulate epistemological and metaphysical propositions about what knowing is and is not, what makes knowing objective, and what reality actually becomes known through the different forms of objective knowing. Because Galileo did not know the difference between practical, common-sense knowing and its objectives and theoretical knowing and its objectives, he made a historically disorienting distinction between primary and secondary qualities of things. This mistaken distinction was picked up by Locke and entered into the empirical philosophical tradition, and eventually was passed on to Kant through Newton's modifications, which further disoriented distinctions between real and apparent motions. One result of this distinction was, if not to discredit common-sense knowing, at least to neglect the study of its central role in human history until the nineteenth-century when thinkers began to focus attention on differing aspects of practical knowing.

A methodical metaphysics must not only critically evaluate the results of the specialized methods of knowing, but also identify the sources of such significant mistakes as Galileo made. Galileo discredited practical, common-sense knowing because he assumed he knew what made knowing objective. Methodical, self-appropriated metaphysicians know that what makes knowing objective is being, and what makes knowing proximately objective is a grasp of the 'virtually unconditioned' or limited absolute as apprehended in the reflective act of judging. Metaphysicians also know that in any correct act of judgment there are three limited objectives: the experiential objective, known by sensing; the intelligible objective known by understanding; and the absolute objective known by judging. In combining those three limited objectives into a single objective judgment, there is a very high probability that empirical objectivity will be overemphasized and given central significance when, in fact, it is the least significant constituent. There is also the much lower probability that the second intelligible objective will tend to assume dominance (some form of idealism), while the third constitutive function will almost always be overlooked or neglected. Only if all three functions and their respective objectives are identified and integrated can we correctly judge what makes a judgment truly objective. Further, self-appropriated metaphysicians will know that human knowers share with animal knowers sensible objectives, and because sensible awareness and the knowing of sensible objects develops quite spontaneously and long before theoretical knowing emerges, there will be the tendency, first, to reduce the tripartite functioning of human knowing to sensible knowing; second, to reduce the tripartite objectivity of objective knowing to empirical objectivity; and, third, to reduce the tripartite reality of experienced, understood, and judged reality to experienced reality.

This reductionist tendency operates in all knowers. Thus, a self-appropriated metaphysician will realize that there will be three types of metaphysicians – empirical, idealistic, and realistic. While there have been any number of major advances in the history of human knowing, the methodical metaphysician will know that there is a special significance to the shift from Newtonian physics to Einsteinian physics, since this shift involved a fundamental change in the basic categories for explaining the spaces, times, and motions of the entire physical universe. By appropriating this shift, which was both a development and reversal of Newtonian positions, the metaphysician can distinguish between the ordinary, sensory-motor frameworks within which animals and humans operate and the strictly intellectual frameworks which mediate and transform in an explanatory manner the descriptive, sensory-motor frameworks in and through which we immediately and spontaneously sense the world around us.

The irony of this shift from Newtonian to Einsteinian world-orders is that our physical universe was reduced from an infinite universe to a finite, limited universe, while the possibility of a potentially infinite and intelligible universe opened up. This example clarifies why a methodical metaphysics depends on a reversal in our ordinary knowing frameworks from a supposedly infinite physical universe to a limited physical universe that exists within the potentially infinite, and knowable, universe of being. A methodical metaphysics, then, depends on a person undergoing a fundamental conversion in explaining why knowing is what it is, and what makes such knowing truly objective. What makes knowing objective becomes known when the knower undergoes a reorientation from an assumed, already known objective to a potentially unlimited, unknown objective.

I defined an authentic knower as a knower who realizes that her identity as an achieved knower is to be continually replaced by a still to be achieved and realized knower. We may now say that an authentic knower is a converted knower who knows the difference between the remote and proximate objective in knowing and how to make this distinction in a methodically normative way. Besides the authentic or converted knower providing a methodical metaphysics, there is the authentic or converted chooser grounding a methodical ethics.

Just as metaphysics grows out of, transforms, and subsumes cognitional questions and answers, so ethics emerges from, transforms, and subsumes metaphysics. Methodical ethics, parallels methodical metaphysics. Cognitive knowing begins with an unknown objective that becomes known through successive, partial objectives; moral knowing begins within an unknown and unchosen objective that becomes known, valued, and chosen through successive partial objectives. The problem of differentiating these partial moral objectives is similar to the problem of differentiating the components of objective knowing. Solving the problem requires moving from descriptive, common-sense moral reasoning to theoretical moral reasoning. This shift from descriptive to explanatory moral reasoning makes possible a distinction between the good as experienced and the good as institutionally ordered, or the difference between a good job and a good economic order, a good class and a good educational system, etc. This explanatory difference also makes possible the further study of the long-term historical trends that are going on within any social order and the short-term trends that sustain or significantly modify these historically conditioned, institutional orders. These orders predispose the members of a cultural community to be morally authentic or inauthentic choosers. Only by establishing this difference between long and short cycles of motivating meanings can we define in a methodical way the difference between authentic and inauthentic choosers. A person makes what seems to be an authentic choice according to the normative practices of their culture, but it turns out to actually be an inauthentic choice according to the transcultural norm that operates within every person. Such a norm operates within the conscious awareness of every cultural chooser insofar as that chooser is oriented to the ultimate moral objective of unrestricted goodness or value.

A moral metaphysics must clarify the way in which the culture provides the mediating structure through which choosers seek their proximate objectives in the various career choices available within their cultural community. Such career choices form cooperative roles within a set of ongoing institutional cycles, and these cycles constitute the performers' participation in seeking an organized objective designed to provide a common good that will benefit each cooperating member. Various cultural symbols mediate the motivating meanings that predispose individuals to choose to cooperate with the other role-players in seeking their common destiny. Since these cultural symbols motivate community members to perform a range of different cooperational schemes – economic, political, social, religious – the crucial question about these institutional schemes is how they scale the ordering of human values and thereby predispose and encourage the members of the society to scale their values in the same way. In other words, since `the order of the soul is the state writ small,' the crucial dialectic is between the proximate scale of values that is operative within any ongoing set of cultural schemes and the remote transcultural objective that orients every cultural chooser in every social order in successive historical periods. To interpret and critically evaluate in an authentic manner, we must mediate the long-term motivational meanings that operate to advance or block the members' development to become more or less morally authentic insofar as they choose personal and collective meanings that will make them more friendly to themselves and to one another. They are thus able to make themselves more responsible to the ultimate goodness that motivates each and every member of their historical community.

Ironically, what the genetic-dialectical mediation of our past historical community reveals is that to be an authentic knower we must commit ourselves to an ever-expanding, practical understanding of better ways to organize and orient cultural communities. For a people to choose to commit themselves to develop and execute more valuable ways of cooperative living requires a willingness that people do not yet have. They are essentially free to live in more reasonable and worthwhile ways, but they are not effectively free to do so, and thus must develop the motivational meanings or willingness in order to develop and execute more choiceworthy ways of seeking their common destiny. What almost inevitably happens is that people do not admit their own moral impotence, but rationalize their lack of effective freedom through various symbolic languages; then they pass on these cultural cover-ups to the next generation, thereby setting up future cycles of disorder. The potential solution to this problem of moral impotence is a religious conversion that grounds a new type of religious authenticity that commits a person or community to transcend every form of human loving and to seek an ever-expanding religious loving.

Such religious conversion involves a response on the part of a person or community to a 'totally other.' While completely transcending the human universe, this 'totally other' is also immanent and effectively present in the personal awareness of every chooser, drawing that person into a more perfect, mysterious communion. This experience of being in the presence of a 'fearful other' who is also mysteriously attractive can take many different forms in different cultures and historical periods, but such historical and cultural variations are not so different that they exclude certain common characteristics which historians of religion have identified. This implies that the notion of an authentic religious conversion can transcend different belief traditions and form a basic challenge for the members of different religious traditions, whether Hindu, Muslim, Jewish, or Christian, etc.

'Religious conversion,' as I am using the term, refers to an experience that is immediately conscious to a person. How individuals or a community come to mediate such experiences will vary with historical periods and different cultural traditions. But there is among these different historical traditions of beliefs seven common characteristics which reveal a transcultural orientation that can summon the culturally different believers to seek, within their own moral and cognitive horizons, a fuller and more perfect response both to knowing and to loving the transcendent source of their experiences, and to develop more morally perfect ways of cooperating with their own and other human communities. Such an authentic conversion is, therefore, primarily a call to practice more morally and reasonably ordered ways of human living. This implies a basic tension, between the present limited personal and communal response of moral and religious practices and the always more perfect response, which lies within the range of any person or community, to an unlimited knowing, valuing, and loving. This same religious conversion also speaks to non-believers since the appeal is not to any religious truths or practices but to conscious experiences that are operative, or may be operative, in the horizon of any knower and chooser.

Thus, the foundation for the method we have been following can be understood as an empirical foundation. The natural sciences in the Renaissance turned away from the deductive method of scholastic reasoning, with its appeal to first principles, and shifted to considering only propositions or theories that could be tested in sensible data. So to the method we have pursued in this study is also empirical, but it is a generalized empirical method because, in addition to appealing to immediate sensible data as scientists do, we have also appealed to the immediate data of our own conscious experiences. This appeal has been directed not primarily to subjects or objects, but to the operations through which subjects and objects are mediated cognitively, morally, and religiously. Furthermore, these operations are dynamically and normatively directed to two quite distinct objects: proximate, limited objects and the remote, unlimited object. The tension between these two objectives has provided empirical norms for testing the authenticity of a person as knower operating through cognitive structures, as chooser operating through evaluative and choosing structures, and as religious lover operating through the whole person.

Notes

Chapter 1

1 Carl Boyer, *The History of Calculus and Its Conceptual Development* (New York: Dover Publications, 1959), 153.

2 Topics treated in this chapter follow quite closely the divisions in chapter 1 of Bernard Lonergan, *Insight: A Study of Human Understanding*, ed. Frederick E. Crowe and Robert M. Doran, Collected Works of Bernard Lonergan, vol. 3 (Toronto: University of Toronto Press, 1992).

3 Bernard Lonergan, *Verbum: Word and Idea in Aquinas* (Notre Dame: University of Notre Dame Press, 1967), 12 ff.

4 *Insight*, 7–13.

5 Frank Lloyd Wright, *An American Architecture*, ed. Edgar Kauffmann (New York: Horizon Press, 1995), 75–80.

6 For a full discussion of abstraction, see *Verbum*, chapter 4. See also Bernard Lonergan, *Topics in Education*, Collected Works of Bernard Lonergan, vol. 10 (Toronto: University of Toronto Press, 1993), 124–32.

7 *Verbum*, chapters 1 and 2.

8 For an excellent introduction to Piaget's thought, see John L. Phillips, Jr, *The Origins of Intellect: Piaget's Theory* (San Francisco: W. H. Freeman, 1969).

9 For an extensive study of the relations between Lonergan's and Piaget's writings, see Walter E. Conn, *Conscience: Development and Self-Transcendence* (Birmingham: Religious Education Press, 1981).

10 *Insight*, 13–19.

11 *Insight*, 19–25.

12 *Insight*, 25–32.

Chapter 2

1 Herbert Butterfield, *The Origins of Modern Science* (New York: Free Press, 1965), 7.

2 Stephen Toulmin and June Goodfield, *The Fabric of the Heavens* (New York: Harper and Row, 1961), 77.

3 Today we know they generated a member of a new species of number – the 'irrational' number. The Greeks named the number 'irrational' because it did not fit into their understanding of what a ratio was, or what we call a fraction. In attempting to solve the problem of how to find the square root of 2, they assumed that there must be two integers such that the product of the first multiplied by itself and the product of the second multiplied by itself stand in the same relation as 2 does to unity. Not only were they unable to find two such integers, but they eventually proved that two such integers could not exist, since such integers would contradict what they already knew about even and odd numbers. They realized they had been searching for an answer that simply did not and could not exist; they realized they had been asking the wrong question – they had an inverse insight. The correct question would have been to wonder just what is a number, but that question would not be posed correctly until the nineteenth century.

4 Euclid, *The Elements*, vol. 1, trans. Sir Thomas L. Heath (New York: Dover Publications, 1956), Books 1 and 2.

5 Euclid, *The Elements*, vol. 2, Book 5, definitions.

6 Appollonius, *Appollonius of Perga Treatise on Conic Sections*, ed. T. L. Heath (Cambridge: Cambridge University Press, 1896).

7 See Jacob Klein, *Greek Mathematical Thought and the Origin of Algebra*, trans. Eva Brann (Cambridge: MIT Press, 1968), Appendix: François Vièta's 'Introduction to the Analytic Art.'

8 René Descartes, *Geometry of René Descartes*, trans. David E. Smith and Marcia L. Latham (New York: Dover Publications, 1954), Book 1.

9 Carl Boyer, *History of Analytic Geometry* (New York: Scripta Mathematica, Yeshiva University, 1956), chapters 4 and 5.

10 Boyer, *The History of the Calculus and Its Conceptual Development*, 158.

11 Patrick H. Byrne, 'Mystery and Modern Mathematics,' in *Lonergan Workshop*, vol. 7, ed. Frederick Lawrence (Atlanta: Scholar's Press, 1988), 1–35.

12 Throughout section 2, I am indebted to two major sources: Bernard Cohen, *The Birth of a New Physics* (Garden City, NJ: Doubleday, 1960), and Toulmin and Goodfield, *The Fabric of the Heavens*.

13 Today, thanks to the science of rockets, we know that the curve is an ellipse and not a parabola.

14 Richard S. Westfall, *The Construction of Modern Science: Mechanisms and Mechanics* (New York: John Wiley & Sons, 1971), chapter 2.

15 Westfall, *The Construction of Modern Science,* chapter 7.
16 For a very clear and helpful discussion of classical time and space, see Milic Capek, *The Philosophical Impact of Contemporary Physics* (Princeton: D. Van Nostrand, 1961), especially chapters 2 and 3.
17 Albert Einstein, *Relativity: The Special and the General Theory* (New York: Bonanza Books, 1961), part 1.
18 Martin Goldstein and Inge F. Goldstein, *The Refrigerator and the Universe* (Cambridge: Harvard University Press, 1993), 51 ff.
19 For a history of the rise of statistical thinking, I refer the reader to Theodore M. Porter, *The Rise of Statistical Thinking* (Princeton: Princeton University Press, 1986).

Chapter 3

1 This chapter attempts to summarize the main contents of chapters 6 and 7 of *Insight.*
2 *Insight,* 181–6.
3 *Insight,* 207–9.
4 Bernard Lonergan, *Method in Theology* (New York: Herder and Herder, 1972), 64–73.
5 *Insight,* 217–18.
6 *Insight,* 191–206.
7 Robert M. Doran 'The Theologian's Psyche: Notes toward a Reconstruction of Psychology,' in *Lonergan Workshop,* vol. 1, ed. Fred Lawrence (Missoula, MO: Scholar's Press, 1978), 93–143.
8 Jean-Jacques Rousseau, *First and Second Discourses,* ed. Roger Masters, trans. Roger D. and Judith E. Masters (New York: St Martin's Press, 1964), 130–4.
9 Max Scheler, *The Nature of Sympathy,* trans. Peter Heath (Hamden: Shoestring Press, 1973), part 1.
10 *Insight,* 218–22.
11 *Insight,* 222–5.
12 Jane Jacobs, *Economy of Cities* (New York: Random House, 1970).
13 Bernard Lonergan, 'Healing and Creating in History,' in *A Third Collection: Papers by Bernard J.F. Lonergan, SJ,* ed. Frederick E. Crowe, SJ (New York: Paulist Press, 1958), 100–9.
14 *Insight,* 225–42.
15 Niccolò Machiavelli, *The Prince* (New York: Appleton-Century-Cross, 1971), chapter 15.

Chapter 4

1 This chapter includes material from chapters 4 and 8 of *Insight.*

2 *Insight*, 89–91.

3 *Insight*, 89–92.

4 *Insight*, 53–62.

5 Morris Kline, *Mathematics in Western Culture* (London: Oxford University Press, 1953); see chapters 22 and 23.

6 *Insight*, 118–20.

7 Charles Darwin, *The Voyage of the Beagle*, ed. Leonard Engle (New York: Doubleday, 1962).

8 The treatment of development in this section is preliminary to a fuller analysis in chapter 6.

9 *Insight*, 115–28.

10 *Insight*, 129–32.

11 *Insight*, chapter 8.

12 *Insight*, 250–3.

13 *Insight*, 253–4.

14 *Insight*, 267–70.

Chapter 5

1 This chapter includes central themes from chapters 9–12 of *Insight*.

2 *Insight*, 271–2.

3 *Insight*, 273–5.

4 *Insight*, 275–8.

5 *Insight*, 279–99.

6 *Insight*, 299–309.

7 *Insight*, 320–5.

8 *Insight*, 319–20.

9 *Insight*, 348–52.

10 *Insight*, 352–7.

11 *Verbum*, 147–51, 183–4.

12 *Insight*, 375–84.

Chapter 6

1 See Lonergan's introduction to *Verbum*.

2 *Insight*, 432.

3 *Insight*, 437–41.

4 *Insight*, 442–4.

5 The title of this section is taken from Bernard Lonergan's 'Mission and the Spirit,' in *A Third Collection*, 23–31.

6 *Insight*, 451–8.

7 Richard C. Lewontin, 'Gene, Organism, and Environment,' in *The Evolution*

from Molecules to Men, ed. D.S. Bendall (Cambridge: Cambridge University Press, 1983), 273.

8 Charles Darwin, *Origin of Species*, introduction by Richard Leakey (New York: Hill and Wang, 1982); see chapter 6, 'Difficulties of the Theory.'

9 R.W. Burkhardt, 'The Development of an Evolutionary Ethology,' in *The Evolution of Molecules to Men*, 429–5.

10 *Insight*, 464.

11 R. May, 'The Evolution of Ecological Systems,' in *Evolution: A Scientific American Book* (San Francisco: W.H. Freeman, 1978), 80–92.

12 *Insight*, 469.

13 *Insight*, 185.

14 *Insight*, 470–9.

15 *Insight*, 553–8.

16 Bernard Lonergan, *Understanding and Being: An Introduction and Companion to Insight*, ed. Elizabeth A. Morelli and Mark D. Morelli (New York: Edwin Mellen Press, 1980), 43–5.

17 *Method in Theology*, 156–8.

18 *Method in Theology*, 158–60.

19 *Method in Theology*, 160–1.

20 *Method in Theology*, 162–5.

Chapter 7

1 In this chapter I will select the major themes of chapter 18 in *Insight* since those themes were transformed by Lonergan's development of a fourth level of the human subject as chooser during the years following the publication of *Insight*.

2 Bernard Lonergan, 'Aquinas Today: Tradition and Innovation,' in *A Third Collection*, 35–55

3 *Method in Theology*, 36–41.

4 *Method in Theology*, 30–4.

5 *Method in Theology*, 41–7.

6 Erik H. Erikson, *Childhood and Society* (New York: W.W. Norton, 1963), chapter 7.

7 *Method in Theology*, 32–3.

8 *Method in Theology*, 64–9.

9 For a very original and suggestive theory of associative feelings, consult Northrop Frye, *The Well-Tempered Critic* (Bloomington: Indiana University Press, 1963).

10 Ernst Cassirer, *Essay on Man* (New Haven: Yale University Press, 1944).

11 See Mircea Eliade, *Myth and Reality* (New York: Harper & Row, 1963).

12 Aristotle, *Nicomachean Ethics*, trans. Martin Ostwald (Indianapolis: Bobbs-Merrill, 1982), Book 2.

13 *Method in Theology*, 47–52.
14 Bernard Lonergan, 'An Essay in Circulation Analysis,' unpublished manu-
    script, part 1.
15 Jacobs, *The Economy of the Cities*; see especially chapter 3.
16 See Jacobs's distinction between efficiency and creating.
17 D.S.L. Cardwell, *From Watt to Clausius* (New York: Cornell University Press,
    1971).
18 *Method in Theology*, chapter 2, 'Stages of Meaning.'
19 *A Third Collection*, 9–12.
20 *Insight*, 619–30.

Chapter 8

1 *Method in Theology*, chapter 1.
2 Throughout this chapter I shall use the word 'god' in lowercase in order to
   avoid any credal associations that the reader may have. My intent is to move
   behind credal meanings of god and focus instead on the sources from which
   such meanings evolve.
3 The themes discussed in this chapter are taken primarily from chapter 4 of
   Method in Theology.
4 Rudolf Otto, *The Idea of the Holy*, trans. John W. Harvey (London: Oxford
   University Press, 1923), chapters 1–5.
5 Abraham H. Maslow, *Religions, Values, and Peak-Experiences* (New York: Viking
   Press, 1970).
6 Eliade, *Myth and Reality*, 1–20.
7 Mircea Eliade, *The Sacred and the Profane: The Nature of Religion*, trans. Willard
   R. Trask (New York: Harper & Row, 1961), chapter 1.
8 Eliade, *The Sacred and the Profane*; see introduction.
9 Mircea Eliade, *Cosmos and History: The Myth of the Eternal Return*, trans. Willard
   R. Trask (New York: Harper & Row, 1954); see especially preface and fore-
   word.
10 Joseph Flanagan, SJ, 'Where the Late Lonergan Meets the Early Heidegger,'
   in *Lonergan Workshop Journal*, vol. 10, ed. Frederick Lawrence (Chestnut Hill,
   MA: Lonergan Workshop, 1994), 83–118.
11 Flanagan, 'Where the Late Lonergan Meets the Early Heidegger.'
12 Eric Voegelin, *Order and History*, vol. 1 (Louisiana: Louisana State University
   Press, 1956); see chapter 13.
13 Voegelin, *Order and History*, vol. 1.
14 Quoted by Bernard Lonergan in 'The Future of Christianity,' in *A Second Collection*, ed. William F. J. Ryan and Bernard J. Tyrrell (Philadelphia: Westminis-
   ter Press, 1975), 149–64.
15 *Method in Theology*, 110–12.

16 *Method in Theology*, 115–19.

17 Bernard Lonergan, 'Philosophy and the Religious Phenomenon,' in *Method: Journal of Lonergan Studies*, vol. 12, ed. Patrick Byrne, Charles Hefling, and Mark Morelli (Chestnut Hill, MA: The Lonergan Institute of Boston College, 1994), 121–46.

18 Karl Jaspers, *The Origin and Goal of History*, trans. Michael Bullock (London: Routledge & Kegan Paul, 1953).

19 Bernard Lonergan, 'The Transition From a Classicist World-View to Historical-Mindedness,' in *A Second Collection*, 1–10.

Bibliography

Appollonius. *Appollonius of Perga Treatise on Conic Sections*. Edited by T.L. Heath. Cambridge: Cambridge University Press, 1896.

Aristotle. *Nicomachean Ethics*. Translated by Martin Ostwald. Indianapolis: Bobbs-Merrill, 1982.

Boyer, Carl. *History of Analytic Geometry*. New York: Scripta Mathematica, Yeshiva University, 1956.

– *The History of Calculus and Its Conceptual Development*. New York: Dover Publications, 1959.

Burkhardt, R.W. 'The Development of an Evolutionary Ethology.' In *Evolution of Molecules to Men*, edited by D.S. Bendall. Cambridge: Cambridge University Press, 1983.

Butterfield, Herbert. *The Origins of Modern Science*. New York: Free Press, 1965.

Byrne, Patrick H. 'Mystery and Modern Mathematics.' In *Lonergan Workshop*, vol. 7, edited by Frederick Lawrence. Atlanta: Scholar's Press, 1988.

Capek, Milic. *The Philosophical Impact of Contemporary Physics*. Princeton: D. Van Nostrand, 1961.

Cardwell, D.S.L. *From Watt to Clausius*. New York: Cornell University Press, 1971.

Cassirer, Ernst. *Essay on Man*. New Haven: Yale University Press, 1944.

Cohen, Bernard. *The Birth of a New Physics*. Garden City, NJ: Doubleday, 1960.

Conn, Walter E. *Conscience: Development and Self-Transcendence*. Birmingham: Religious Education Press, 1981.

Darwin, Charles. *Origin of Species*. Introduction by Richard Leakey. New York: Hill and Wang, 1982.

– *The Voyage of the Beagle*. Edited by Leonard Engle. New York: Doubleday, 1962.

Descartes, René. *Geometry of René Descartes*. Translated by David E. Smith and Marcia L. Latham. New York: Dover Publications, 1954.

Doran, Robert M. 'The Theologian's Psyche: Notes toward a Reconstruction of Psychology.' In *Lonergan Workshop*, vol. 1, edited by Fred Lawrence. Missoula, MO: Scholar's Press, 1978.

Einstein, Albert. *Relativity: The Special and the General Theory.* New York: Bonanza Books, 1961.

Eliade, Mircea. *Cosmos and History: The Myth of the Eternal Return.* Translated by Willard R. Trask. New York: Harper & Row, 1954.

– *Myth and Reality.* New York: Harper & Row, 1963.

– *The Sacred and the Profane: The Nature of Religion.* Translated by Willard R. Trask. New York: Harper & Row, 1961.

Erikson, Erik H. *Toys and Reason.* New York: W.W. Norton, 1977.

– *Childhood and Society.* New York: W.W. Norton, 1963

Euclid. *The Elements.* Vol. 1, translated by Sir Thomas L. Heath. New York: Dover Publications, 1956.

Farrell, Thomas J., and Paul A. Soukup, eds. *Communication and Lonergan: Common Ground for Forging the New Age.* Kansas City, MO: Sheed & Ward, 1993.

Flanagan, Joseph, SJ. 'Where the Late Lonergan Meets the Early Heidegger.' In *Lonergan Workshop Journal*, vol. 10, edited by Frederick Lawrence. Chestnut Hill, MA: Lonergan Workshop, 1994.

Frye, Northrop. *The Well-Tempered Critic.* Bloomington: Indiana University Press, 1963.

Gleick, James. *Chaos: Making a New Science.* New York: Viking Press, 1987.

Glendon, Mary Ann. *The New Family and the New Property.* Toronto: Butterworth, 1981.

Goldstein, Martin, and Inge F. Goldstein. *The Refrigerator and the Universe.* Cambridge: Harvard University Press, 1993.

Hacking, Ian. *The Emergence of Probability: A Philosophical Study of Early Ideas about Probability, Induction, and Statistical Inference.* London: Cambridge University Press, 1975.

Jacobs, Jane. *Economy of Cities.* New York: Random House, 1970.

Jaspers, Karl. *The Origin and Goal of History.* Translated by Michael Bullock. London: Routledge & Kegan Paul, 1953.

Kammen, Michael. *A Season of Youth: The American Revolution and the Historical Imagination.* New York: Oxford University Press, 1978.

Kearney, Richard. *The Wake of Imagination.* London: Hutchinson Press, 1988.

Klein, Jacob. *Greek Mathematical Thought and the Origin of Algebra.* Translated by Eva Brann. Cambridge: MIT Press, 1968.

Kline, Morris. *Mathematics in Western Culture.* London: Oxford University Press, 1953.

Lewontin, Richard C. 'Gene, Organism, and Environment.' In *Evolution from Molecules to Men*, edited by D.S. Bendall. Cambridge: Cambridge University Press, 1983.

Lonergan, Bernard. 'An Essay in Circulation Analysis.' Unpublished manuscript.
– *Insight: A Study of Human Understanding.* Edited by Frederick E. Crowe and Robert
    M. Doran. Collected Works of Bernard Lonergan, vol. 3. Toronto: University of
    Toronto Press, 1992.
– *Method in Theology.* New York: Herder and Herder, 1972.
– 'Philosophy and the Religious Phenomenon.' In *Method: Journal of Lonergan Stud-
    ies*, vol. 12, edited by Patrick Byrne, Charles Hefling, and Mark Morelli. Chestnut
    Hill, MA: Lonergan Institute of Boston College, 1994.
– *A Second Collection.* Edited by William F. J. Ryan and Bernard J. Tyrrell. Philadel-
    phia: Westminister Press, 1975.
– *A Third Collection: Papers by Bernard J. F. Lonergan, SJ.* Edited by Frederick E.
    Crowe, SJ. New York: Paulist Press, 1958.
– *Topics in Education.* Collected Works of Bernard Lonergan, vol. 10. Toronto: Uni-
    versity of Toronto Press, 1993.
– *Understanding and Being: An Introduction and Companion to Insight.* Edited by
    Elizabeth A. Morelli and Mark D. Morelli. New York: Edwin Mellen Press,
    1980.
– *Verbum: Word and Idea in Aquinas.* Notre Dame: University of Notre Dame Press,
    1967.
Machiavelli, Niccolò. *The Prince.* New York: Appleton-Century-Cross, 1971.
MacIntyre, Alasdair. *Three Rival Versions of Moral Inquiry: Encyclopedia, Genealogy, and
    Tradition.* Notre Dame: Notre Dame University Press, 1990.
Marx, Leo. *The Machine in the Garden: Technology and the Pastoral Ideal in America.*
    London: Oxford University Press, 1964.
Maslow, Abraham H. *Religions, Values, and Peak-Experiences.* New York: Viking Press,
    1970.
May, R. 'The Evolution of Ecological Systems.' In *Evolution: A Scientific American
    Book.* San Francisco: W.H. Freeman, 1978.
McCarthy, Michael H. *The Crisis of Philosophy.* New York: State University of New
    York Press, 1990.
McEvenue, Sean E., and Ben F. Meyer, eds. *Lonergan's Hermeneutics: Its Development
    and Application.* Washington: Catholic University of America Press, 1989.
McShane, Philip. *Randomness, Statistics, and Emergence.* Notre Dame: University of
    Notre Dame Press, 1970.
Montagu, M.F. Ashley. *Culture and the Evolution of Man.* New York: Oxford Univer-
    sity Press, 1962.
Otto, Rudolf. *The Idea of the Holy.* Translated by John W. Harvey. London: Oxford
    University Press, 1923.
Pattee, Howard H., ed. *Hierarchy Theory: The Challenge of Complex Systems.* New York:
    George Braziller, 1973.
Phillips, John L., Jr. *The Origins of Intellect: Piaget's Theory.* San Francisco: W.H. Free-
    man, 1969.

Porter, Theodore M. *The Rise of Statistical Thinking.* Princeton: Princeton University Press, 1986.

Ricoeur, Paul. *The Symbolism of Evil.* Translated by Emerson Buchanan. New York: Harper & Row, 1967.

Rousseau, Jean-Jacques. *First and Second Discourses.* Edited by Roger Masters; translated by Roger D. and Judith E. Masters. New York: St Martin's Press, 1964.

Salthe, Stanley N. *Evolving Hierarchical Systems.* New York: Columbia University Press, 1985.

Scheler, Max. *The Nature of Sympathy.* Translated by Peter Heath. Hamden: Shoestring Press, 1973.

Shea, William. *The Naturalists and the Supernatural: Studies in Horizon and an American Philosophy.* Macon, GA: Mercer University Press, 1984.

Snell, Bruno. *The Discovery of the Mind.* New York: Harper & Row, 1960.

Taylor, Charles. *Sources of the Self: The Making of the Modern Identity.* Cambridge: Harvard University Press, 1989.

Toulmin, Stephen, and June Goodfield. *The Architecture of Matter.* New York: Harper & Row Torchbooks, 1962.

– *The Fabric of the Heavens.* New York: Harper & Row, 1961.

Tracy, David. *Plurality and Ambiguity: Hermeneutics, Religion, Hope.* San Francisco: Harper & Row, 1987.

Voegelin, Eric. *Order and History.* Louisiana: Louisana State University Press, 1956.

Waldrop, M. Mitchell. *Complexity: The Emerging Science at the Edge of Order and Chaos.* New York: Simon & Schuster, 1992.

Westfall, Richard S. *The Construction of Modern Science: Mechanisms and Mechanics.* New York: John Wiley & Sons, 1971.

Wright, Frank Lloyd. *An American Architecture.* Edited by Edgar Kauffmann. New York: Horizon Press, 1995.

Index

Abraham, 234, 238, 243–5, 247, 249, 250, 253, 258

Absolute: foundation, 212; norm, 184; objective, 264; objectivity, 143, 232; space and time, 6, 59–61

Abstract, abstracting, 14, 19, 20, 24, 25, 28–31, 36–8, 43, 52–6, 59, 65, 67, 70, 85, 87, 90, 96, 100, 105, 111, 113, 115, 116, 127, 138, 139, 155, 160, 191, 204, 205, 232, 238, 240; as enriching, 52; and understanding, 20

Adaptation, 102, 169, 246, 247; assimilation and accommodation (Piaget), 23, 45, 71; Darwinian, 168, 169

Aggregate(s): chemical, biochemical, 79; coincidental, 44; higher things, alternative world-orders emerge from lower, 118, 163; insights emerge from sensible, 108; numbers, spaces, times, 44, 97; as spatiotemporal frame, 99

Algebra, 5, 24, 25, 34–46, 56, 57, 61, 103, 104, 108, 167, 183, 200

Already-out-there-now-real, 114, 115, 155

Analogy (*see also* Metaphysics): and generalization, 128; as nominal

understanding, 139; and tripartite structure, 160, 162, 176, 178

Anima: conscious vs unconscious shadow (Jung), 80

Antigone, 77, 179

Appropriation. *See* Self-appropriation

Aquinas, Thomas, 12

Archimedes, 40

Aristotle, Aristotelian, 8, 9, 11, 12, 18, 19, 26, 27, 28, 31, 46, 47, 48, 52, 55, 59, 65, 66, 67, 68, 98, 100, 111, 128, 138, 141, 149, 150, 182, 194, 195, 202, 209, 210, 211, 226, 257, 262

Augustine, 10, 236

Authentic, authenticity (*see also* Conversion): cognitionally, intellectually, 15, 211, 252, 260; as continuing struggle, 232; as developing, 178; grounded in transcultural methodical metaphysics and ethics, 265; identity, 225; judging, 189; lover, 235; meanings and values, 257; moral chooser, 210–13, 223, 225, 229, 233–6, 266; as restricted vs unlimited, 178; scale of values, 204, 206; subjectivity/objectivity, 141

ence and mathematics, 42, 54, 60, 74, 91, 103; truth of, 122

Invariant, 61–3; and changing statistical frequency, 105; in classical insight, 160; and classical law, 50, 61, 96, 186; limited, 135; and structure of human knowing, 13

Inverse insight (*see also* Empirical residue): and absolute space/time, 60; in Greek mathematics, 27, 30; and knowing, objectivity, reality, 193; notion or, 26, 27; and reasonableness, 28; in statistical thinking, 67; and way scientists wonder, 53, 144

Irrational: numbers, 44; in policies, social order, history, 93; religious experience as, 238, 242

Isaiah, 253

Isomorphism (*see also* Analogy; Structure), 191

Israel, 244–50, 252, 255

Jacobs, Jane, 83, 216, 217

James, William, 238

Jeremiah, 253

Joule, James, 63

Judaism, 250

Judging (*see also* Chooser; Knower and chooser; Reality; Reflective understanding; Truth): common-sense vs scientific, 127–31; correctness of, 126, 128, 136–8, 141–7, 151, 155, 184, 188, 209, 231; criterion of, 126, 136; defined, 126; elements of, 121–7; of fact, 198–202, 228; in interpretation/evaluation of history, 179, 181, 186–8; and 'Is it so?' question, 122–6, 136, 138, 182, 197, 208; as limited absolute, 136–8 (*see also* Virtually unconditioned); and love, 202–6; norms for, 87, 94, 98, 128; objectivity of, 143–7, 155, 178; and self-appropriation, 75;

truth known through, 183, 184; of value, 198, 207–9, 233, 264

Jung, C.G., 80, 82

Kant, Immanuel, 9, 32, 98, 223, 242, 264

Kepler, Johannes, 5, 51–5, 58, 97, 130

Kierkegaard, Søren, 9, 235, 246

Knower and chooser, 75, 80, 200, 201, 205, 210–13, 221–5, 228, 229, 234, 235, 251, 258

Knowing (*see also* Insight; Judging; Objectivity; Questions; Reality; Self-appropriation; Understanding; Virtually unconditioned): and cognitional theory, 193; defined, 130; and deliberating, 125, 194, 196, 235; and experience, 123–5, 130; as identity, 141; and judging, 122–5, 130, 137, 146; vs meaning, 120–1; and self as knower, 131–6; as tripartite structure, 134, 136, 141, 146, 151, 152, 153, 156, 160, 162, 176, 186, 190, 193, 209, 264; ultimate objective of, 156; and understanding, 123–6, 130, 137, 237

Knowing, choosing, loving, 12, 15, 206, 234–6, 257, 260, 262

Lagrange-Euler mechanics, 63

Lavoisier, Antoine, 63

Law(s): basic, 56, 64; classical, 55, 63, 68, 98, 99, 111, 112; genetic, 105, 112; public, 126; statistical, 68, 69, 98, 99, 101, 111, 112

Leibniz, G.W., 6, 33, 41, 183

Limit (*see also* Potency and limit): in definition, 20–2, 38, 39; and empirical residue, 30; and inverse insight, 30

Limited absolute, 126, 135, 136, 137, 184, 198, 207, 208, 211

Locke, John, 32, 263

Logic, 104, 223; and cognitional theory, 231; and discovering self as authentic